Between the Murray and the sea

Tom Austen Brown Studies in Australasian Archaeology

Peter Hiscock, Series Editor

The Tom Austen Brown Studies in Australasian Archaeology series publishes new research on the archaeology of Australia and the adjacent regions. It aims to develop our understanding of Australasia's human past, with particular focus on the archaeology of Aboriginal and Torres Strait Islander people during both prehistoric and contact periods.

Animal bones in Australian archaeology: a field guide to common native and introduced species
Melanie Fillios and Natalie Blake

Between the Murray and the sea: Aboriginal archaeology in southeastern Australia
David Frankel

Between the Murray and the sea

Aboriginal archaeology in southeastern Australia

David Frankel

SYDNEY UNIVERSITY PRESS

First published by Sydney University Press

© David Frankel 2017
© Sydney University Press 2017

Sydney University Press
Fisher Library F03
University of Sydney NSW 2006
AUSTRALIA
sup.info@sydney.edu.au
sydney.edu.au/sup

A catalogue record for this book is available from the National Library of Australia

ISBN 9781743325520 paperback
ISBN 9781743325537 ebook

'The 41st year of 1968' by Les Murray (from *Taller when prone*) is reproduced by permission of the author, care of Margaret Connolly & Associates Pty Ltd.

'The shellfish gene' by Peter Porter (from *Collected poems, vol. 2*) is reproduced by permission of the author's estate, care of Rogers, Coleridge & White Ltd, 20 Powis Mews, London W11 1JN.

'Bora ring' by Judith Wright (from *Collected poems*) is reproduced by permission of HarperCollins Publishers Australia.

Cover image: 'Murray River' by Chris Fithall, 2014. Licensed under Creative Commons, CC BY 2.0. Sourced from Flickr.

Cover design by Miguel Yamin.

Contents

List of figures

List of figures

List of figures

Acknowledgements

Primary acknowledgement is due to the Traditional Owners of the lands discussed in this book.

My debt to the many colleagues on whose work I have drawn is obvious. It takes much effort – often physical, always challenging and sometimes emotional – to find ancient remains and to draw out their stories. Archaeology is always unfinished business. This book, dealing as it does with Aboriginal Australia, intersects with Australia's other unfinished business of reconciliation. I hope that in exploring aspects of Aboriginal life in both ancient and more recent times it can contribute to a better understanding of its richness, diversity and resilience, and in doing so pays appropriate respect to Traditional Owners and their Elders, past and present.

I would like to thank Peter Hiscock, as editor of the Tom Austen Brown Studies in Australasian Archaeology, and Agata Mrva-Montoya and Denise O'Dea of Sydney University Press for their assistance in preparing this book. Many others responded generously to my requests for information, comments or illustrations: Jim Allen, Robert Bednarik, Ilya Berelov, Caroline Bird, David Clark, Dan Cummings, Peter Davies, Neale Draper, Christine Eslick, Nick Evans, Joanna Fresløv, Jillian Garvey, Ben Gunn, Jo Kamminga, Sharon Lane, Susan Lawrence, Martin Lawler, Roger Luebbers, Jane Lydon, Ian McNiven, Janine Major, Christina Pavlides, Gary Presland, Tarmo Raadik, Tom Richards, David Rhodes, Lynette Russell, David Thomas, Ben Watson, Cathie Webb and John Webb.

Especially thanks are due to my wife Lena who encouraged me to take on this task, put up with my distraction while working on it and read each chapter as it was completed. Without her support neither this book, nor any of my others, could have been written.

Preface

In this volume David Frankel synthesises the archaeological and ethnographic evidence for Aboriginal lifeways in southeastern Australia, up until the early period of contact with Europeans. Such regional syntheses are now critical for understanding Australia's human past. They provide an opportunity for researchers to offer novel and detailed reviews of the existing evidence while profiling the differences in cultural systems across the continent. Fundamental questions about how cultural systems evolved in different parts of the continent, and whether those trajectories were parallel or divergent, can be based on comparisons of regions. Cultural change in Australia has sometimes been assumed to be directional, inevitably trending from simple to complex, but here Frankel seeks to evaluate the evidence for the range of adaptations, and not to presuppose the nature of change. He views the long-term cultural sequences of each region as a consequence of many individual adaptations that built outcomes without necessarily being planned. This provides a conceptual framework for comprehending geographic differences.

Cultural diversity underpins the Indigenous past of Australia. It is apparent in early historic observations and ethnographies, and it is revealed in the archaeological record of earlier times. Diversity is not surprising given the very different environments that people lived in, and archaeologists have often employed biogeographic distinctions as the basis for exploring cultural differences, even if those environmental conditions need not have acted alone to create the cultural variation. Frankel takes advantage of these possibilities by structuring his chapters geographically, thereby emphasising the difference in lifeways and culture history in the various landscapes of southeastern Australia as well as the different evidence upon which those narratives are constructed.

Between the Murray and the sea reveals the Aboriginal settlement of very different landscapes across southeastern Australia. Broad riverine corridors, rugged sandstone mountain ranges, wide sandy coastlines, lengthy peninsulas of sand, large islands, extensive eucalypt scrubland (mallee), and rocky lake districts are only some of the settings in which past peoples lived. Frankel explains the evidence for different settlement patterns and economies in each landscape, and in the process describes the varied evidence that archaeologists have at hand to infer those ancient activities. Caves and rock shelters are rare and long archaeological sequences few. In many parts of the southeast, archaeologists are confronted with landscapes of gently flowing rivers and rolling hills, gently sloping plains, bounded by sandy beaches interspersed with rocky headlands. Archaeologists working in these locations have examined diverse signals of past behaviour: stone walls, channels and mounds of earth, painted walls, scatters of stone artefacts on the ground surface, collections of meal debris by the sea, and so on. To explain how archaeologists interpret such things Frankel weaves the stories of modern archaeological investigations into his account of what may have happened in the past. He explains how previous interpretations sometimes arrived at conclusions not required by the evidence, and how other ways of interpreting the archaeological material are more plausible. Avoiding unwarranted speculation in this way he provides a narrative that is grounded in his concerns about the effects of scale and resolution on the interpretations we make of the past.

The result is a carefully crafted and impressively illustrated depiction of the economic and social lives of past Aboriginal peoples who lived in the diverse landscapes that existed between the Murray and the sea. This depiction will be valuable to both specialists and non-specialists alike, as the book provides a foundation for thinking about the remarkable variety of ways Aboriginal foragers adapted to the lands of southeastern Australia.

Peter Hiscock
October 2017

Introduction: Jigsaws and the past

Tourism Victoria's long-running 'jigsaw' campaign took the diversity of the state as its key motif (Figure I.1). This also provides an appropriate theme when exploring the area's past. In this book, I reflect on this variability in geography and ancient Aboriginal society, raising some critical issues in how we can understand the past. Like other people, archaeologists often seek broad patterns when writing stories from isolated and patchy fragments. But we need to find the right focus so that we do not force disparate pieces of evidence into the wrong frames, while at the same time not losing ourselves in trivial detail. It's a question of scale: of leaves, trees and woods.

The cultural and historical frames – those straight edges surrounding the generally more familiar archaeologies of settled farmers, of city-dwellers and of states – appear self-evident, especially where written documents are available. They are harder to establish for hunter-gatherer societies with their very different relationships to land, to animals and to one another. The edges are always blurred. The material traces, too, may be more varied and difficult to appreciate. And then there is the question of time. For, unlike Tourism Victoria's jigsaw, we are not dealing with a contemporary map of one complex landscape, but with a series of maps of ever-changing landforms and environments. Our diversity has many dimensions.

We are also at the mercy of available evidence. Most pieces of our puzzles are missing. 'Probable', 'possible' and 'on current evidence' could preface every statement, recognising, as we must, that new evidence, new techniques and new concepts continually challenge, if they do not change, our understanding of the past. Often, when giving general talks on local archaeology, I lead off with a simple question to the audience: 'When do you think people first came to Australia?' Inevitably, when talking to Indigenous groups, someone will immediately assert 'We have always been here!' This is, as often as not, a challenge to test my reaction. But others will bid larger or smaller ages: 40,000 years … 60,000 years … 120,000 years. I then show a diagram like Figure I.2, commenting that 'it depends on how old *you* are'. Nothing more simply and clearly demonstrates how archaeological knowledge changes with new research. What was 'true' when I was a student was no longer true when I began teaching, and what I said then has, in turn, been replaced by new evidence. Archaeological information is contingent, not absolute: changeable, not fixed. But at no time can we go beyond it. Ideas, beliefs and

Figure I.1 Tourism Victoria's 'jigsaw' logo emphasises
diversity and integration.

speculations are possible, but from a disciplinary perspective they must always be grounded solidly on the available evidence, even though we know that our understanding will and must change.

The pieces of our puzzles are also mixed: not only do we have the specific archaeological evidence of sites and artefacts but other types of information and varied perspectives must also be considered. Some are more technical, such as research on changes in climate and landscape; some are social, especially the interests of Aboriginal people regarding how their ancestors can and should be studied; some are framed by what we know of Aboriginal life at the time of European invasion, and others by more general ideas we have about society and social systems.

All these influence the way we decide what sort of stories to tell and how to tell them. Should we highlight the dramatic and unusual or stay with the more mundane aspects of everyday life? Should we look for broad narrative histories linking developments across regions and millennia or focus on specific events? Should we look to anthropology to help identify economic and social systems and the ways in which people created meaningful and successful lives in the past? Should our explanations emphasise social factors or should we view changes primarily as responses to environmental circumstances?

Personally, I prefer local and shorter-term scales of observation, analysis and explanation. This naturally promotes a view of diversity. It also affects the organisation of this book, as does the structure of the archaeological record, itself as varied as the landscapes of the past. Different questions, different explanations and different narratives arise from this diversity of material. I have therefore chosen to present aspects of this varied archaeology by region rather than by time or topic, and often with an eye to the environmental setting.

My focus is on the lands enclosed by the sweeping arm of the Murray River as it meanders from its source in the Snowy Mountains to the sea nearly a thousand kilometres away, taking in all of Victoria and southeastern South Australia (Figure I.3). But this area cannot be entirely isolated from the rest of Australia, and

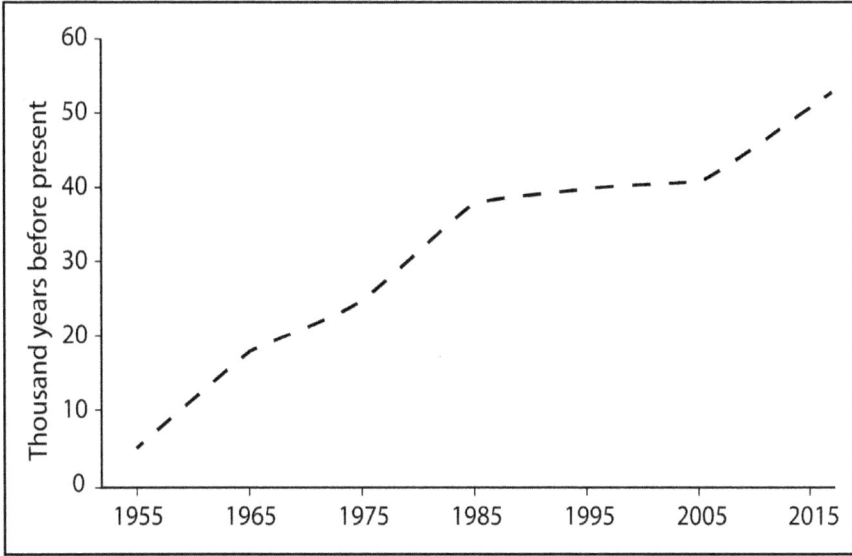

Figure I.2 Earliest dates available to Australian archaeologists over the last 60 years.

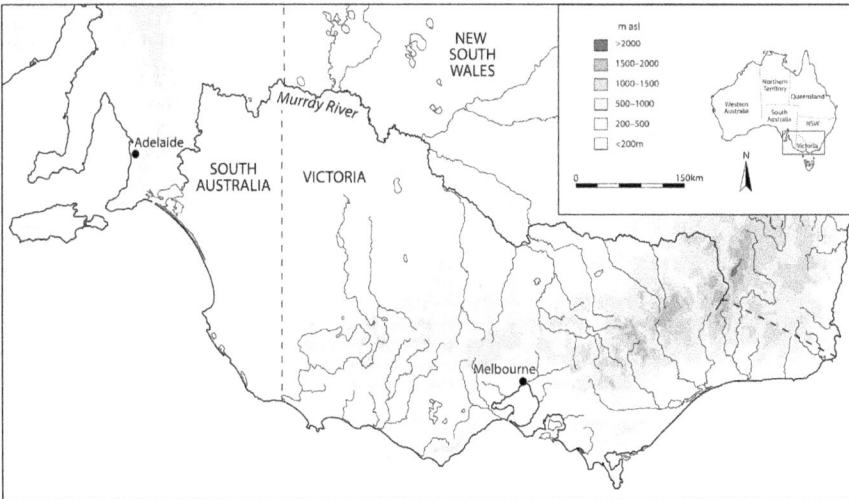

Figure I.3 Southeastern Australia.

the Murray cannot provide an absolute or strict boundary: our jigsaw has fuzzy edges indeed.

It is a varied region, with many different environments. There are the high steep hills and deep valleys of the Australian Alps to the east, with their winter snows and fast-flowing rivers. The hills drop away as we move westward, but still divide the north- and south-flowing rivers of central Victoria. But further west again the land is flat and increasingly dry. The arid mallee in the northwest is bounded by the riverlands, where the Murray provides a ribbon of richness as it winds its way towards the sea. The coasts of the south and west are far from uniform, with long stretches of open beach and estuary alternating with sections of rugged cliffs. The adjacent plains vary from dry limestone to lava-strewn volcanic plains, and swamps and wetlands.

The social context

This book presents one view to the past, seen through an academic, archaeological filter. I am – as all non-Indigenous archaeologists in Australia are – acutely aware of sensitivities involved in writing about dispossessed First Nations' history and heritage. It would be inappropriate, even presumptuous, for me to speak for Aboriginal Australians, but such technical expertise as I have justifies, I believe, this attempt to present my view of sites and circumstances. And, from discussions with members of local communities, I have every reason to believe that this view, and the archaeological evidence that lies behind it, is appreciated and welcomed, especially when it is not seen to preclude alternative voices and understandings.

Many Victorian Aboriginal people are keen to reconnect with their heritage: working with archaeological evidence is one way to do this, often as active participants in the field and with responsibility for managing sites. But this involvement is generally structured within a framework of cultural heritage management, which emphasises, as it must, the documentation and assessment of sites in advance of development. In doing so, it often pays too little attention to research and its potential for creative analysis and broader understanding – or indeed to other ways of seeing the world:

> The Wathaurong Community regard the focus on 'artefacts' and 'sites' to be a European approach to Aboriginal heritage. To the Wathaurong, a locality or place has more importance than the artefacts on it, because of the spiritual connection to the land itself. The natural context of a place is an integral part of its heritage and this context can often extend beyond the boundaries of an archaeological site. (quoted in Richards 1998: 80)

Aspects of archaeology

Archaeologists will draw on many lines of evidence, often integrating elements from fields as diverse as art history and geology, linguistics and genetics, anthropology and pollen analysis. While the primary questions must, I believe, come from archaeology itself, developments in and information from these other areas continually open up opportunities and recast approaches and explanations.

The archaeological record is surprisingly problematic. There are many different types of sites, each with its own particular potential for analysis. Some, such as rockshelters, provide a focus for repeated, if intermittent, use over centuries or millennia, allowing us to trace changes, continuities and discontinuities. At the other extreme are sites that may have been used for very short periods, in some cases for only single events. Sites such as quarries give information on industrial activities while coastal shell middens provide insights into one aspect of subsistence economies. Burials inform us of customs, genetics and demography; mounds about housing or cooking. All across the country, in almost every lot or paddock, are scatters, sometimes sparse, sometimes dense, of stone tools. These, the most common manifestation of the Aboriginal past, are the hardest to deal with. More often than not there is no way of knowing how old they are, or indeed how many different episodes of activity over how many centuries they may represent.

Then, too, we deal with the residues of innumerable small events: the chipping of a piece of stone, the discard of a shell, the burial of a relative. Each event tells a story, but as we move from observing single items and actions and seek out repeated patterns of behaviour, the stories become broader, now telling of local customs and traditions, of communities rather than of individual people. It is also a question of time, for our ability to measure and divide up time forces us away from the personal and human towards abstract systems, processes and grander narratives. It is all too easy to refer glibly to centuries or millennia, spans of time beyond our easy understanding, telescoping together the lives of countless generations:

> The problem is our tide-warped mensuration.
> We live not long, our scale is planetary;
> Just single soldiers of a warrior nation,
> Time-truncated, ex-explanatory.
>
> I can't be pictured but in diagram,
> Yet this one shell's to me a satrapy—
> (Peter Porter, 'The shellfish gene')

The way our knowledge continually develops has already been noted. But it is worth emphasising that it is also very much the creation of archaeologists. As we uncover we also structure the material traces left by past peoples into frameworks of our own devising. Although apparently self-evident, every aspect related to the discovery, identification and description of these remains is to some extent affected by the background, training and ability of researchers, each with an individual style. While some researchers have had the luxury of investigations designed to investigate particular questions, most fieldwork today is framed by heritage management concerns, where archaeologists are employed by developers to assess the significance of areas in order to mitigate the impact of development. The circumstances in which the work is carried out affects the detail and comparability of the documentation they produce.

Modern archaeologists will grapple with issues related to the ways in which objects are discarded and sites are formed, and to how both things and their buried contexts will change over time as natural and cultural events transform them. We also recognise that researchers are only the latest in this series of transformations as they bring material back from the archaeological context into a new social environment where it can serve different purposes. Understanding our own impact on the archaeological record is a crucial aspect of assessing and interpreting it. What we know is bound up with how we know. This is not, of course, to suggest that it is all a matter of opinion and invention. Archaeology as a self-critical and self-conscious discipline remains a powerful, if not the only, way to find out about the human past and to test our understanding of it.

In this book we will see how these different types of evidence, artefacts and sites provide varied opportunities to explore ancient worlds.

Landscapes, taskscapes and persistent places

The land is key. But there are many ways in which it can be understood. There are the physical facts: topography and landforms, rocks and soils, climate and water, plants and animals. These can readily be defined and described. Then there is the social dimension: how people perceive, structure and relate to the world they live in. This is harder to discern, but constitutes an essential aspect of our archaeological stories.

Nothing more clearly illustrates how the same places mean different things to different people than 19th-century Victoria. For the first decades of the century, the only people present were Indigenous hunter-gatherers who understood, managed and exploited their land and its resources following long-standing customs and traditions. From the 1830s to the 1850s, European settlers saw this world differently. They were primarily concerned with the value and utility of land for agriculture and especially for grazing domesticated animals, with the local economy linked to a wider, British world of commerce and manufacture. From the 1850s, concepts of the landscape and its value drastically changed with the discovery of gold, the consequent influx of people from all around the world and the massive impacts they had on the environment. Land once judged important for the availability of wild plants and animals, then for farming or running cattle or sheep, was now assessed in terms of its mineral resources. As these were worked out, new patterns of economy and settlement developed towards the end of the 19th century. In this way, places which have the same location on a map can be very different places in social, economic and metaphysical terms.

It is often easiest, or at least more straightforward, for archaeologists to discuss mundane aspects of the material remains they deal with and to give priority to technology and subsistence economy when talking of lands, resources and activities. But we know that Aboriginal people today give emphasis to the importance of Country, linking conceptual and physical worlds in fundamental ways. There is no reason to suppose that it was different in the distant past. But

Figure I.4 Two views of the South Gippsland Hills: on the left during clearance of the rainforest trees and scrub in the 19th century (Korrumburra and District Historical Society 1998); on the right as it appears today.

identifying specific attitudes and beliefs that shaped ancient society is far from easy – some would say impossible. Others regard this as an essential starting point. We may, on occasion, think of how the land itself, or land previously occupied, exerts an influence of its own on more recent people. Particular places become *persistent places* with a continuity of association, use and reuse, as explained by Howard Morphy with reference to a different area of Aboriginal Australia: 'People do not move in and take over a country by imposing new myths: rather they move in and act as if they are taken over by the new country' (Morphy 1995: 186). We can also explore how people perceived and lived 'on country' by defining *taskscapes* of interrelated actions taking place in time as well as in space (Ingold 1993).

I often drive over the South Gippsland hills which lie between the coast and the Latrobe Valley. The views are wonderful as one looks across the rounded hills and deep valleys with only occasional lines of windbreaks dividing the open pastures. It is hard to envisage what the area was like in the late 19th century. But some sad monuments give a clue. Near Thorpdale are signs commemorating the 'World's Tallest Tree', a mountain ash some 114 metres high which was felled in 1884. It was one among thousands of similarly massive trees forming the Great South Gippsland Forest, for these now open hillslopes were covered by a dense temperate rainforest, entirely removed by settlers, assisted by the occasional devastating bushfires which swept through the miles of ringbarked, dead trees.

There are many such examples of the dramatic transformations brought about by the vigorous attacks on vegetation and the land itself during the 19th century. Alongside universal broad-scale clearance for agriculture, miners sluiced away whole hillsides and filled river valleys of central Victoria with toxic sludge. The landscapes we see today can be a poor guide to how things were 200 years ago. And even less of a guide to the far more distant past.

Aboriginal life through European eyes

There is a wide variety of information about Aboriginal life in 19th-century Australia as seen through the eyes of European settlers, missionaries and officials. These ethnohistorical sources provide us with important information on individuals and groups, on languages and dialects, on customs and techniques, which fleshes out the material remains and gives us a picture of what Aboriginal society was like in the recent past (Frankel and Major 2017).

In this book I have used many extracts in this way. The understanding and knowledge of European observers naturally varied, and their accounts are not always reliable. And, of course, there are obvious limitations inherent in any descriptions provided by foreign observers of a society suffering the massive traumas of displacement and dispossession. Nevertheless, the written accounts, along with photographs and drawings, artefacts in museum collections and the traditions and knowledge retained by Aboriginal people today can give life to archaeological evidence.

The ethnohistorical accounts can be used in different ways. They are least problematic where they give descriptions of particular activities – hunting kangaroo, catching eels and netting birds – or where they describe tools, clothing and techniques. Accounts of ceremonies, social and economic interaction and recreation remind us of the rich and complex nature of everyday life and of the many activities that have left little or no material, archaeological trace.

Things become more difficult when broader questions are asked. One concerns the extent and location of Aboriginal language groups, tribes or clans. This requires a close reading and careful assessment and integration of numerous comments, notes and traditions (Clark 1990; Wesson 2000). Any analysis of these structures and boundaries is not only of academic interest but is also important to Aboriginal communities today, helping to establish formal and sometimes legal associations to land. A closely related issue, of particular interest in much archaeological discussion, involves estimates of population numbers: how many Aboriginal people were there immediately before Europeans arrived in the region?

This question – and indeed all consideration of the ethnohistorical accounts – becomes crucial when set into the long-term history of Aboriginal people. It helps us form a view of the size, distribution and behaviour of Aboriginal people early in the 19th century, seeing aspects of society as it was at the time of the catastrophic destruction by Europeans. But how far back in time can we project this view and read the archaeological record with these ideas firmly in mind? Equally, recognising that things were not always as they were in 1800, we must ask how these particular social and economic customs came into being. Here we have to be careful not to see past events as leading inevitably towards the ethnographically described systems. Such teleological views can blind us to the inherent diversity and contingency in human history. I think we should see long-term histories as comprising numerous adaptations, changes and choices, sometimes made out of necessity, resulting, more by accident than design, in later systems.

This book, then, explores some of these diverse pathways and developments, with each stage legitimate in its own terms, but each destined to evolve into something new as part of a dynamic process of continual change.

1
The first three quarters

The rapid global spread of our immediate ancestors is an amazing story. Within the last 150,000 years, anatomically modern humans – that is, people just like us – evolved in Africa and spread out to colonise the world: we are all their descendants. Adaptability, flexibility and innovations in tools, techniques and social behaviour were the keys to their success. Some of these people travelled east through India and then southward to reach the coasts of Southeast Asia. There they had boats to move along the coasts and to sail offshore to catch deep-water fish. By 65,000 years ago, some sailed even further, becoming the first to reach Australia.

Lower sea levels, 60 to 80 metres below those of today, meant that the northern coastline of Australia was then far to the north. The Torres Strait and Gulf of Carpentaria together formed a vast plain, so that the island of New Guinea was part of an expanded greater Australian continent, which we call Sahul. The extended coastlines made open ocean distances shorter than they are today, but even so these colonists needed to sail far out of sight of land to arrive safely. Several routes have been suggested. Those coming straight from Timor would have brought people more directly onto the northern coasts. An easterly route from Sulawesi had the advantage of shorter journeys between intermediate islands on the way to the shores of New Guinea. In any event it is likely that many – even perhaps very many – two-way voyages took place over centuries and involved dozens, if not hundreds, of people, sufficient to establish viable populations at points along these coasts.

New arrivals found most plants and all animals different from those they left behind. Some things would have been more familiar, especially on the coastal fringe, where there would have been less immediate pressure for major adjustments to their new homes. However, once communities were established, it took little time for people to move around and across the continent – continuing the rapid expansion characteristic of their immediate ancestors, now encouraged by the patchy and limited distribution of resources. Well before 40,000 years ago, there was widespread, if low-density, occupation everywhere in Australia, especially along the most favourable stretches of coast and those inland regions served by major river systems.

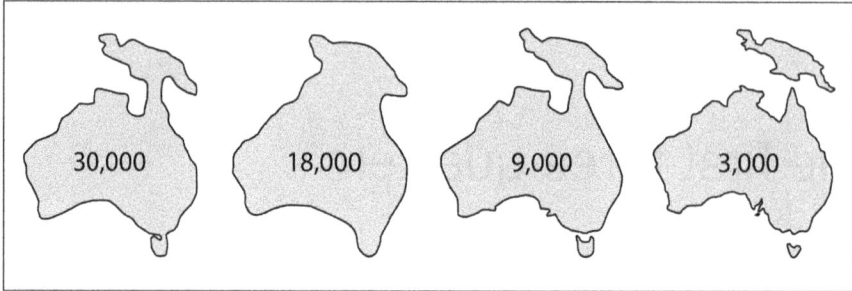

Figure 1.1 The changing shape of Australia as sea levels rose and fell over the last 30,000 years.

The earliest Australians adjusted and adapted to the different places they encountered whether they were tropical, arid, temperate, coastal, inland, riverine or highland. But the world was never constant. It, too, changed around them, even though the changes – changes on a global, continental and far-reaching scale – were imperceptible, too slow to be recognised from one generation to the next.

The most obvious of all these changes was the rise and fall of sea levels as alternating warmer and colder conditions froze or released the world's oceans. The coldest, driest and windiest conditions experienced by people in Australia were between 23,000 and 18,000 years ago at the height of the last Ice Age (the Last Glacial Maximum) with temperatures six to ten degrees below those of today. The sea was 125 metres below its present level and the coasts were far from where they are now (Figure 1.1). Equally important were the effects of this great drought on the inland. Parts of southeastern Australia that are now well watered, with woodlands and rainforest, were then more likely to be open grasslands; what are now semi-arid areas, perhaps covered with mallee scrub, were deserts (Figure 1.2). Across many areas new dunefields developed, resulting in the well-known sand sheets of central Victoria. Inland rivers had reduced flows, or dried up completely, and the lakes they fed became barren pans. The process of warming after this made life easier for people, and it is likely that populations increased. But it was not a steady, uninterrupted improvement, with varied local effects of colder episodes, such as one between 14,500 and 12,500 years ago. After that the climate continued to improve – at least from a human perspective. It became warmer and wetter, with increased vegetation cover and, as a consequence, a greater availability of useful plants and animals. It would be convenient to think of this as compensating for the significant loss of land as the sea rose to reach, and then even exceed, its present level by 6000 years ago. Each local area would have responded differently to the major continental trends, which provided new challenges and opportunities for people in all areas (Canning 2009).

There is, as yet, barely any archaeological evidence of the first three-quarters of the time people were in Victoria and South Australia. There are only half-a-dozen sites that are over 25,000 years old, and hardly a dozen more to fill the next 10,000 years – and most of these have minimal evidence beyond their age (Figure 1.3). But there is no reason to suppose that there were not more people around during all these

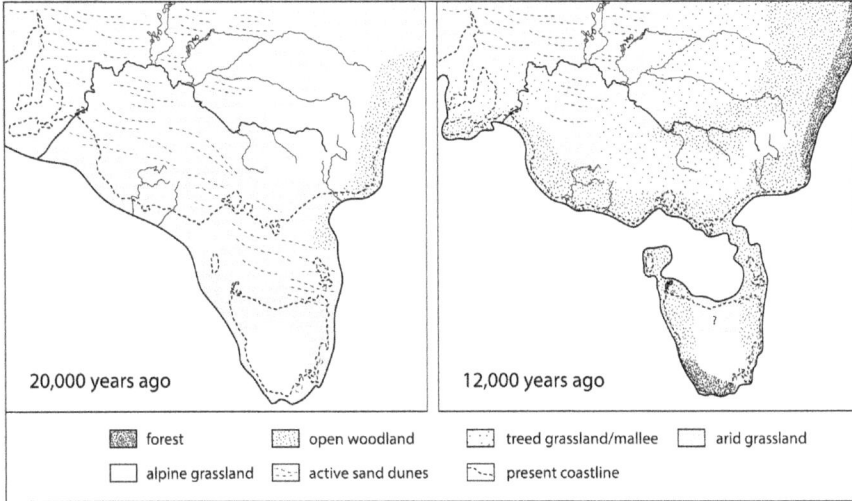

Figure 1.2 Land and vegetation at the height of the last Ice Age (left), and as the climate improved and sea levels rose (right) (after Ross 1986).

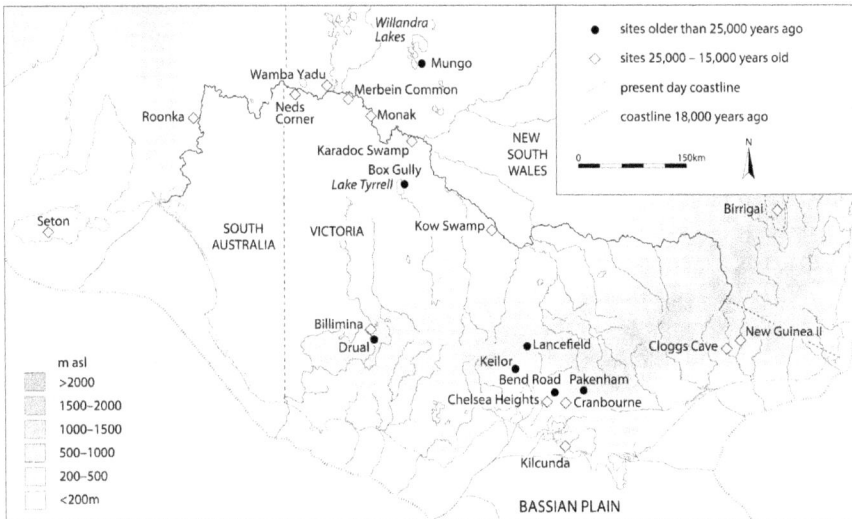

Figure 1.3 Locations of the few archaeological sites more than 15,000 years old.

Figure 1.4 Looking west from the eroding dunes across Lake Mungo.

immense periods of time. Certainly, they were present immediately to the north and south. Several sites in Tasmania show that people crossed the land bridge from Victoria as soon as it was exposed by lower sea levels about 43,000 years ago, while some of the best evidence that we have comes from Lake Mungo and the Willandra Lakes, only 100 kilometres north of the Murray River. This World Heritage area has become the best-known archaeological place in Australia, both because of the quality and quantity of evidence and because of its haunting scenery (Figure 1.4).

The fortuitous circumstance of recent erosion of the ancient dunes beside the long-dried-out lakes provides a vast archaeological landscape with many different facets. The crescentic dune (or lunette) that formed on the eastern margins of the lakes documents a complex sequence of changes in water availability, the environment and the ways in which people used the country over tens of thousands of years (Stern 2015; Stern et al. 2013). Two of these ancient people have become particularly famous, for their remains are among the oldest known in Australia. One, known to us as Mungo 1 (or Mungo Lady) was cremated and the other, Mungo 3 (Mungo Man), was buried on the shores of the lake some 40,000 years ago (Bowler et al. 2003). But we cannot say exactly when or how their ancestors first reached this area several thousand years before that. Perhaps they moved from the southern coast, up the Murray, Lachlan and other rivers, including the now extinct ancient course of the Willandra River. Equally - if not more - likely they were part of a broader spread southward, across the Murray-Darling drainage basin from northern New South Wales or Queensland.

Figure 1.5 Box Gully, Lake Tyrrell, 2011 (photo: Aboriginal Victoria).

Northwest Victoria

Our first early site south of the Murray is in many ways in a similar setting to those around the Willandra lakes. As at Mungo and other ancient lakes, Lake Tyrell in the Victorian Mallee has a crescentic lunette on the eastern shore which formed when the lake held fresh water (Macumber 1991). Suggestions of early occupation (Ross 1981) were confirmed in 2001 when Aboriginal Affairs Victoria ran one of its Aboriginal Community Heritage Projects in the area. Local Traditional Owners assisted in the limited excavation – just two 1x1 metre squares – dug into the extensive dune (Richards 2004; Richards et al. 2007) (Figure 1.5). They only found seven flaked stone tools: not much to show, just sufficient to confirm that people were there when the dunes formed between 32,000 and 26,000 years ago, a little before the lake, and the region as a whole, began to dry out during the Last Glacial Maximum. There were many more fragments of animal bone. Some of these may have been from animals which happened to die naturally on the spot, but others were burnt in a way that could only have been done by people. They show that people camping on the dune ate a wide range of small mammals, reptiles, birds and freshwater shellfish.

In Gariwerd, nearly 250 kilometres south of Lake Tyrell, the Drual rockshelter was used at about the same time (as discussed in Chapter 2) but we cannot say if these two sites were in any way directly connected with one another. To the northwest, several shell middens beside the Murray River have provided dates of between 25,000 and 15,000 years ago. It is more than a coincidence that these sites were used when occupation ceased at Lake Tyrrell, for people retreated to the major water systems from increasingly inhospitable areas as the climate changed for the worse (Williams et al. 2013). But even the river corridor itself was far less attractive, rich and productive than it is today (Pardoe 1995).

In the Maribyrnong valley

James White's pick struck something solid as he dug into the yellow silts in the Hughes Soil Pit near Keilor in October 1940. It proved to be an incomplete human skull, immediately exciting scholarly interest both locally and around the world, for it was demonstrably very old and fed into long-standing debates on the origin of Aboriginal people. For many years this Aboriginal ancestor continued to be a key player – or perhaps an academic football – in the slowly developing field of Australian archaeology, especially as he was then the earliest person known on the continent.

The site itself is on the northern fringes of Melbourne, increasingly surrounded by housing development. As the climate fluctuated between periods with greater or lesser water flows along the Maribyrnong and its tributaries a succession of deposits of silt and clay were laid down in the river valley. For tens of thousands of years people camped away from the more exposed basalt plains in the deep valley beside the river, their discarded artefacts covered by these sediments.

Over the last 70 years, many archaeologists and geomorphologists have worked to disentangle the complex series of sedimentation and the formation of river terraces at several places along the Maribyrnong River (Figure 1.6). A long-running research project by Alexander Gallus with volunteers from the Archaeological Society of Victoria approached the sequence of deposits near the junction of the Maribyrnong and Dry Creek from the side, where they were exposed in a vertical cutting (Gallus 1974; see also Presland 1998) (Figure 1.7). In the 1970s, a joint project by the Victoria Archaeological Survey and Paul Ossa from La Trobe University took a different approach, digging a large hole down from the surface. It was no easy task to dig carefully through many metres of thick, heavy and often rock-hard clays, in the hope of coming upon a sufficient number of artefacts associated with dateable material (Burke 1990; Munroe 1998) (Figure 1.8).

At the very surface they found many examples of recent types of small stone blades and scrapers made primarily of fine-grained silcrete. These come from recent occupation of the area by Wurundjeri people. There was little in the silts immediately below, but a cluster of slightly larger scrapers and notched implements lay beside a hearth – perhaps all from one episode of activity about 15,000 years ago, within a thousand years of the time when the famous burial took place. Animal bones in these silts are mainly from those animals of the dry woodlands that would have been present on the surrounding plains at that time (Marshall 1974). Deeper down, in the clays deposited in the order of 30,000 years ago, there was a different range of animals, including many now extinct species. The evidence that people were there at this earlier time is far more equivocal, with only a few stone tools found in these sediments.

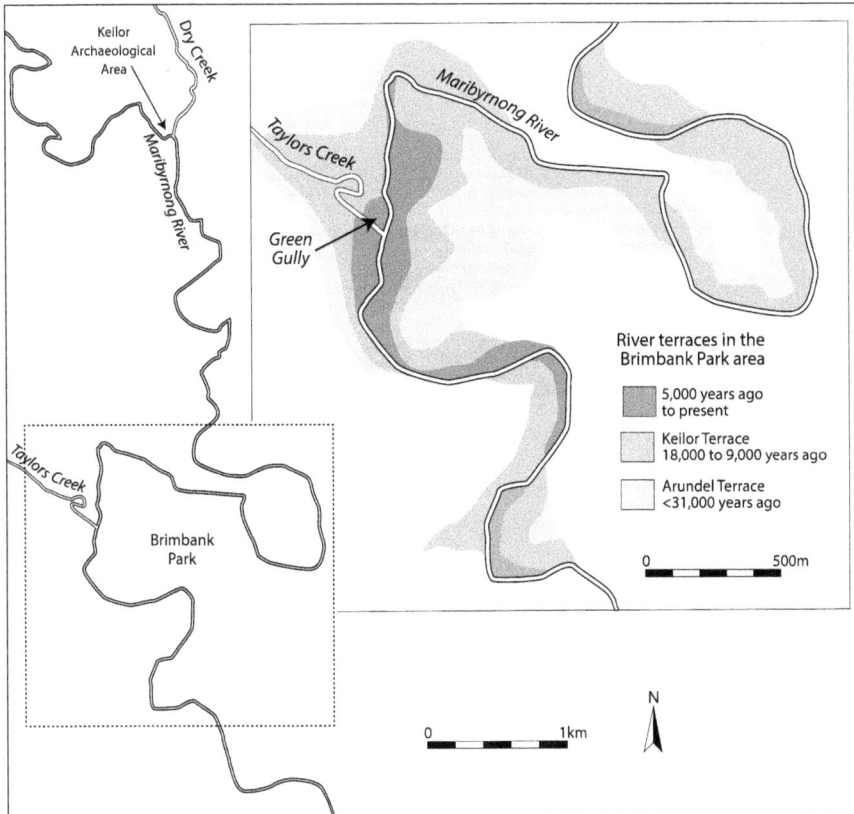

Figure 1.6 Early sites at Keilor and Brimbank Park in the Maribyrnong valley (after Tunn 1998: figure 2).

Three kilometres downstream, the Maribyrnong winds through Brimbank Park. Rather than concentrating on one particular spot, John Tunn surveyed the complex landscape as a whole, connecting the artefacts he found with the sequence of river terraces of different ages (Tunn 1998). He was thus able to trace activities at different locations. While the oldest evidence comes from the formation of the Arundel Terrace, which began 31,000 years ago, the greatest number of findspots and artefacts found are associated with the Keilor Terrace of between 18,000 and 9000 years ago.

More recently, two smaller excavations at Green Gully and a larger space opened up so that a mechanical digger could shift the otherwise intractable heavy clays at the site of the nearby sewage treatment plant, revealing well-preserved hearths, some with fire-shattered stone and quartzite artefacts (Tunn 2006; Canning et al. 2010). These finds reinforce the impression that the valley was a particularly favoured place for several thousand years after about 16,000 years ago. The worst of the cold and arid climate of the last Ice Age was over. More water

Figure 1.7 Exposed sediments cut by the Maribyrnong River at Keilor. Archaeological excavations in the 1970s took place within the long shed.

Figure 1.8 Excavations in progress at Keilor, 1979.

flowed through the Maribyrnong system, providing habitat for plants, animals and the people who made use of them.

The people camping in the sheltered valley near the river at this time generally made their stone tools from quartzite, producing both larger and smaller scrapers, which contrast with the array of silcrete microliths characteristic of the last few thousand years found widespread on the surface and in the upper layers of excavations. Apart from this obvious difference, the small number of the earlier artefacts, separated as they are by centuries if not millennia, makes it hard to see a distinctive or neatly uniform approach to manufacture or design in this area. This applies equally at other early sites, but it is nevertheless clear that there was a diversity across Victoria in local patterns of raw material selection and the tools made from them (Bird and Frankel 1998).

An inland swamp

Fifty kilometres north of Keilor is Lancefield Swamp. The archaeological evidence of early activity beside the water is scanty indeed – just two quartzite tools found in deposits laid down sometime between 30,000 and 24,000 years ago (Gillespie et al. 1978). While the tools may in fact be far more recent, the site is important in other ways, for the swamp is full of many thousands of bones of now extinct animals, mainly *Macropus titan*, a giant kangaroo. These were washed in at intervals between 80,000 and 45,000 years ago, perhaps from mass die-offs during periodic droughts (Dortch et al. 2016).

When people first arrived in Australia there was a range of animals far larger than those we have today. These megafauna included giant browsers, grazers and carnivores like the leopard-sized thylacoleo. All mammals larger than 100 kilograms, with their sonorous names – diprotodon, sthenurus, procoptodon – as well as many smaller ones became extinct tens of thousands of years after people arrived. So too did the giant emu-like genyornis and the magalania, a frighteningly large goanna as big as any crocodile. The timing and cause of their extinction is hotly debated. How could so many varied species disappear from a continent as large and diverse as Australia? Should it even be seen as a single or closely associated set of events? What, if any, was the role of people, either directly through hunting or indirectly through the effects of extensive burning? Or did changes in climate, or perhaps a greater rapidity of changes to environments, have these drastic effects?

People did not kill or eat any of the animals at Lancefield, for the bones are all far older than the tools (Dortch et al. 2016; Horton and Wright 1981; van Huet et al. 1998; van Huet 1998). But, equally, there is no reason to suppose that hunters would not or could not have taken animals of any size (Hamm et al. 2016). What is more interesting is that these extinctions of both large and small creatures, whenever or however they happened, removed a significant, doubtless valuable, part of people's world.

Southern sand sheets and wetlands

> On the Western Port plains there is a basin of water – never dry, even in the
> hottest summers – which is called *Toor-roo-dun*, because the Bun-yip lives in
> that water. *Toor-roo-dun* inhabits the deep waters, and the thick mud beneath the
> deep waters, and in this habit resembles the eel. The natives never bathe in the
> waters of this basin. A long time ago some of the people bathed in the lake, and
> they were all drowned, and eaten by *Toor-roo-dun*. (Smyth 1876: I, 436)

The township of Tooradin, named after this mythical creature, is near the eastern
shore of Western Port Bay, land now drained and known, among other things, as
a major producer of asparagus. But before drainage works began in the middle of
the 19th century, this was all part of the great Koo Wee Rup Swamp, an extensive
area of wetlands, covered with thick, almost impenetrable swamp paperbark with
mangroves along the shoreline. But 20,000 years ago, during the Last Glacial
Maximum, it was quite different. Western Port was then a lowland through which
the Lang Lang, Bass and Bunyip rivers flowed slowly from the surrounding hills
and out onto the exposed Bassian Plain (Bird 1993). Later, as the bay filled,
extensive peat swamps and wetlands extended across to French Island, which,
together with Phillip Island, was then a low rise. Similarly, the Carrum Swamp to
the northwest developed beside Port Phillip Bay once it too was filled by rising
seas. Between these two low-lying areas the land is slightly higher, much of it
covered by the Cranbourne Sands, a complex of sand sheets and dunes, of raised
ridges and intermediate swales.

Many archaeological heritage assessments have been carried out in the area
because of urban development at Pakenham, Cranbourne and the Mornington
Peninsula. These have documented numerous diffuse scatters of stone artefacts,
almost all of relatively recent age, where Bunurong people camped beside the rich
swamps and watercourses. But several studies also provide tiny glimpses into a far
older landscape of the time before and during the most arid period of the Ice Age.
The area was then far inland, on the northern side of the exposed Bassian Plain
which stretched out across to Tasmania.

The oldest artefacts come from Bend Road, Keysborough, where archaeological
work was carried out in conjunction with the construction of the Eastlink tollway
between Mitcham and Frankston (Hewitt and Allen 2010; Allen et al. 2008). A team
from La Trobe University led by Jim Allen explored the dunes beside the Carrum
Swamp (Figure 1.9). As well as uncovering relatively recent artefacts (discussed in
Chapter 3), their excavations down into the lower layers came upon a small handful
of tools which, despite the complex changes to the dunes, can be dated to at least
35,000 to 30,000 years ago, earlier than the tools from Keilor. People continued to
use the area occasionally from then on, even during the coldest, driest periods. There
is equivalent evidence from Chelsea Heights, a little to the west, where artefacts have
been found below what was later to become the Carrum Swamp (Wheeler et al.
2014). Only 16 artefacts were found in the very small area excavated, but sufficient to
show that soon after the dunes formed about 30,000 years ago people were camping
on the site, just as they were at Bend Road.

Figure 1.9 Excavations during construction of the Eastlink Freeway at Bend Road, Keysborough.

In 2004, David Rhodes found a deeply buried circular scatter of charcoal, possibly from a fireplace, on a rise above wetlands on the Koo Wee Rup floodplain near Pakenham which provided a date of 25,000 years ago (Rhodes 2004). The associated tools are broadly similar to the contemporary ones from Bend Road and those from Keilor: larger, heavier and made from a wider variety of types of stone than the small tools characteristic of the last few thousand years. A fourth site, not far away at Cranbourne, also tested as part of a heritage management study, has provided sufficient traces in the dunes beside former swampland to show, once again, that people were using the area about 20,000 years ago, at the height of the last Ice Age (Lawler and Berelov 2013).

This cluster of early sites does not mean that this was an unusually dense focus of activity immediately before or during the Last Glacial Maximum. It is largely a result of the intensity of archaeological exploration and the nature of the sediments tested. Occupation in this part of Victoria was widespread beyond the particular circumstances of the Western Port and Port Phillip sunklands, as we have seen at Keilor, 50 kilometres to the northwest. A similar distance in the opposite direction, over the hills which cut off the sunklands from the present day coast, brings us to Kilcunda. Through salvage excavations carried out in connection with the construction of the desalination plant we find intriguing hints that people also camped near the Powlett River 20,000 years ago (Kayandel Archaeological Services 2009). Their territory may well have extended down from the higher ground southward onto the dry, sparsely vegetated and windy Bassian Plain, along and around the now submerged lower reaches of the Powlett River.

Eastern ranges

Two caves far to the east – New Guinea II Cave beside the Snowy River and Cloggs Cave above the Buchan – round out what little we have in the way of early sites south of the Murray. We can think of them as highland – or at least upland – sites, especially when the sea levels were 100 metres or more below those of today. Neither has very early evidence, but both were used, if only intermittently, at and after the height of the last Ice Age.

Paul Ossa spent four seasons during the 1980s excavating near the main entrance to New Guinea II Cave and on the steep slope outside (Ossa et al. 1995) (Figure 1.10). A narrow passage leads further back into the 150-metre long main cave itself, with a stream running through it. Here there are sets of wavy parallel marks in the soft limestone walls, somewhat similar to those seen at Koonalda Cave on the Nullarbor and in caves in southeast South Australia, although some are animal scratchings rather than cultural symbols (Chapter 4). It was an awkward place to work, with massive blocks of roof-fall on the surface and throughout the accumulated sediments; these had to be broken up using drills and wedges before they could be removed. Largely because of these blocks there was no neat stratigraphic sequence, but rather a patchy and confused series of layers. Nevertheless, Paul was able to establish that people began to use the site at some time between 25,000 and 21,000 years ago.

Only a couple of hundred stone tools were found, made from different types of stone available as cobbles washed up on the banks of the river or from local limestone. Five bone tools were used for tasks such as piercing skins. Although hundreds of thousands of very small fragments of animal bone were recovered, most are those of small rodents and the like. The parts present and patterns of breakage indicate that they were the prey of owls, not the remains of people's meals. Other bones were heavily chewed by carnivorous mammals such as the Tasmanian tiger and Tasmanian devil (which later became extinct on the Australian mainland). A few bones, however, were charred: clearly the work of people.

While all of this confirms that people did visit the cave, it also shows that this was neither regular nor often. It was a place used rarely, possibly by people on occasional forays up the river valley, perhaps from their more usual territory lower down and closer to the now submerged coastal fringe – although that may not have been so attractive an area (Bowdler 2010).

Cloggs Cave, set in a high cliff overlooking the Buchan River, is in many respects similar (Flood 1980, 2010) (Figure 1.11). In her excavations Josephine Flood found recent tools, dated to the last 1000 years or so, in the area immediately outside the cave and in the uppermost layers within it. Below there were larger tools, and below these again layers with no artefacts at all (Figure 1.12). These earliest deposits, which built up more than 25,000 years ago, contained bones from several locally extinct species: the cave was then a home to rock wallabies or a carnivore's den, used by Tasmanian tigers or Tasmanian devils, while other bones

Figure 1.10 New Guinea II Cave.

were dropped by owls. By 20,000 years ago, people also began to use the site, but, as at New Guinea II, only on rare occasions. The focus of their lives would also have been 30 to 40 kilometres down the river to the south, closer to the extended coastal plain. By the time the sea began to approach its present level the cave was no longer used in the same way.

The early use of Cloggs Cave is matched by evidence on the other side of the Snowy Mountains in the Australian Capital Territory. The small, camped shelter, set between two boulders at Birrigai, was occasionally, perhaps only fleetingly, visited between 25,000 and 19,000 years ago: a somewhat surprising use of an area above the tree line during some of the coldest periods (Flood et al. 1987). While there is only this minimal evidence of the early use of the highlands on the mainland, things were different far to the south in Tasmania (then, of course, still part of the one landmass). Here the climatic extremes did not prevent, but rather encouraged, regular use of sub-glacial areas. There is abundant evidence from several sites that people in southwest Tasmania took advantage of a particular combination of circumstances in these areas to develop a pattern of seasonal movements into higher country based on hunting wallabies and, to a lesser extent, wombats (Pike-Tay et al. 2008).

Figure 1.11 Looking up the Buchan River. Cloggs Cave is near the top of the cliff in the centre of the photo (arrowed).

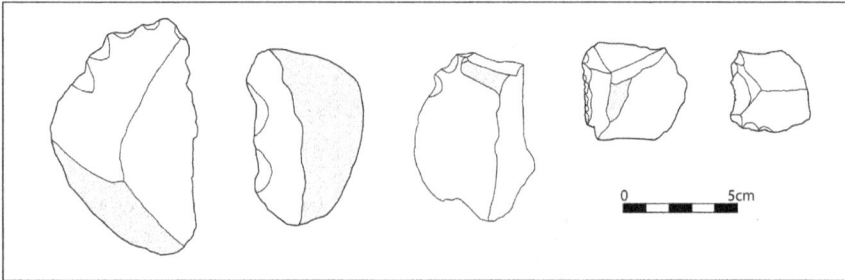

Figure 1.12 Stone tools from the lower layers at Cloggs Cave (after Flood 1980: figure 57).

So little for so long

People were in Australia for over 20,000 years before the first evidence of their presence is seen in Victoria and even much longer in southwestern South Australia. Indeed, the first three-quarters of the history of our area is barely represented in the archaeological record. Where once individuals such as the man from Keilor was the oldest known person in Australia we now find that, like his contemporaries at Kow Swamp (Chapter 6), he is closer in time to us than to the Mungo Lady and Mungo Man.

Why is this so? Is it simply a matter of the accident of discovery, of research intensity and strategy – remembering how recently most evidence has come to light? Are we looking in the wrong places or in the wrong way? Was the focus of people's lives along the ancient, now submerged, coastline? Or is this a true reflection of a small, scattered population seldom using and reusing particular places in such a way as to leave identifiable concentrations of rubbish behind them?

Sometimes a lack of evidence encourages us to assume or create broad generalised ideas about times and places no matter how long or extensive they may be. But what little we have of early Victoria cannot be easily treated in this way. The few sites described here clearly differ in type, location and setting. The types of stone in each area are invariably local, and the tools and techniques used to make them show no consistency across the state. And they are also far from contemporary – unless we stretch 'contemporary' to cover events thousands of years, or hundreds of generations, apart. So we have no grounds for seeing any commonality; rather, the impression is of diversity, reflecting local adaptations or behaviour as the earliest known Victorians made the best they could of the environments in which they lived.

2
Time and place at Gariwerd

The story of Gariwerd takes us into Jardwadjali country and also into a fundamental aspect of Aboriginal society – the intimate interplay between social, cultural and physical landscapes. We can trace links between site use, stone tools, the environment and art that reflect long-term changes in local conceptual and ideological associations alongside more mundane economic systems. Here, as elsewhere, it is possible to say that while the physical location of sites and features remained the same, their place in the environment changed.

Gariwerd (the Grampians) is a dramatic series of sandstone mountain ranges rising up to 700 metres above the surrounding plains (Figures 2.1, 2.2). It is a rugged and romantic place, with steep east-facing escarpments and shallow slopes running down again to the west. Between the high ridges are long, narrow valleys with rivers running out to the north and south and swampy flats where drainage is more restricted. The complex terrain is reflected in the richness and diversity of vegetation, fed by a higher rainfall than across the surrounding plains.

The ranges were, of course, affected by the major continental-scale changes in climate. About 18,000 years ago, at the height of the last Ice Age, when all of Australia was at its coldest and driest, the much expanded arid zone covered a far greater area. Gariwerd would have been on its southern edge (Figure 2.2) (Dodson et al. 1992). The higher escarpments were then treeless and covered by heath or scrub, while in the sheltered valleys there was open grassland with a scattering of trees. But throughout this arid period the ranges were relatively well watered, diverse and attractive compared to the very dry, barren plains.

As warmer and wetter conditions began to develop around 10,000 years ago, there was a general increase in water availability. Vegetation change followed rapidly, with a succession of casuarina-dominated woodlands, followed by increases in eucalypts and grasses. By 7000 years ago the open red gum woodland with grassy understorey was already established in the Victoria Valley. Today the ranges are clothed in dense vegetation and are often inaccessible except to the most dedicated bushwalkers. However, Aboriginal people in the past did move into and through the area using tracks such as those seen by Charles Hall in 1841, which were

Figure 2.1 Looking northeast over Halls Gap.

Figure 2.2 Gariwerd today: rugged topography and thick vegetation.

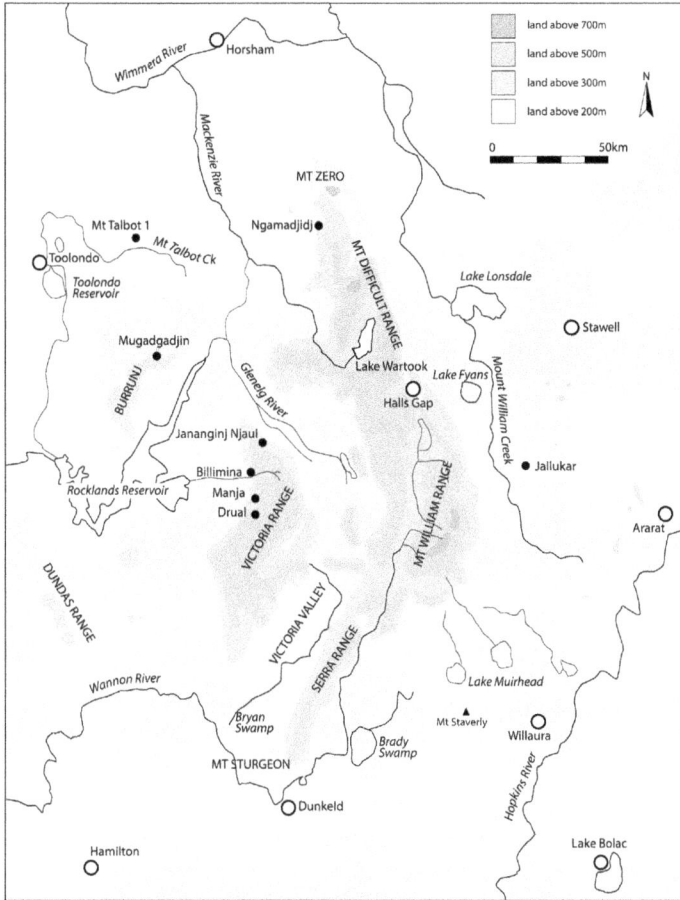

Figure 2.3 Gariwerd and surrounding areas.

formed by the natives in travelling over any particular pass. There was one across the Grampian Range, leading up a wild romantic glen over onto the source of the Glenelg ... another through the tea-tree scrub of the Wannon, near Mount Sturgeon ... (Bride 1898: 272)

Regular burning may also have kept the valleys, and perhaps other areas, more open than they are now – although this would have been more difficult during a wetter period, 7000 to 5500 years ago, when the ranges may have been far more inaccessible.

The geological structure created numerous overhangs and shelters which characterise the archaeology of the area. Gariwerd is also famous as having the densest concentration of rock art in Victoria, with over a hundred art sites recorded (Gunn 1983, 1987). Most of these are small, with only a handful of painted marks. But there are larger rockshelters with many individual motifs. The

Figure 2.4 Ngamadjidj shelter.

most extensive is Billimina, perhaps the most visited Aboriginal site in Victoria. Unfortunately, this means it is necessary to protect the art from vandalism – graffiti began to appear even by the 1890s, and too many people have not learnt better behaviour since. Most of the other well-known shelters also have strong protective grilles: the best one can say about them is that they do their job, for the only one that is at all pleasing to the eye is at Ngamadjidj (Figure 2.4).

Surprises at Billimina

The airy sheltered space at Billimina lies beneath a massive sandstone formation jutting out near the top of a steep-sided spur in the Victoria Range. The natural roof curves high over a flat floor about 90 square metres in area (Figure 2.5). Twelve metres of the back wall are covered with paintings up to a height of 2.7 metres above the present surface.

There are nearly 3000 individual motifs painted in red ochre, with a handful that are white and yellow: the majority are simple lines, some of which may be arranged in groups, 45 simple human (or human-like) figures, animal tracks and other small designs (Figure 2.6).

This extensive panel of art attracted European interest from the mid-19th century, explaining the long succession of names given to the shelter: Red Rock, Painted Rock, Blackfellows Rock, Glen Isla Rock and Glenisla I. In 1990, the Aboriginal

Figure 2.5 Billimina shelter during Victoria Archaeological Survey excavations, 1975 (photo: Aboriginal Victoria).

Figure 2.6 Paintings on the back wall of Billimina shelter.

organisation Brambuk Inc. and the Koorie Tourism Unit of the Victorian Tourism Commission set out to replace names such as these (Clark and Harradine 1990). 'Billimina shelter' was adopted for this site after the traditional name for Cultivation Creek, which runs through the valley below.

The first European to visit Billimina was Samuel Carter, the holder of Glenisla station, who came across it while looking for stray cattle in 1859 or 1860. His Aboriginal companions denied all knowledge of the site and its art: is it that they could not or would not tell him anything? By the end of the 19th century, Billimina was the subject of one of the first formal studies of rock art in Australia, and the start of a long history of academic interest in the site. This focused on the paintings until excavations were attempted by successive staff from the National Museum of Victoria in the 1950s and 1960s. Little came of their efforts. In 1975, Peter Coutts and the Victoria Archaeological Survey returned to the site, recorded the art in detail and excavated an extensive area beneath it (Coutts and Lorblanchet 1982). But that was not the end of the story. In 1980, Benn Gunn recorded the art yet again, and new digital technologies are now being used to create 3D images (Almeida and Lovett 2016).

In the 1990s, Caroline Bird and I had developed a particular interest in the area through scrambling over the steep, rocky slopes of nearby Mount Talbot in search of sites, and through her excavations at a small rockshelter. We felt that the full potential of the previous excavations had not been realised, and were encouraged to set up a project in conjunction with local Aboriginal communities and Aboriginal Affairs Victoria to reanalyse and fully publish the finds (Bird and Frankel 2005; Frankel and Bird 2013).

The excavators in 1975 opened up a chequerboard of 13 1x1 metre squares along the back wall and extending out across the shelter. As in other Gariwerd shelters, the deposit is shallow, ranging in depth from about 50 centimetres at the back to 1 metre further out. Typically, looser, darker, more organically rich soils overlie consolidated and compacted clays from which the organic material has been leached out. At the time of the excavations the few radiocarbon dates which could then be obtained indicated that the site had been used for less than 2000 years. The idea that Gariwerd was not used until so very recently had significant implications for how all archaeologists understood its place in western Victorian history. The short duration also discouraged attempts to look for changes within the site, which was seen as having similar artefacts throughout its occupation. Caroline and I wanted to confirm the dating and to see if we could identify any variation through time. To do so we needed far more radiocarbon dates. Fortunately, soil samples had been kept in storage by Aboriginal Affairs Victoria, which we could use. In the two decades since the excavations, new radiocarbon dating techniques had been developed, so that extremely small samples of charcoal could be used, whereas before substantial amounts were needed. We submitted 15 samples from several sites for dating. To our surprise – shock might be a better word – these showed that the shelter was used consistently for at least 11,000 years, five times as long as anyone had imagined (Bird et al. 1998). And, as there were no samples from the very compacted lowest layers, we are confident that it was used for many thousands of years before that. Almost by accident, we had entirely

Figure 2.7 Looking across the valley toward Drual, in the exposed rocks on the right of the centre of the picture.

changed the way we should view the history of the site and the ranges as a whole. This was reinforced by evidence from Drual.

Drual

The rockshelter at Drual is smaller and far less accessible than Billimina, especially as it is off the tourist route and to reach it one needs to struggle up a steep climb through dense tea-tree, sawgrass and prickly acacia scrub. It is not as well protected from the weather as the overhang at Billimina, and perhaps it always needed additional windbreaks to make it comfortable. The floor slopes a great deal, and archaeological deposits only accumulated in a small area towards the western end of the shelter.

The 57 individual motifs were painted on the back wall, both above the archaeological deposit and off to one side. Some are red, others white, and Benn Gunn has argued that the colours and motifs used show distinct periods of painting. The earliest are red 'human' figures and emu tracks, followed by large simple white designs and then later emu tracks (Gunn 1983).

The excavations in 1975 revealed up to 70 centimetres of deposits, which, like those at Billimina, have compacted soils below the looser more recent upper layers. The original radiocarbon dates suggested occupation from about 2000 years ago, as at Billimina. Once again, our new, more extensive program of dating, with the ability to use material from the lower deposits, transformed understanding of the

Figure 2.8 Drual rockshelter.

site. People were there 26,000 years ago, even before they were using Billimina. We could now see that the ranges were used during the driest and least hospitable period of the last Ice Age.

Other sites

Caroline and I also re-examined the finds from several other shelters excavated in the 1970s: Mugadgadjin (formerly Black Range 2), Manja (Cave of Hands), and Jananginj Njaui A and B (Camp of the Emu's Foot). Each has a distinct suite of paintings and archaeological deposits of varied depth and age. None turned out to be anywhere near as old as Drual and Billimina. Additional dates from Caroline's own excavations at Mount Talbot 1 and from Ngamadjidj (Cave of Ghosts) show these sites were in use by 5000 years ago (Bird 1987; Gunn 2003).

Sequences and strategies in stone tools

Although we have only a patchy archaeological record, with an irregular representation of periods at different sites and sets of artefacts that vary considerably in integrity and duration, we were able to define nine assemblages, or sets of objects. These fall into two main very broad chronological groups. The Early group includes tools from the oldest deposits at Drual and Billimina, made and discarded before about 5000 years ago. A Late group (after about 5000 years

Figure 2.9 Mugadgadjin shelter.

ago) includes finds from all the sites; for two of them, very recent (Final) material of the last 1000 years could also be separated.

As we have seen, Drual has the earliest archaeological evidence in the region, with basal radiocarbon dates of greater than 25,000 years ago. It would have been good to separate out shorter periods within its Early deposits, but this was not possible, so over 15,000 years of discarded artefacts have to be lumped together. The Late Phase at Drual also conflates thousands of years of activities, spanning the last 5000 years. The Early Phase at Billimina, too, incorporates artefacts from a very long period, perhaps 10,000 years, if not more. At this site the Late (about 5000 to 1000 years ago) and Final (within the last millennium) phases can be differentiated. These chronological divisions form the basis for defining assemblages of stone tools and their analysis.

Stone tools have many stories to tell, opening up leads into separate but interrelated aspects of ancient society. The presence of different types of stone tells us about how widely people ranged across their territory and how they were connected to others. The choice of which rock is also determined by the types of tools to be made, and these together are linked to techniques of manufacture. The forms and function of tools, and waste products from their manufacture, show what people were doing in different places or at different times.

One striking feature of the Gariwerd stone tools is the diversity of rock types selected. Up to a dozen types of stone were used, each with different qualities for both manufacture and use. They can be grouped according to where they are to be found, some within Gariwerd and others from the surrounding region.

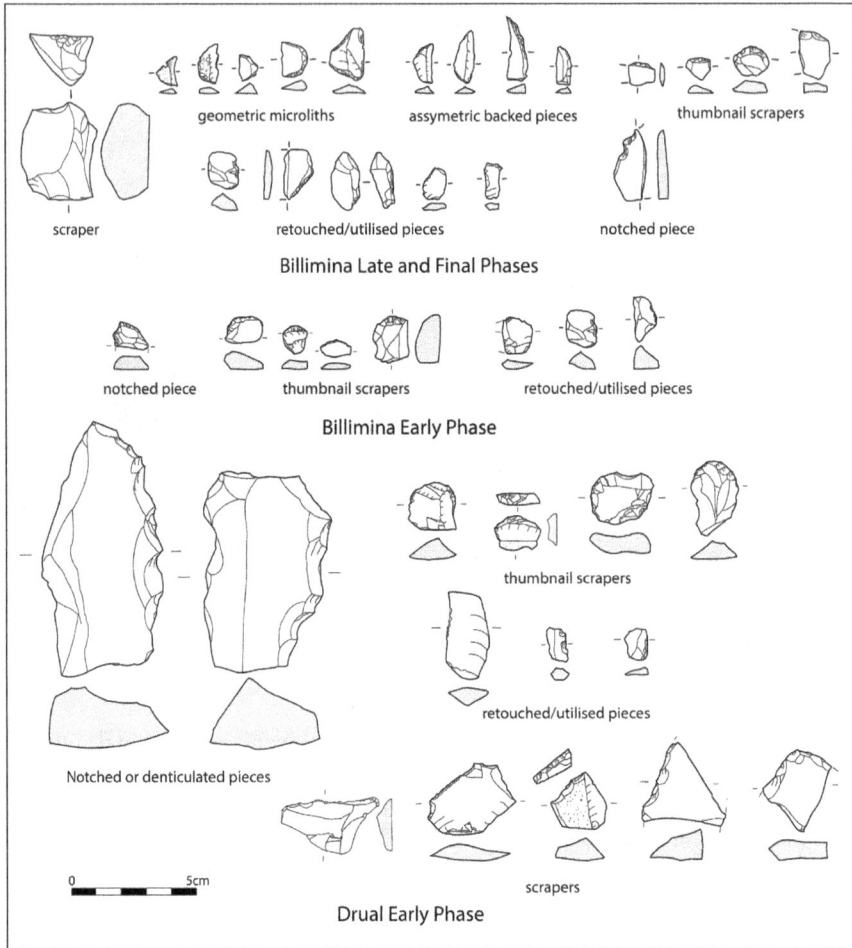

Figure 2.10 Stone tools from Billimina and Drual.

Quartz is generally the most common type of stone, making up more than 50 per cent of artefacts in all sites except Manja. Within this there are two groups: sites with less than about two-thirds (67 per cent) quartz, and those with 80 per cent quartz or more. This could result from differences in technology or the ways in which quartz shatters. It is not chronological. The other types of stone used also vary from one assemblage to another. The earlier assemblages tend to be more diverse, including stone from different places, both east and north of the ranges; the most recent are dominated by Grampians Group rock types, local to Gariwerd. A similar domination of Late and especially Final assemblages by local stone is seen at Billimina and most other sites. At Mugadgadjin, there is a slightly different pattern, perhaps related to its location in the Burrunj (Black Range) outlier on the western fringe of Gariwerd. Here, silcrete from much further north of the ranges is dominant in the Late Phase, signalling that this may have been part of a different land-use system, linked more to the semi-arid Wimmera and Mallee to the north and not dissimilar to social patterns seen in the 19th century.

The quantity of artefacts discarded at sites during the later periods varies. This reflects differences in the activities carried out or how frequently each place was used. Unfortunately, Billimina is the only place for which relative rates at which tools were discarded can be estimated for more than two phases. Here a decline in intensity of site use from sometime after 7000 years ago was followed by an increase in the last millennium.

All the Gariwerd assemblages showed the use of the same general approach to working stone, with most variations related to the demands imposed by different raw materials. The clearest change in technology is the appearance in the Late Phase (after about 5000 years ago) of specialised types of cores made on large flakes, which can be associated with the production of small blades which were then blunted or backed along one edge. These backed tools were inserted into wooden hafts and used for a variety of tasks (Robertson et al. 2009; Fullagar 2016). Among other things, they are often regarded by archaeologists as spear barbs: in one unusual burial, numerous barbs were found embedded in a man killed and buried in the Sydney suburb of Narrabeen (Fullagar et al. 2009). These backed blades form part of a suite of small tools which become most common across much of Australia after about 4500 years ago, although there are many earlier examples and their presence reflects individual site histories and local traditions (Hiscock and Attenbrow 1998; McNiven 2000a).

The tools in Gariwerd fall into two broad groups: backed tools and edged tools. Local quartzite from the Grampians Group was preferred for the former and quartz, volcanic glass or silcrete for the latter. Backed tools are not found in the Early Phase, but only occur during later periods, as elsewhere. About half the edged tools are 'informal' – not made to any specific design. These were made using all types of raw material in all periods. Most of the rest are scrapers, including both larger examples with convex or straight retouched edges and small convex, 'thumbnail' scrapers, which make up the largest category of formal or deliberately designed tools. These were only made of quartz, fine-grained siliceous materials and volcanic glass.

The types of tools made and used also provide some insights into site function. The ratios of backed to edged tools vary from one backed to more than four edged tools at Jananginj Njaui B to two backed for each edged tool at Late Phase Billimina and at Jananginj Njaui A. Differences like these can be explained in a variety of ways. For example, at Graman, in northern New South Wales, Isabel McBryde (1977) noted a coincidence in the occurrence of backed pieces and animal remains: the proportions of backed pieces (which she saw as spear barbs) and macropod bones increased at the same time. She suggested that this was due to an increase in hunting tools, directly related to the availability of different animal species. This, in turn, was related to changes in the local environment. The shift between the Late and Final Phases at Billimina may signal a similar change.

However, another concept can also be developed. The higher levels of maintenance tools (that is, tools such as scrapers used for general purposes including making wooden items) are more likely to indicate a variety of domestic activities. Conversely, higher proportions of extractive tools (used for hunting) can

Figure 2.11 Rock art in Gariwerd: red paintings, dry-pigment drawings and white paintings.

indicate a more specialised use of sites. If we assume that hunting was primarily carried out by men, then this raises the possibility that high proportions of spear barbs were the mark of men's sites, while more generalised, maintenance tools indicate occupation and activities of family groups.

These two modes of explanation are, of course, not mutually exclusive. The change at Billimina may not be simply an economic one reflecting a change in the local resources, but may also be related to the broader site function, moving from a special purpose (possibly a men's) site in the Late Phase to a more generalised, multi-purpose site in the Final Phase.

We have, therefore, several significant changes taking place in different aspects of tool manufacture and use. At the broad scale there was the change from Early to Late phases with an increasing use of local, Grampians Group raw material in the place of more varied stone types brought in from further afield. At a more specific scale there are differences showing the more restricted use of sites (possibly by men) and later a more general use of sites for varied purposes by whole family groups.

Sequences in art styles

We can now turn to rock art. Close study of overlapping or superimposed motifs has allowed Ben Gunn to set out a relative chronology with three distinct phases (1987, 2008). The earliest, Art Phase A, is characterised by red paintings; the intermediate, Art Phase B, by red and black drawings; and the most recent, Art Phase C, by white paintings. Absolute dating is difficult, but several lines of evidence confirm the relative sequence.

The red paintings of Art Phase A may have been made between about 3500 and 1600 years ago. These paintings are, as the name implies, typically in red ochre, with bars as the dominant motif. Simple human figures, lines and emu tracks are common while red hand stencils and handprints are also found. Phase A sites occur in local clusters, each with a major site surrounded by several smaller sites. Most sites have one particular dominant motif. With the exception of the ubiquitous bars, motif types also seem to cluster in different parts of the ranges. As most motifs of this phase can be constructed from combinations or variations of bars and emu track motifs, Ben Gunn has argued that they form a 'tightly interconnected system' and that the distinctive patterns of distribution indicate that it was closely linked to particular places. The symbols in the art could therefore directly relate to mythology tied to named places.

Art Phase B red and black drawings are probably about 1000 years old. These fine line drawings in red ochre and charcoal have a similar range and proportion of motif types as those of the earlier, red paintings of Phase A, with the exception of emu tracks, which are rare. There is, however, less structural similarity between motifs, while the human figures appear more animated and less stylised. There is little specialisation in distribution, although there is a concentration of sites with drawings at the north end of the range. Here, Ben Gunn speculates that the freer drawing style and looser structure indicate that similar art was also produced on other media, such as bark.

Art Phase C white paintings probably date from about 800 years ago and may have continued to be produced into the 19th century, probably into the contact period. The range of motifs is similar to the earlier phases, although bars are rare. The motifs are not structurally linked as they were in the red paintings of Phase A, and the technical execution is generally comparatively crude. These sites tend to occur singly rather than in clusters. They are also located around the periphery of the ranges in easily accessible locations. This contrasts with the earlier art, which was more widely distributed and often less accessible.

While indicating strong continuity, Ben Gunn's analysis and characterisation of the phases allows their interpretation not only as stylistically distinct periods of artistic activity but also as serving different ends, related to the social context within which the art was produced. Seen in this way, the art of Phase A can be regarded as tightly controlled and associated with particular locations, perhaps carried out in specific ritual contexts, while Phases B and C represent a more casual production of publicly accessible art. This explanation fits well with the differences in site use suggested by the stone tools. A similar sequence may also be seen in the northeast of Victoria, at sites such as Mudgegonga 2 (Chapter 9).

Out of the shelters: Lake Wartook

In 1885, Samuel Carter (we've met him before at Billimina) joined John Dickson Derry in advocating the construction of the Wartook dam on the Mackenzie River. By 1889 it had been built, extended and improved, initiating one of the largest water supply systems in Australia, where water from Gariwerd is now carried to a vast area of country and more than four dozen towns. While working on the project, John Derry

> found the site of a stone axe factory, marked by heaps of chips lying around large boulders, which appeared to have been used as anvils, at Wartook, in the Northern Grampians, near Horsham. (Worsnop 1897: 99)

By 1997, maintenance work was needed on Derry's old dam wall, so the water was released, exposing land that had not been seen for a hundred years. Extensive

Figure 2.12 Exposed shores of Lake Wartook.

scatters of stone tools were revealed on the muddy surface, still lying where they were when the slowly rising waters had gently covered them more than a century before. Although Derry's 'axe-factory' could not be found, this exposure provided a unique chance to see another side of the archaeology of Gariwerd, for normally the dense vegetation makes it difficult, and more often than not entirely impossible, to find open-air sites – the scatters of stone tools that typify campsites and activity areas (Bird 1989; Edmonds 1995). The evidence from Lake Wartook counterbalances any impression that the use of the ranges focused entirely on shelter sites and was always associated with rock art.

When Ben Gunn drew my attention to the newly exposed surface at Wartook it was obvious that the chance should not be missed (Figure 2.12). Fortunately, one of our La Trobe students, Jacinta Essling, was also sufficiently excited by the prospect and made this the subject of her honours thesis (Essling 1999). As we walked across the muddy flats of the exposed lake bed, stone tools seemed to be everywhere – too many, indeed, to be able to record them all before the dam was refilled (Figure 2.13). We did not find the 'large boulders' noted by Derry, but Jacinta and later Ben Gunn (2003) were able to document numerous scatters of stone-flaking areas where tools were made – and hearths, one of which provided a radiocarbon date of about 4000 years ago. Although the rest of the finds cannot be dated in this way, it is likely that none are significantly older.

A wide array of chipped stone artefact types was identified, similar to those in Late Phase assemblages from the shelters: cores, the flakes struck off them, and finished tools including backed blades and thumbnail scrapers. There were also small anvils, used when making stone tools, and small grindstones for milling

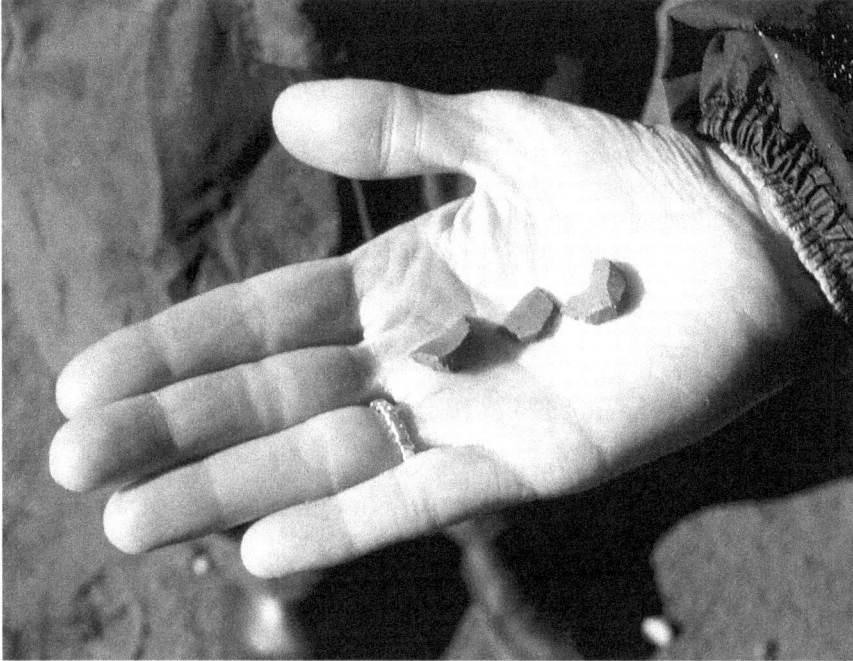

Figure 2.13 Small stone tools from the shores of Lake Wartook.

seeds or crushing ochre for painting. As we have seen in the shelters, quartz was the most common type of stone, but there were also other local types. Some, such as tachylite or volcanic glass, was brought to Wartook from elsewhere in Gariwerd, if not further away, perhaps from sources in Dja Dja Wurrung country, north of Ballarat (Smith and Kerr 2016).

We are lucky to have this insight into the way people were living in the valley, close to the river. The variety of tools suggests that these archaeological remains would have been the kind of residues from many different activities, similar to the abandoned campsites that George Augustus Robinson visited in 1841, when he

went in quest of the tribe. Passed hurriedly over wooded and rocky ranges and anon through gullies, my guides following admirably on the trail of the blacks. Saw numerous bark huts, similar to those made by the natives of Van Diemen's land. Entered a lofty and close stringy-bark forest, about west from Mt William, with bare room to squeeze our horses through. Under the highest bluff of the Victoria on the banks of a rapid stream 8 feet in width [probably a tributary of the Glenelg], we found the camp, but the natives were gone. Numerous weapons and articles of aboriginal industry lay in the huts and emu shells about the fibres. The *Xanthorrhea Humilis*, the buckcup of the natives, was scattered profusely at and around the camping place. The young roots are eaten by the aborigines, the dried stems are attached to the spears called Haramal; and, from this wood, the natives also in their pristine state procured fire. We left their property, as we found it untouched, with the addition of a few blankets, handkerchiefs, and other articles, and small coronation medals which I had distributed generally to the tribes. Finding the natives would neither personally appear or answer, I thought it fruitless to waste further time and returned, purposing hereafter to communicate with these tribes. From a point east of the Grampians, near the camp of the natives, the water fell over large blocks of coarse granite, forming a cascade fringed with woodbines and overhanging shrubs. The numerous indications seen led me to suppose that this secluded spot was the favorite resort of the blacks ... (Kenyon 1928: 155–56)

Into the 19th century

The people whose camps Robinson passed by, or perhaps their near kin, may even have been those who left some unusual things for Ben Gunn to find in three small sites near to one another on the ridge above Cultivation Creek in the Victoria Range (Gunn 2009). Two slabs of bark were found in one shelter, 29 modified wooden sticks and two pieces of cut bark in a second, and 18 pieces of bark and four wooden sticks in the third. These were not ancient wooden artefacts, like the wooden boomerangs, digging sticks and spears at Wyrie Swamp (Chapter 4), but are very recent indeed – the bark slabs were clearly cut using a steel axe. Even so, wood or bark seldom survives, so these items are of special interest.

Ben Gunn interprets all these items as related to the same type of activity: curing animal skins. The bark slabs are the size and shape of those known to have been used when pegging out possum skins, in preparation for making cloaks, as discussed at Glen Aire (Chapter 3). They remind us very directly of the many tools and products we normally do not see in the archaeological record. But, more than that, they are evidence of some of the last traditional activities in the shelters in Gariwerd before the Jardwadjali were dispossessed of their country.

Changing places

Putting together the various lines of evidence, from art, archaeology and environment, we can see a complex story of cultural adaptation and change over 26,000 years, with varied strategies of land use and regional associations. Here we can trace the way in which new cultural taskscapes developed within this ever-changing natural landscape. The first people we know to have visited Drual did so before the onset of the most arid period at the peak of the last Ice Age. We also have traces of people using the Mallee at the same time.

Lake Tyrrell, 200 kilometres to the north of Drual, is today the largest salt lake in Victoria within what is now a semi-arid land of parallel sand ridges, dunes and saline lakes covered in mallee scrub. But at that time it was less inhospitable. The lake was full and people camped on the crescentic 'lunette' or clay dune formed on its eastern shore. Stone tools excavated at Box Gully, along with the bones of the small animals the people hunted, are from between 32,000 and 26,000 years ago (Richards 2004; Richards et al. 2007) (Chapter 2). Box Gully and Drual – or

Figure 2.14 Gariwerd today (top) and as it might have been 18,000 years ago, looking similar to the red centre (bottom).

at least these two regions – could well have been part of the same broad cultural territory. But then the climate changed. It was increasingly colder and drier, the flow of water became less reliable and the lake levels fluctuated before drying up completely. True desert had come to the Mallee. Use of the area declined as people retreated south to better-favoured places like Gariwerd and north to the Murray River, where freshwater shell middens, such as those at Karadoc Swamp, Merbein Common and Monak, have been dated to between 25,000 and 20,000 years ago.

Eighteen thousand years ago Gariwerd would have stood out from an arid sand plain, much as the ranges of central Australia do today. During this harsher arid period it became a refuge as the core territory for groups making less frequent, less intensive and more wide-ranging use of the dry surrounding plains, a pattern for which we can find parallels in arid central Australia (Smith 1989, 2013; see also Williams et al. 2013). Their forays away from the richer and more reliable resources of the ranges are marked, archaeologically, by the acquisition of raw materials that they collected and brought back to their core territory.

As conditions improved, with more reliable water supplies in the semi-arid regions to the north and the development of wetlands in the surrounding plains, it became possible for people to spend more time, if not most time, away from Gariwerd. With warmer conditions and increased rainfall towards 10,000 years ago, the ranges became more heavily vegetated and the plains less dry. At later times, changing rainfall increased water availability both in the ranges and in the rivers, creeks and lakes of the surrounding plains. From a human point of view, the place of Gariwerd in the perceived and useable environment must have changed significantly in response to these fluctuations, as seen in the use of different types of stone.

Further changes can be linked to the increased stress brought about by a drier episode from about 5500 to 2000 years ago, when there was less intensive use of Billimina. It, and other shelters, may have been visited only on particular occasions. If the red paintings of Art Phase A were painted at this time, they may be associated with the use of shelters by men out hunting and engaged in more esoteric, religious activities involving rock art. Meanwhile, more general use of the ranges continued with open-air camps in the valleys and beside swamps and watercourses, as seen at Lake Wartook.

The use of the ranges changed again in the last millennium. Many smaller, remote shelters, perhaps now more difficult to reach with the growth of denser vegetation, were no longer used at all. Larger shelters, especially on the periphery of the ranges, became places for general domestic, rather than special, activities. The relative isolation of Gariwerd from other areas is signalled by the greater use of local raw materials and a decline in the use of silcrete and other fine-grained material from beyond the ranges, in spite of their better flaking qualities for producing regular, designed tool types. While Gariwerd became more isolated and more inward-looking, things were different in the surrounding plains. In the southwest Wimmera, the focus of occupation was on lakes and swamps and spread along the lines of rivers (Chapter 7). In some areas the lack of stone led people to draw on sources in the northern and western parts of the ranges and further afield, one facet of the long-distance, open social connections appropriate in relatively poor regions. This broader inclusive strategy was not so necessary in and around Gariwerd itself, where rivers and wetlands developed, and where fish weirs

> were numerous at the time of my residence [1841–42], and had apparently been much more so, judging from the traces left by them in the swampy margins of the river. At these places we found many low sod banks extending across the shallow branches of the river, with apertures at intervals, in which were placed long, narrow, circular nets (like a large stocking) made of rush-work. Heaps of muscle shells were also found abounding on the banks, and old mia-mias where the earth around was strewed with the balls formed in the mouth when chewing the farinaceous matter out of the bulrush root. (Charles Hall in Bride 1898: 271)

In the 19th century, Jawadjali people continued to use their traditional lands as long as possible, perhaps the more inaccessible areas of Gariwerd again providing a refuge for them, this time from the European settlers who took over their country. A hundred and fifty years later they again have control of their heritage, displayed to advantage at the Brambuk Cultural Centre in Halls Gap.

3
Along the Victorian coast

Coasts are complex and capricious. The shoreline is immediately at the mercy of waves and weather, and over the long term by changes in sea level which affected its very location and form. As anyone whose holiday has been spoilt by wind and storms can appreciate, frequent bad weather would certainly have limited the use of beaches during the winter in the past as much as in the present. But, even at other times, tidal variations as well as uncertain weather suggest opportunistic use rather than longer-term planning. Where there were concentrations of other plants and animals in wetlands adjacent to the back dunes, these would have been the main attraction, with shellfish providing only an occasional supplement to those primary resources. Coastal economies could therefore never have been more than one part – often only one minor part – of broader patterns of land use. Although always linked to their hinterland as one component within each local regional system, it is worth dealing with much of the coastal zone together to highlight common aspects as well as significant variations (Fresløv and Frankel 1999). In this chapter I will concentrate on the south-facing coasts of Victoria; the nature and history of the southeast of South Australia will be considered in Chapter 4.

Some of the variability in archaeological evidence – and of course the behaviours that led to its formation – can be attributed to the nature of the coast itself. The Victorian coast today is far from uniform (Bird 1993). There are long stretches of sandy beaches, such as Discovery Bay to the west and the appropriately named Ninety Mile Beach in Gippsland to the east, where Mallacoota and the Gippsland Lakes can be seen as akin to the nearby coastal New South Wales, apart from a greater exposure to prevailing westerly winds. Here we find lagoons and lakes close to the steep woodland slopes of the Snowy Mountains. The central coastline is broken into by the two major embayments of Port Phillip and Western Port with mudflat and low wave-energy shores. Elsewhere, low cliffs flank smaller coves, some with sandy beaches, others with extensive rock-platforms.

Of course, all this coastline is relatively recent. When the Ice Age sea level was as much as 125 metres below the present level it exposed a low, flat plain between Victoria and Tasmania (Lambeck and Chappell 2001; Lewis et al. 2013). King, Flinders and other islands were then low hills. Some 14,000 years ago, Tasmania was completely cut off and the coasts on either side of Bass Strait began to assume

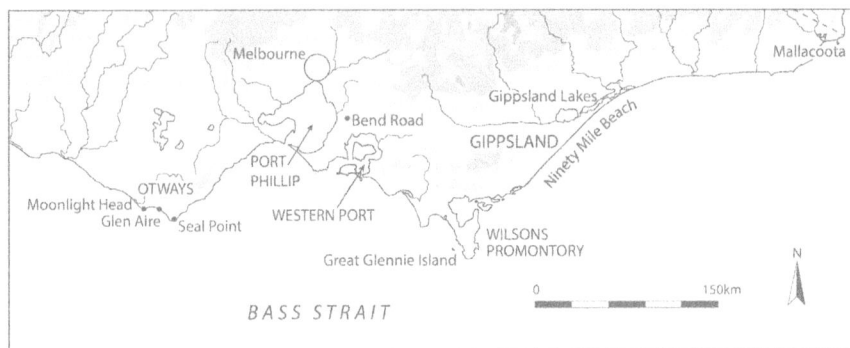

Figure 3.1 Central and eastern coasts of Victoria.

their present form, although as the sea was at times 1 to 2 metres above its present level this was – and still is – a work in progress. The impact of the loss of land and the reshaping of the coast on people remains unclear, especially if these areas were relatively unattractive (Bowdler 2010). Did these events, as is sometimes suggested, cause major disruptions? Did the sea encroach too slowly for people to be aware of it, or were the effects sometimes swift and dramatic enough to be remembered in oral traditions and myths for many generations (Nunn and Reid 2015)?

Shell middens

The shell-mounds in Victoria are, as a rule, never opened by anyone. Few people know that they were formed by the natives; and there is therefore no wanton injury done to them. In one or two places I have seen a shell-mound cut through where a track to the coast has been formed; but the old middens are not interfered with; and future archaeologists will find abundant fields for their research, in all parts of Australia, when more attention is given to the habits of the natives and a deeper interest is felt in their earlier history. (Smyth 1878, I: 242)

The word 'midden' is rarely used in modern English – apart from in archaeology. Originally from Old Norse, it refers to dumps of refuse, especially the remains of meals. For archaeologists it is generally reserved for the heaps and scatters of shells which provide the most obvious and most common evidence of past activity along coasts and rivers. But this single label hides a great diversity. Elsewhere in Australia, middens can be of great size, most impressively in the tropics at Weipa, where mounds may be hundreds of metres long and up to 10 metres in height, the result of numerous episodes of shellfish harvesting from among the mangroves over many generations. No such rich resources were available in Victoria, and here most middens are small or, even where they can be traced over many metres within beach dunes or along nearby cliffs, they generally comprise thin and patchy layers of shells. Many have been documented, although the distribution of known sites

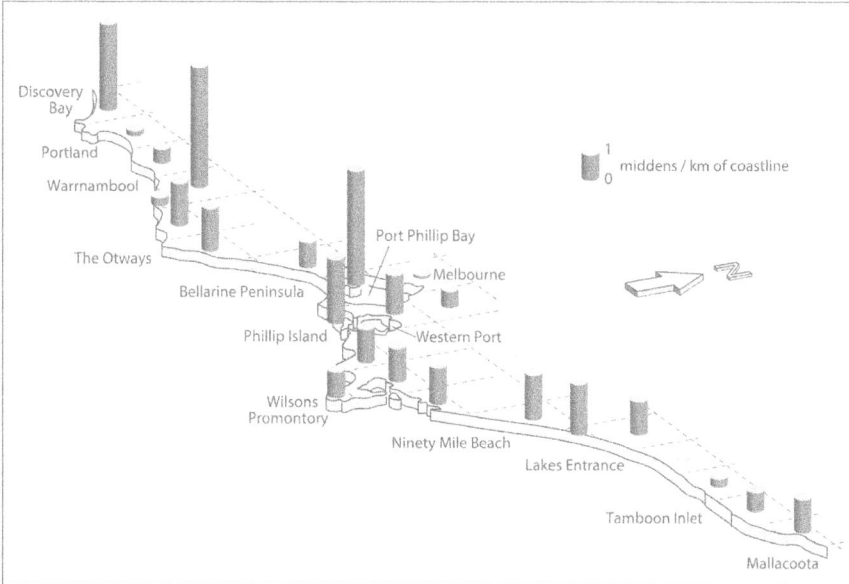

Figure 3.2 Numbers of middens recorded along the coast of Victoria.

(Figure 3.2) is a little deceptive as this is to some extent a product of the intensity of archaeological research.

When, and to what extent, was the coast important? Simple questions, but surprisingly difficult to answer. And to do so we need to take a brief detour into aspects of archaeological practice. Some years ago I prepared versions of Figure 3.3 (Frankel 1991a; Bird and Frankel 1991a; Fresløv and Frankel 1999; see also Frankel 1991b). This is one way of counting the number of shell middens along the Victorian coast at different times – there are others! You can read this diagram in different ways. The most obvious is to read it from right to left, telling a story of a massive increase in the number of sites during the last 3000 years, suggesting a greater use of the coast. Alternatively, it can be read the other way round. Archaeological sites are fragile, none more so than coastal shell middens. From left to right the diagram illustrates the decay and disappearance of middens through time, less of a story about people than about erosion. But wait … it is not even as simple as that. This diagram shows the number of *dated* middens; that is, sites selected for excavation and analysis. Imagine yourself as an archaeologist with a choice of excavating one of two middens. One has thick, undisturbed layers of shell; the other is a scanty scatter. The former is certainly the more attractive for addressing interesting questions of collection and consumption. Regular choices of the better-preserved sites creates an inherent bias against more poorly preserved and probably older examples.

And, as we will see, while middens are conspicuous and numerous, they only represent one small part of coastal economies. Some middens are the product of

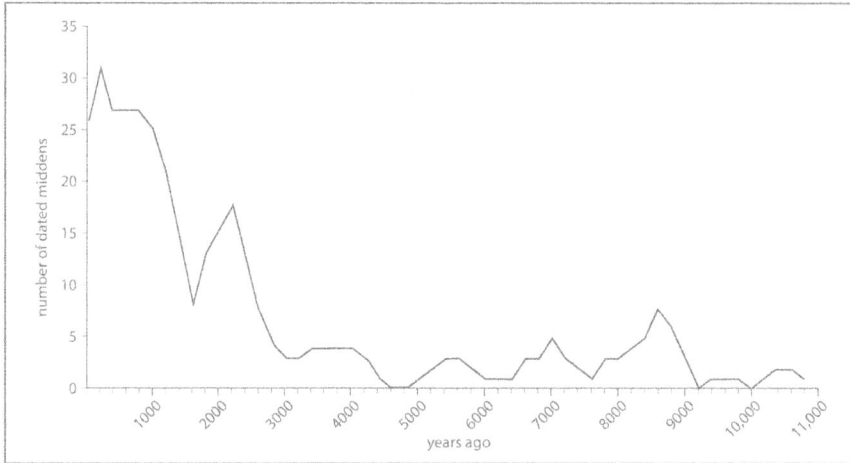

Figure 3.3 Number of dated middens on the Victorian coast (after Fresløv and Frankel 1999: figure 2).

only occasional and brief visits to the seashore, but even those representing longer or greater use of marine resources must be set within a broader context, where people drew on the richer and more varied plants and animals in adjacent wetlands and larger inland estates and territories.

However, middens are especially useful to us through their potential for exploring aspects of economy and decision making at a fine scale, something not so easily done with other types of sites. To illustrate this, and their general variability, it is worth looking closely at a few examples. We can start with three sites in the Otway Ranges – Gundbanud country (Scarlett 1977; Clark 1980: 184–91; Niewójt 1990) – where the sandstone and mudstone cliffs of the rugged coast drop sharply to the sea. Small isolated beaches and rock-platforms lie at the base of the cliffs, washed over at high tide, while inland the steep rounded hills were covered with temperate rainforest, difficult of access.

Picnics at Moonlight Head

Alec Neave, a local dairy farmer in the Otway Ranges, directed Ron Vanderwal and me to the midden at Moonlight Head. We stood on the cliffs above the site, looking out over a calm blue sea surrounding extensive rock platforms, doubtless rich in shellfish (Figure 3.4). It seemed an ideal, if not idyllic, place for a summer excavation, a chance to introduce students to fieldwork and to begin a program of research on the Victorian coast (Zobel et al. 1984; Frankel 1991a). The midden itself was very unusual, at the base of steep cliffs, close to the sea and rock-platforms but – as we later discovered to our cost – swept by storms and high water. But it had something not often seen: rather than the typical diffuse scatters

Figure 3.4 Cliffs, beaches and rock platforms of the Otway coast at Moonlight Head.

or layers of shells, the closer confines of the more sheltered area at the foot of the cliff provided a specific place where returning visitors had discarded the remains of their meals, building up nearly 2 metres of deposit. This would provide the chance to trace a history of activity by generations of Gudabanud people.

It was a dramatic place to work, with the constant roar of wind and water. Even reaching the site was itself a daily challenge, both to bring in equipment and then each day to clamber up or down the cliffs and dodge the incoming surf to reach the site itself, especially during wilder weather or at high tide. No one could ever have been sure enough of access to the rock-platforms to rely on or plan visits to the site ahead of time. It was well used, but only when unpredictable circumstances allowed.

The face of the deposits had been cut into by the sea, exposing the superimposed layers of deposit, mainly thin bands of shell and charcoal. This provided a guide, although often an unreliable guide, to assist us as we attempted to remove each identifiable layer in turn (Figure 3.5) – not always with perfect success. For middens such as this were not neatly constructed, but made up of a hodgepodge of discarded refuse, evened off and redistributed by feet and bottoms of later visitors, walking, sitting, eating and tossing aside empty shells on top of earlier dumps (Figure 3.6).

However, we could separate two dozen or more individual layers in some of the deepest parts of the midden. Later radiocarbon dating shows that the site was used for about 800 years from about 1000 years ago. As we excavated we collected all the shells, divided them into the different species and counted and weighed each – a long and tedious process. But we were then in a position to trace changing

Figure 3.5 Excavations in progress at Moonlight Head midden.

patterns of shellfish collection and consumption over some 800 years. Shellfish species differ in size, habits and habitat. The main rock-platform types we had to deal with were limpets (such as *Cellana*), mussels (*Austromytilus rostratus*), chiton (*Polyplacophora*), turbo (*Turbo undulata*) and abalone (*Haliotis rubra*). The first three are found on the rocks in the intertidal zone, exposed at low tide. These mussels are generally smaller than most species of limpets and live in groups rather than singly. Turbo, often larger again, prefer greater depths, as does abalone. Collectors therefore can make practical, economic decisions based on the relative size, abundance, aggregation and ease of collection, balancing energy, time and

42

Figure 3.6 Stratigraphic section through the Moonlight Head midden showing layers of accumulated shells.

risk against food value. Is it better to collect smaller limpets from on top of the rocks or to dive for the much larger abalone at greater cost and risk of coming up empty-handed (or perhaps never at all)? Is a generalised approach better than concentrating on one or two species?

Figure 3.7 gives one summary view of the data from Moonlight Head, where the relative proportions of each shellfish species are shown for each of four main periods, each perhaps conflating the activities of seven or eight generations (A as the earliest, D as the most recent). Mussels and limpets were always most frequently collected. But as turbo are generally larger, they contributed more to the

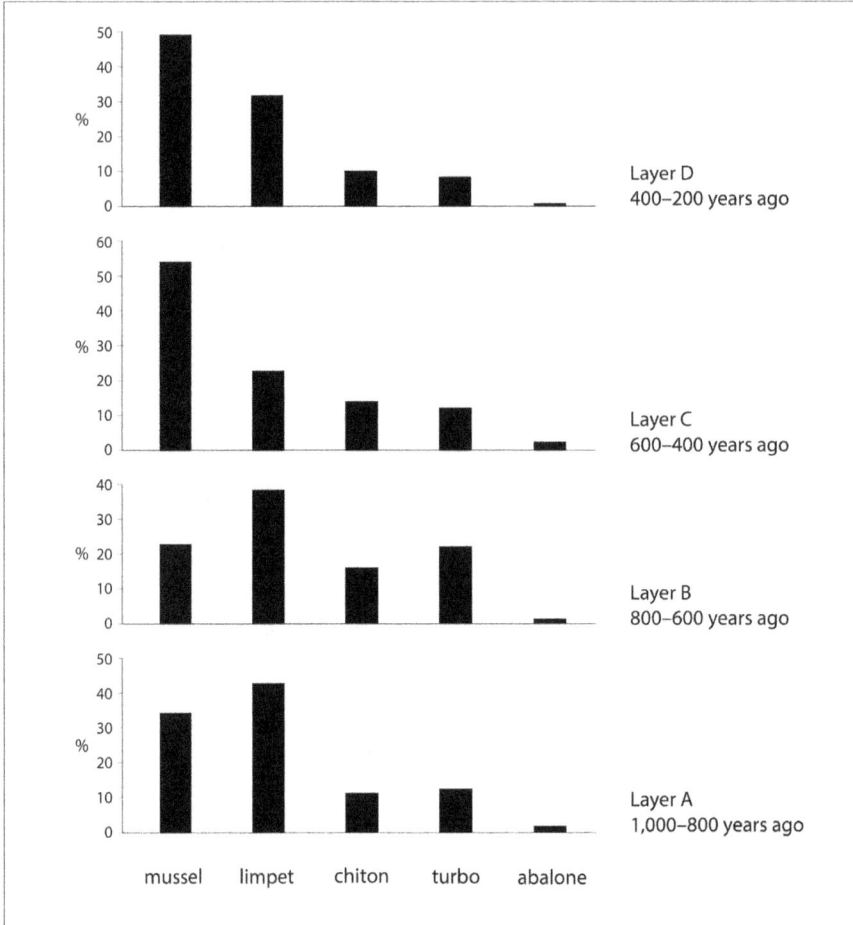

Figure 3.7 Relative proportions of different types of shellfish deposited during four periods at Moonlight Head.

diet than the simple numbers suggest. Over time Gundbanud people using the site gradually changed some aspects of their collection strategy, with an initial move to a more diverse approach between about 800 and 600 years ago, after which time there was a far greater concentration of the more easily gathered mussels.

As one might expect at such a specialised place, bones of land animals were very rare, but with more possum and wallaby in the more recent periods. Perhaps the site was now used in a slightly different way, with people bringing other food down to the shore, and spending less time or energy on shellfish gathering. Few fish bones were found. This matches observations at other sites along the open coasts of Victoria, suggesting fishing in these waters was never a major activity. Only two seal bones were found at Moonlight Head. Perhaps these were from seals washed up on the shore, providing a very rare bonus once every century or two.

Living at Seal Point

Our second midden is about 30 kilometres east of Moonlight Head, and quite different in character. In 1878, Philip Chauncy noted the presence of

> some very large shell-mounds ... especially near Cape Otway where the largest is about three hundred feet long, forty or fifty feet wide, and sixteen feet high. It must have taken ages for the fish-eating natives of the coast to build up such heaps. (Chauncy 1878: 234)

A century later, when Harry Lourandos first saw one such midden at Seal Point site, he recorded a spread of shells over an area 400 metres in length and up to 100 metres wide, overlooking extensive rock-platforms (Lourandos 1980a, 1983, 1997; Mitchell 1988). Over the next few years he returned to Seal Point to excavate a series of small squares towards the eastern end, attracted both by its size and the presence of shallow circular depressions which reminded him of ethnohistorical reports from western Victoria and similar features he was familiar with in Tasmania, where they are understood to be associated with huts and shelters. Harry focused on this higher area of the midden, where he uncovered 80 to 150 centimetres of complex and uneven layers of midden material. This part of the site was used from about 1420 years ago. There is some slight trace of earlier activity, but with coastline eroding several centimetres a year (Gill 1997), older middens along the cliff-tops would have long since disappeared. The place was then frequently visited; perhaps, like Moonlight Head, until early in the 19th century. But the very size of the midden means that the less substantial areas within it could have been used to a greater or lesser extent at different times. The circular hollows suggest the presence of huts set into or surrounded by accumulating dumps of shell. Particular features, such as hearths or more compacted layers of fragmented shells, allow us to imagine where people walked, cooked and warmed themselves.

As at Moonlight Head, a variety of shellfish were eaten, but here at Seal Point turbo were always much preferred to limpets and mussels. Abalone, despite their abundance in the deeper waters off the rock-platforms, were relatively rarely collected – again because of the greater difficulty and risks involved in gathering them. Fish and crayfish remains, although perhaps slightly more common than at Moonlight Head, were still comparatively rare, for sea-fishing was never a major activity on the high wave-energy coasts of Victoria.

Hunting was more important. Possums were especially targeted, but, although fewer in number, the larger wallabies probably contributed just as much to the diet. Koala, bandicoot and marsupial mouse provided some occasional variety. And, of course, animals provided more than food. Bone, sinews and skin were all made use of in many ways.

Then there were seals. Seal bones were found in all parts of the excavation, although not in great quantity. This may be because such heavy animals were butchered on the spot, and only some bones carried back home. Two species of seal were present. Earlier, most were elephant seals while later on fur seals became more common. Both species include female and male seals of varied ages. Where did the seals come from and were they a regular target for Gundbanud hunters?

Seals were once common in Bass Strait before 19th-century sealing caused a catastrophic collapse in their numbers. Offshore islands were always their favoured habitat, but there is nothing to suggest that people in western Victoria visited islands, or had the watercraft to do so – although, as we will see later, east of Port Phillip and Wilsons Promontory canoes were used both on lakes and estuaries and for short forays to nearby small islands in search of shellfish, birds and seals (Gaughwin and Fullagar 1995). At Seal Point, the animals must have been attacked when they hauled ashore nearby. But it is unclear whether they did so as members of breeding colonies or whether these were isolated events.

People do not live on meat alone: all these and other animals from the land and sea would only have provided one – perhaps not even the most regular – part of a broader diet. While no direct evidence of plant food survives, the stone tools give some clues. Sandstone pounders or pestles and associated mortars, Harry Lourandos argues, were used for processing fibrous rhizomes of bracken fern, to make a 'kind of bread … roasted in hot ashes, and beaten into paste with a stone' (Dawson 1881: 20; see also Gott 1982). Half of the chipped stone at the site was made of flint nodules washed up on the beach, here as along most of the western coast of Victoria (Scott-Virtue 1982). These and other tools made of quartz and quartzite were used for a variety of purposes – butchery, woodworking and the like. One example of a ground stone hatchet head was found, one of a small handful from formal excavations, although many hundreds have been collected over the years from all across the state. The Seal Point example comes from a quarry at Berrambool on the Hopkins River – demonstrating the interconnections or movements of groups of people (for further discussion of that site and the importance of similar stone and its distribution, see Chapter 10).

Unlike Moonlight Head, where the midden was created by occasional and opportunistic visits, Seal Point gives the impression of a place used more regularly for longer periods of time, serving as a base from which people could go out daily to hunt, gather and harvest from different areas around.

Working at Glen Aire

Our third site in Gundbanud country is different again. Glen Aire II is a small rockshelter overlooking the open valley and estuary of the Aire River, near the base of the substantial high ridge which blocks it off from the sea, about a 3 to 4 kilometre walk away. Here, in 1960, John Mulvaney carried out one of the first professional archaeological excavations in Victoria. Shelter I had recently been almost entirely destroyed, but Shelter II was better preserved and provided over 2 metres of deposits, with the sole radiocarbon date indicating use during the last 500 years (Mulvaney 1962).

There are numerous open middens along the nearby beaches but people also brought shellfish that they collected from the rock-platforms back to the landward side of the ridge, where the shells were later discarded all along its lower slopes as well as in the rockshelters (Head and Stuart 1980) (Figure 3.8). As at Seal

Point, there were also fish and animal remains. Possum was more common than kangaroo, wallaby and pademelon, but even more common were the bones of Pacific black duck.

The tools tell an interesting story. They also provide an example of how changing techniques of analysis provide different insights and give new views on the past.

When John Mulvaney analysed the stone artefacts he had excavated, only a small proportion (seven out of 2278 pieces of stone) were identified as tools on the basis of shape and other characteristics visible to the naked eye. This suggested to him that carefully manufactured 'formal' tools, such as backed blades, were no longer in fashion when the shelter was used and that wooden and bone tools became increasingly more important than stone in the recent past.

Subsequently, Richard Fullagar undertook a new study of finds from Glen Aire (Fullagar 2011). He was able to bring new techniques to bear, particularly microscopic studies which could identify traces of use through damage to the edges of tools or the build-up of residues. He was thus able to show that a large proportion of artefacts which had previously been regarded as waste flakes had, in fact, been used. Such amorphous tools do not conform to clearly identifiable types. Rather, it was the nature of the working edge that determined usefulness. Even so, the tools display limited signs of use, suggesting that they were seldom resharpened but were readily discarded. Often, especially when high quality stone was rare or especially sought after, more interest was taken in preparing and looking after tools. Here, the availability of coastal flint and other suitable stone allowed a strategy where sharp flakes were struck off cores, selected, sometimes modified by fine retouch on the working edge before or during use, and then casually tossed aside.

The stone tools at Glen Aire were used for several different tasks. The most common was to make bone tools from marsupial leg bones. Graving tools were used for scoring grooves along the bone, examples of which can also be seen on some of the excavated marsupial bones. Small stone wedges were then hammered into the grooves to split the bones apart before the pieces were cut or scraped down to form points or other shapes. Stone scrapers were used for cleaning skins; awls and drills for boring holes into shells or softer material; a few other types for cutting, sawing, or when mounted in a handle, for heavier woodworking. Pounders or pestles were used for processing plant food. A ground edge hatchet hints at heavier woodworking tasks such as cutting bark or making footholds when climbing trees after possums.

The particular use-damage caused by different tasks is hard to identify with bone tools, especially as these could be used in many ways (Webb 1987; Pickering 1979). One spatula showed traces of having been used to prise shellfish off rock, while wear patterns on others were less distinctive. But we can imagine their use in contexts like that described by William Thomas writing about people on the Yarra:

> The opossum rug called *Waller-wal-lert*. It hung loosely about the body, had a knot at each upper corner, and was fastened by a small stick thrust through holes made with a bone needle – *Min-der-min*. It could be cast off in a moment. It was carried when travelling, but in camp it was usually kept in the miam. In making

Figure 3.8 Looking east over the Aire basin. Glen Aire II is to the right of centre (arrowed).

an opossum rug some skill and knowledge are employed. In the first place it is necessary to select good, sound, well-clothed skins. These, as they are obtained, are stretched on a piece of bark, and fastened down by wooden or bone pegs, kept there until they are dry. They are then well-scraped with a mussel-shell or a chip of basalt, dressed into proper shape and sewn together. In sewing them the natives worked from left to right – not as the Europeans do – and the holes made with the bone awl or needle, and instead of thread they used the sinews of some animal – most often the sinews of the tail of the kangaroo. (Smyth 1878, I: 271)

It is not hard to visualise all of this going on at Glen Aire, where we have the material remains of the entire production sequence: hunting and collecting the raw material, making tools and then using them to prepare skins and turn them into the possum skin cloaks so often worn in Victoria.

The Aire basin was rich in plants, animals and especially birds, with fish and shellfish available on the nearby coast, making it a favoured locality – incorporated into a complex taskscape as people made use of this range of resources from different areas (Figure 3.8). The landward side of the ridge where the shelters were located would have been a choice place for camping, for it was relatively sheltered from prevailing winds and close to the wetlands where ducks could be taken and wetland plants collected. Larger animals could be hunted in the coastal heath or captured in woodland. Nor was it far from the rock-platforms along the coast where shellfish could be gathered. These could have been carried home or eaten on the spot, forming the numerous middens found along the dunes. We need to see these sites not as individual archaeological sites but as part of a broader system

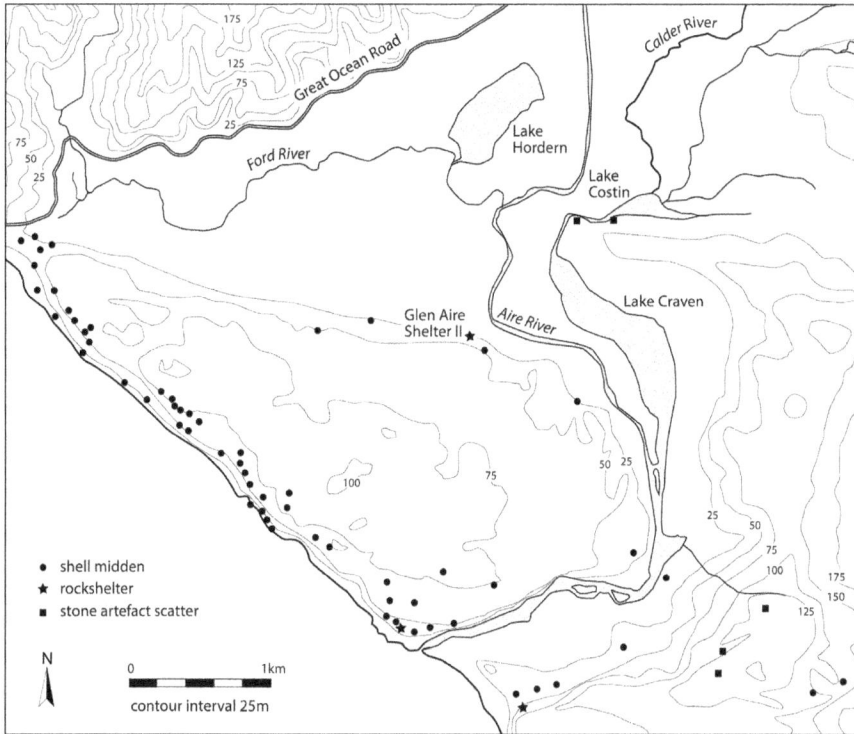

Figure 3.9 Location of Glen Aire II shelter and other sites in the vicinity (data from Head and Stuart 1980).

of interrelated activities. Similarly, the rockshelters, the focus of the excavations, should not be seen in isolation. As a general rule Aboriginal people did not camp in tight clusters, but often people would be spread out over a broader area, setting up huts, shelters or shades for themselves, perhaps divided according to their age, sex or family connections (see Figure 3.15). The Glen Aire II rockshelter was just one convenient natural sheltered space, used, as we have seen, for particular purposes, although not, of course, to the exclusion of other, more general activities – nor need it have been the only spot where these craft activities took place.

Finally, we end the story of Glen Aire II on a tragic note. In the upper deposits of the site lay the skeleton of a young Aboriginal man in his 20s. This was not a customary burial, but something different, something that happened when Aboriginal people were no longer able to use the site or area as they had done for centuries. Although there is no direct evidence, it is even possible, as John Mulvaney has suggested, that these are the remains of a man shot during a reprisal for the murder of a surveyor at Blanket Bay in 1846 (Mulvaney 1962: 7; for accounts of this event, see Stuart 1981: 83; Clark 1990: 187; Clark 1995: 121–23).

Beaches, lakes and estuaries of east Gippsland

The coast of east Gippsland could hardly be more different from that of the Otways. From Wilsons Promontory east to Mallacoota are long stretches of sandy beach. Behind the barrier dunes of Ninety Mile Beach lies a series of large freshwater lakes and lagoons fed by many rivers – the La Trobe, Thompson, Mitchell, Nicholson and Tambo – which run down from the steep slopes of the Great Dividing Range across the coastal plain. Further east, past where the Snowy River reaches the sea, there are fewer bodies of open water until the extensive estuary at Mallacoota. All these provided rich and varied environments for the several clans of Gunai/Kurnai people.

Ethnohistorical accounts describe the wide range of plants, animals and birds that were used. Fishing in the lakes was especially important. Writing from Lake Tyers, John Bulmer noted that:

> In summer their days were spent chiefly in fishing for eels and fat mullet (*Pert-pang*). They camped at the entrance to the lakes, where they were plentiful at this season ...
>
> In summer his nights would be spent in getting eels and other fish, as at night they can be more easily taken. He would go into the shallow water with a torch and a spear; the fish would be attracted to the light, and they would fall easy prey to the spear ...
>
> In summer they fished mostly on the coast, or at the mouths of rivers which run into the sea, as at this season the fish were either going to or returning from the sea. In winter they would more likely procure fish in the rivers with grass nets, and often with hooks of bone with a line made of the bark of the *Yowan* or lightwood. I believe they found the bone-hook as good for fishing as the hooks supplied by Europeans, though no doubt it would be very troublesome to make it, as it had to be scraped out with flint and shells ...
>
> The women would also go away in large numbers in canoes to fish ...
> (Smyth 1878: I, 141–42)

At Mallacoota, Peter Coutts and colleagues from what was then the Victoria Archaeological Survey carried out surveys and small excavations in and around the estuary. At least 150 middens were identified. They must all have been developed during the last 4000 years when the sand bar blocked the inlet and it began to take on its present form. Each of the few middens investigated in detail has evidence of hunting a variety of large and small animals, and each displays a slightly different array of shellfish and fish reflecting local availability (Coutts et al. 1984; Richman 1996, 1999; Weaver 1985). As modern fishers know, different species of fish are to be found in particular areas, so it is no surprise that snapper, which avoid freshwater, are only found at Captain Stevensons Point nearer to the inlet mouth and are not present further up the inlet, while only bream, wrasse and leatherjacket were excavated at Fisheries Point. At that site, as might be expected, almost all shells are of estuarine species, especially mud ark (*Anadara trapezia*), blue mussel (*Mytilus edulis*) and oyster (*Ostrea angazi*). A handful of others, such as turbo, were brought into the site from the rock-platforms a few kilometres away.

In the Goanna Bay midden at Top Lake, much further again up the inlet, there was a more restricted range of fish and shellfish, especially when compared to the wide array of species noted at Captain Stevensons Point.

Further west along the Gippsland coast near Jack Smith and other lakes, the archaeology again shows differences in site types, shellfish collection and artefacts. Many of these can be associated with the way in which the present barrier dune and lake systems developed over the last 4000 to 5000 years (Hotchin 1990; Bird 1993). A broad sequence can be seen in the middens along Ninety Mile Beach. Middens of about 4000 to 3000 years ago have estuarine shellfish associated with microlithic tools made from imported stone. During the last millennium the middens along the stabilised barrier dune are characterised by pipi (cockle) shells (*Donax deltoides*) – a species found in great abundance along rough surf beaches. These middens still have tools similar to earlier ones, but at this time were more commonly made from local raw materials. These most recent pipi-middens on the foredunes appear to have far fewer stone tools, which were now made using locally available cobbles rather than finer quality silcrete brought in from elsewhere.

Along this and other stretches of coast, such as nearby Wilsons Promontory, shellfish collecting largely reflected availability of species in response to local changes in coastal geomorphology and ecology (Coutts 1970). Many other aspects of life were not so directly determined by the environment, although it always provided a context limiting or encouraging particular lifeways and the adoption of new technologies. One, probably recent, innovation was the introduction of the fish hook. Although fish may have been taken using bone or wooden gorges with two pointed ends elsewhere in Victoria, hooks were only used in the sheltered waters of the Gippsland coast. Here several European observers, like John Bulmer, refer to fishing with hooks as well as with nets and spears. An example of an 'ancient' bone fish hook that he collected was illustrated by Smyth (1878: 391, Fig. 226) and is now in Museum Victoria (Massola 1956: 5, Plate 3; Vanderwal 1994: Fig. 12; Gerritsen 2001: 19–20, Fig. 3; see also Clark 1998b: Figs 6.6, 6.8) (Figure 3.10).

Along the coast of New South Wales, fish hooks appear in the archaeological record only during the last millennium: a new introduction thought to have spread southward from Queensland (Walters 1988; Gerritsen 2001). The adoption of this new technology has been linked by some archaeologists to changes in social structure and to the gender division of labour, giving women the ability to fish where previously this was the preserve of spear-using men (Bowdler 1976; Walters 1988). Quite apart from such broader issues, the timing of the introduction of hooks to Gippsland is far from clear, for no hooks have been found in any of the archaeological sites. Unlike the shell hooks of New South Wales, hooks in Gippsland were made of wood or bone. There is no reason why bone hooks should not survive, even if wooden ones would not. So we are left with a puzzle – or, indeed, two puzzles: when were hooks adopted, and why, if they were copied from those of their northern neighbours, did Gunai/Kurnai people not use shell?

Canoes, like fish hooks, were unknown on the Victorian coast west of Port Phillip Bay, although they were used in the Coorong and along most of the Murray River (Draper 2015) (Chapters 6 and 7). But they were important to people living beside sheltered waters for fishing and for transport. Today, the revival of the old

Figure 3.10 A bone fish hook from east Gippsland (Smyth 1878: fig. 226).

skills is particularly significant for Aboriginal people in Gippsland. Steaphan Paton recently documented the manufacture of a canoe under the direction of Elder Albert Mullett (Paton 2013). The photographs of the project give modern images which illustrate well the 19th-century account by John Bulmer:

> A more robust canoe was made in Gippsland from the bark of suitable trees available in the district – the stringy bark (*yangoro*) and the mountain ash (*yowork*). They secure a long sheet of bark from either of these trees and turning it inside out, they carefully make the ends thin by peeling off the rough part of the bark. By the assistance of a little fire they lift up the ends and carefully fold them together just as you would fold a bag for tying. They secure the end with a string made from the bark, and with two pieces of the bough of the tree they bend in to the end to form a rib. The canoe, called *gree*, a word expressing all of a man's goods, is now finished. The Gippsland canoe was fairly safe … I have seen one made big enough to carry three bags of flour and three men. Indeed it was wonderful to see the number of men, women and dogs which could get into a large canoe.
>
> The canoes were propelled with a long stick, *gendook*. This could be used both sitting and standing. This serves as a propeller in shallow water, but when they are crossing a lake they squat down, with a piece of bark about 6 inches long in each hand. With these they paddle along very quickly. (Vanderwal 1994: 57; Frankel and Major 2015: 199)

Figure 3.11 Great Glennie Island. Wilsons Promontory can be seen in the background (photo: Jim Allen).

Of course, there is no direct archaeological evidence of bark canoes, but some idea of how long they have been used in the area comes from offshore islands – people were visiting Great Glennie Island, 7 kilometres off the west coast of Wilsons Promontory, at least 1850 years ago (Head et al. 1983).

To the islands

> Rounding the Cape once more, the journey was boisterous but feasible and so we proceeded into a world of rolling seas and seals, with albatrosses skimming the wave tops with their drooping narrow wings. The stacks and islands all around us were for the most part engirdled by great cliffs, which plunged precipitously down to depths of 25 fathoms (45m) and more onto the floor of the Bassian Plain. (Jones and Allen 1979: 4)

So Rhys Jones and Jim Allen described their visit to Great Glennie Island in 1968. They returned in 1980 to excavate within a rockshelter they called GG1. There they dug through five main midden deposits of shellfish and animal bone which provided evidence of occasional visits over the last two millennia (Jones and Allen 1985; Head et al. 1983; Gaughwin and Fullagar 1995; Fullagar 2015). While the materials found in the successive layers are different from one another, no clear line of development can be seen, not surprisingly when the island was so rarely visited. Seal and sea bird were important at all times, but fish only so in the latest

Figure 3.12 Rhys Jones during excavations at Great Glennie cave (photo: Jim Allen).

layers, which also had the greatest density of shellfish. Could the increase in fish be related to the introduction of fish hooks? While quartz could have been collected on the island, the flint must have been brought across, but some changes can be seen. Coastal flint was always most common, but quartz was also used, especially in the earlier periods when tools were used for butchery, and for working on skin, bone and plants. The decline in its use matches that seen on the mainland sites at Wilsons Promontory, as do other aspects of the stone tools. On the mainland at Yanakie, backed tools, most common at earlier times, were absent during the last millennium, when tools are far less carefully made. The waste products indicate that the earlier visitors to the island carried prepared tools with them, which they used intensively enough to form use-polish on the working edges. Later on blocks of stone were brought to the island and tools knapped there for more immediate use, which may have included more woodworking than at earlier times.

Although obviously planned and deliberate, forays to Great Glennie were probably infrequent and short, involving only a few people. They were not, therefore, an integral part of normal life or subsistence economy. We are left to wonder what, apart from seals, encouraged people to make the occasional hazardous crossing to this island. Can we get a clue from other adjacent islands?

To the east of Wilsons Promontory there is a large group of sandy barrier islands in the sheltered waters of the Nooramunga Marine and Coastal Park. Historical accounts coupled with the very small number and size of archaeological sites found on the islands suggests that Aboriginal people only used them to a limited extent, even though only short voyages were involved (McNiven 2000b). This is understandable when one considers that there would have been far fewer resources on the islands than on the richer, more diverse environments of the mainland. In spite of the seasonal presence of mutton-birds and their eggs, these islands were never economically significant. Why then were they visited at all? Here, Ian McNiven (2000b: 26) has argued, the islands were socially important, particularly when they served as havens in special circumstances, as described by Alfred Howitt:

> Snake Island was the place of refuge of the Brataualung, not only in cases of elopement, but when raids were made on them by other clans of the Kurnai ... There can be no doubt that the old people of the Kurnai winked at this practice of marriage by elopement. In by far the greatest number of cases they themselves had obtained a wife or husband in this manner, and yet when their daughter married in the same way they were furious at it, and punished her with severity. (Howitt 1904: 278–79)

Around the bays

When George Bass explored the Victorian coast in 1797, he sailed his small whaleboat only as far as the large bay, which he named Western Port – a somewhat confusing name as it lies east of the adjacent, larger, Port Phillip Bay. Here the wide, shallow valleys leading down to the Bassian plain were filled as the sea rose to its present level by 7700 years ago before continuing to rise another 1 to 2 metres, flooding as much as 10 kilometres up the rivers and covering the low-lying shoreline. By 4000 years ago, the waters receded more or less to their present position (Sloss et al. 2007; Lewis et al. 2013; Holdgate et al. 2011). As recent research has shown, from about 2800 years ago sediment blocked the entrance to Port Phillip, allowing the shallow bay to dry out. Then, perhaps a thousand years ago, this barrier was broken and the sea flooded back through the Rip (Holdgate et al. 2011).

This flooding of the bay was remembered for a millennium in local Aboriginal oral traditions. Several versions were recorded by Europeans in the 19th century, one by Georgiana McCrae:

> 'Plenty long ago ... men could cross, dry-foot, from our side of the bay [in the east] to Geelong [in the west].' They described a hurricane – trees bending to and fro – then the earth sank, and the sea rushed in through the Heads, till the void places became broad and deep, as they are today. (McCrae 1934: 176)

Another account was included in William Hull's testimony to a Select Committee of the Legislative Council in 1858:

> The blacks say that their progenitors recollected when Hobson's Bay was a kangaroo ground. They say – 'plenty catch kangaroo and plenty catch possum there;' and that 'the river (Yarra) once went out at the Heads, but that the sea broke in, and that Hobson's Bay, which was once a hunting ground, became what it is. (Quoted in Fison and Howitt 1880: 270 n. 1; see also Holdgate et al. 2011: 157; Fels 2011: 285–57)

The two large embayments, Port Phillip Bay and Western Port, present us with different coastal environments, but, as elsewhere, reinforce the need to recognise that the coasts were never more than one part of Aboriginal territories, economies or patterns of land use. Shell middens are found along the shorelines where these were accessible. As might be expected, these are made up of calm water, soft shore shellfish such as mud arks (*Anadara trapezia*), mussels (*Mytilus edulis panulatus*), mud oysters (*Ostrea angasi*) and top shells (*Austrocochlea*) as in equivalent environments such as those described above at Mallacoota Inlet. However, historical accounts again remind us that these archaeologically conspicuous middens reflect only a minor part of people's lives. Wetlands and swamps were always more favourable and favoured by people as they moved seasonally around their country. The Bunurong, for example, not only travelled around the shores of Western Port and the Mornington Peninsula that divides the two bays but spent more time further inland, as noted by William Thomas in 1850:

> It is with regret that I am not prepared to state precisely where the reserve of the Coast 'or Boonurong' tribe should be situated ... A few years back when shifting from Melbourne their regular route was natural, shifting gradually along the Coast to the nine mile beach, Mt Eliza, (Berringwallin) Mount Martha, (Nerngallin) Arthurs Seat, (Wongho) Point Nepean (Monmore) Cape Schanck (Tuornangho) Sandy Point (Yollodunnho) then to the index & returning in land by Mahoon (Western Port plains) to Dandenong the whole circuitous route of their Country ... (Byrt 2004: WT 3084; Fels 2011: 245)

Movements such as these were often just as much for social interaction, attending ceremonies and maintaining connections with other groups of the Kulin nation, as they were for economic, subsistence needs, which are always so much more easily seen in the archaeological record (Sullivan 1981; Gaughwin and Sullivan 1984).

The recent, rapid spread of development east of Melbourne has prompted numerous archaeological surveys designed to locate sites, mitigate adverse impacts and to predict the most likely areas where sites might be expected. Most sites are scatters of stone tools and vary in extent, density and age. One example is at Bend Road, where Jim Allen and a team from La Trobe University carried out large-scale salvage excavations along this section of the Mitcham to Frankston tollway, which was being constructed in 2006 as a key part of the road system to the east of central Melbourne (Hewitt and de Lange 2007; Allen et al. 2008; Hewitt and Allen 2010). The Carrum Carrum Swamp once covered some 50 square kilometres between Dandenong and Frankston, before the Paterson 'river' was cut in the late 19th century to drain the area for agriculture. It was a complex area of permanent water, swampy marshland and extensive alluvial flats: an area rich in birds, fish, yabbies, eels and edible plants. The Bend Road site lies on one of the low dune ridges surrounding the low-lying swamp, one of many conveniently located places to camp.

The heritage significance of the locality had been identified in earlier assessments, leading the road contractor to fund the archaeological project. The La Trobe team were fortunate in being able to excavate a larger area than is common with most heritage management work, and to invest in specialist dating and the

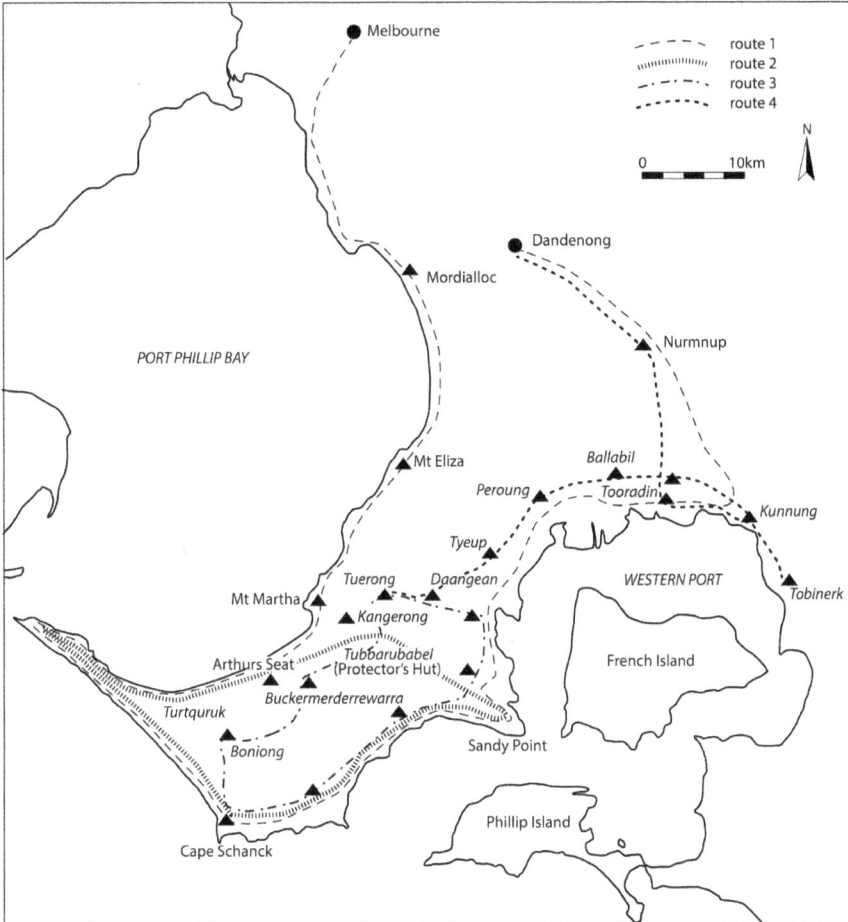

Figure 3.13 Four routes of movements on the Mornington Peninsula (after Sullivan 1981: figure 3).

detailed analysis of the finds. In all, they excavated 31 square metres carefully by hand and used a mechanical excavator over a total of 120 square metres. In the lower layers of the dunes they found some of the earliest evidence of occupation in Victoria, from a time when Bend Road was far inland on the southern side of the exposed Bassian Plain (Chapter 1). The more recent layers with stone tools are only about 4000 to 2000 years old, when the swampland developed at about the time when waters of the bays had dropped to where they are today. Bend Road was then only about 8 kilometres from the shores of Port Phillip Bay. Tracing later activity was not possible due to the effects of modern ploughing and other disturbance, so it is not known what effect the drying out of the bay between about 2800 and 1000 years ago (Holdgate et al. 2011) might have had on the swamp and the way people used the area.

Figure 3.14 Excavations seen in the centre of the photograph during construction of the EastLink freeway at Bend Road, Keysborough.

A total of 8236 pieces of stone were found, discarded at different times over two millennia and spread unevenly across the excavated areas. Concentrations, including in many cases fragments that could be fitted together, suggest that these were places where tools were occasionally made – individual events taking place within broader areas of occupation. Again, we may think of a spread of activities and small camps across a broader occupation locale, as described and sketched for Alfred Howitt by William Barak (Figure 3.15) (Howitt 1904: 773–77; see also Fels 2011: 136–37).

Fine-grained silcrete was by far the most common raw material for making small tools at Bend Road between about 4000 and 2000 years ago. The array of asymmetrical backed points, geometric microliths and thumbnail scrapers are types characteristic of the last 4500 years, as discussed in Chapter 2. Quartz replaces silcrete as the most common raw material in the later deposits at Bend Road when backed tools were no longer found. Whether this was as part of a more general trend, as seen, for example, at Wilsons Promontory and beside the Gippsland Lakes, is an open question. There was, at the same time, a decline in the density of artefacts recovered. This may well be because this part of the Carrum Swamp was used less than before because dense tea-tree scrub invaded the area, making access more difficult. But it could equally well be simply because of a slight change in where people were camping, so that they left fewer traces in the specific areas excavated.

Many other Aboriginal places have been found on the sandy rises beside the former Carrum Swamp. One large concentration of stone tools was discovered

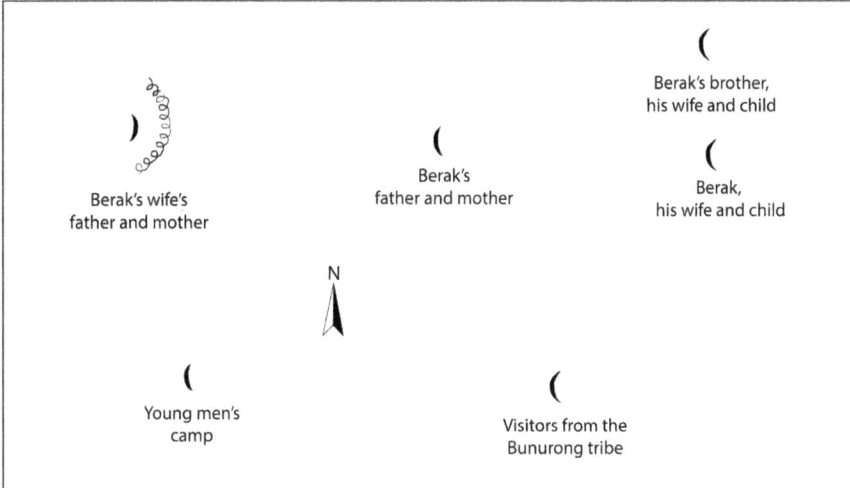

Figure 3.15 Layout of a campsite as drawn for Alfred Howitt by Berak (William Barak) (after Howitt 1904: diagram XXXIII).

near Lyndhurst (Filihia et al. 2016). Excavations, again as part of a heritage management study, came across numerous hearths, some as old as 11,000 years, although most were far more recent, from a time when the area was not far from the waters of Port Phillip Bay. The majority of the more recent chipped stone tools are similar to those of the same age at Bend Road. But there were also examples of grinding tools used for processing plant foods or crushing ochre (pieces of which were also found at the site) and used, as likely as not, for decorating both objects and people. Once again we see a complex archaeological site, where people camped intermittently over many millennia and carried out all their many everyday tasks.

4
Either side of longitude 141°E

In 1914, after many decades of legal wrangling over its exact location, the border between Victoria and South Australia was finally established – a few kilometres west of where it should have been along longitude 141°E. Here we will ignore this arbitrary, and once contentious, divide. Although affecting their lives once in place, it had no meaning for the Buandik and other Aboriginal communities of the area. To the east, the sand dunes of Discovery Bay sweep from Port MacDonnell, past the mouth of the Glenelg River to Cape Bridgewater 50 kilometres away. To the west, the coast curves northward with a series of bays and beaches exposed to the prevailing westerly winds. This is riverless limestone country, where water percolates through the pervious rocks. But there are many large freshwater lakes and wetlands in the low-lying swales between the series of ancient dune ridges that are a major feature of the area: successive barrier dunes left marooned inland as the land tilted upward over the last two million years.

Koongine Cave, December 1985. I am taking a video of Ken Mulvaney as he crouches at the bottom of a 1x1 metre square excavation just inside the entrance. He extracts one large piece of stone, hamming it up a little for the camera, and begins to gently flick off the attached soil. As he turns the tool over in his hands his self-conscious commentary gives way to a surprised 'it ... it's beautiful!' And, indeed it is (Figures 4.2, 4.3). He is particularly excited because it is rare to have such moments: although nothing can compare to the pleasure of fieldwork, the process of excavating is normally one of slow, patient, often tedious care.

This tool, as we later find out, was made, used and disposed of – or perhaps just left aside and forgotten – by someone 10,000 years ago. It is a classic example of a stone tool industry we call the Gambieran, as it is found in the general vicinity of Mount Gambier. These are sizeable woodworking tools, made from large flint flakes struck off their cores to provide the basic shape and then neatly and uniformly retouched or chipped around the convex working edge. Unfortunately, their size and general appearance made them particularly attractive to enthusiasts, who collected vast quantities in the early part of last century (Warren 1985; Griffiths 1996). By the 1940s, Stanley Mitchell proudly noted that 'at least 1000 implements have been collected' from Hoods Drift, one of many favoured localities in the Kongorong Hills (Mitchell 1949: 175), while Tom McCourt found 3000 on a few hundred acres

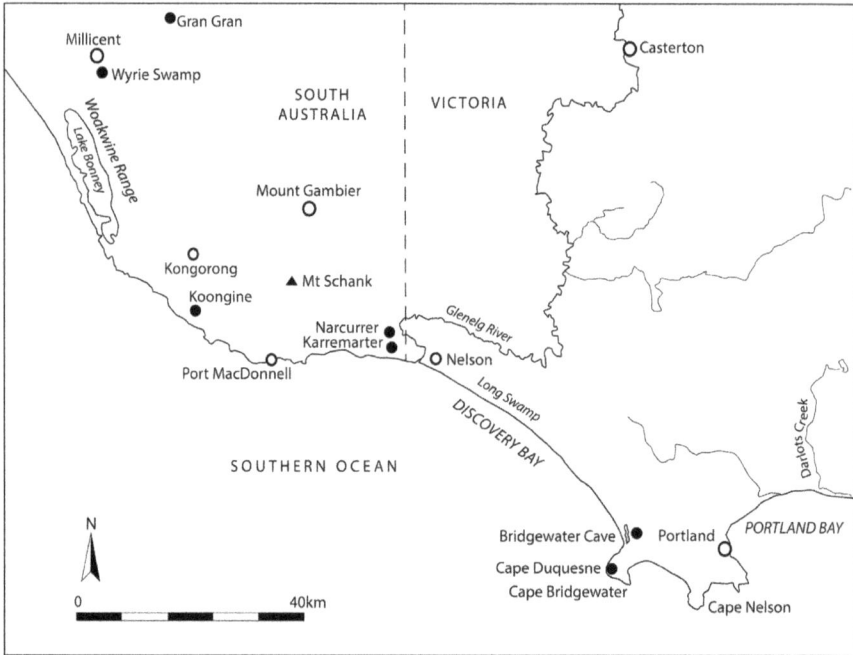

Figure 4.1 Location of sites in South Australia and Victoria.

Figure 4.2 Ken Mulvaney at Koongine Cave, 1985.

Figure 4.3 Large Gambieran flint
scraper from Koongine Cave.

near Beachport (McCourt 1975). Equivalent numbers were picked up by many others (Campbell et al. 1946). Only a very small proportion of these are now in museums and still available to us; for example, David Clark was only able to study 333 that finally made their way into the National Museum of Victoria (Clark 1979).

As these flint tools were highly patinated (chemically altered by the old, consolidated terra rossa soils on which they were found), they were generally considered to be older than the microlithic or smaller tools found by the same collectors on the more recent dunes. This was only confirmed when examples were properly excavated from dateable contexts, as at Wyrie Swamp and Koongine. But where did all this flint come from?

Mining at Gran Gran and Karlie-ngoinpool

The flint (or chert, as some prefer to call it) from which these thousands of tools were made forms as veins or nodules within limestone. Where these outcrop on exposed ridges or jut out of the walls of caves, pieces can be readily struck off. But mining larger quantities of high quality stone required far more arduous work − many hours of difficult, backbreaking effort.

Deep underground in Gran Gran Cave, Robert Bednarik (1992) has traced the way people extracted flint from along 65 metres of an exposed seam (Figures 4.4, 4.5). The tool marks show how, in one place, massive amounts of limestone overburden had to be removed to gain access to the seam, the miners working right-handed to drive in long, sturdy, pointed stakes to split and lever away the overlying rock. Then, in the dark, confined space, perhaps lit by flickering firelight, two or three men (in all probability it was men who did these tasks) worked closely together.

Figure 4.4 Entrance to Gran Gran Cave.

Figure 4.5 Marks made on the sloping roof of Gran Gran Cave by very long wooden wedges during flint mining (photo: R.G. Bednarik).

While one held a wooden wedge in place his partner struck it to remove the desired blocks of flint. In nearby Karlie-ngoinpool Cave, individual nodules were extracted by gouging out limestone from above them before wedges were inserted

Figure 4.6 Mining and art at Karlie-ngoinpool Cave, where flint nodules have been removed or battered. Deeply carved petroglyphs can be seen below them (photo: R.G. Bednarik).

below to lever away the flint (Figure 4.6). At times, these miners resorted to more aggressive battering to chip off pieces. In this way almost all the nodules within reach and up to several metres above the floor were extracted and taken away to be turned into tools.

In addition to the evidence of quarrying, these caves also have a particular form of wall-marking, with parallel series of finger marks or fluting impressed into softer surfaces. There is no reason to suppose the two activities were not closely related. These markings are reminiscent of those found in Koonalda Cave, far below the surface of the Nullarbor Plain, where stone was also quarried over 20,000 years ago. The Koonalda markings are 1500 kilometres and 15,000 years away from those near Mount Gambier. Could they still both belong to a very ancient, widespread tradition, somehow symbolically, if not psychologically, linked to the underground mining (Bednarik 1986, 1999)?

Figure 4.7 Excavations in progress at Wyrie Swamp, 1973 (photo: Roger Luebbers).

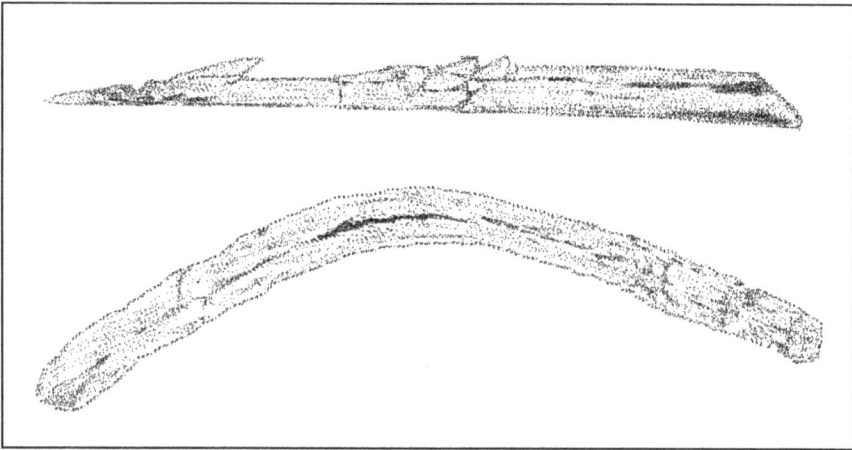

Figure 4.8 Wooden boomerang and spear from Wyrie Swamp.

Beside the wetlands at Wyrie Swamp

Roger Luebbers came to Wyrie Swamp more by accident than by design. Commercial quarrying of high quality peat for gardening began there in the 1960s. Workmen soon found pointed sticks and boomerangs preserved in the lower peaty mud. But their importance was not fully realised until Roger was shown some in 1973. He immediately realised their significance and set out to excavate at the swamp to find and date additional wooden implements and establish their relationship with Gambieran stone tools from the site (Figure 4.7) (Luebbers 1978).

It was certainly no easy job to work in waterlogged conditions and to extract fragile wood from a matrix of clinging fibrous peat, but the excavators came away with nearly three dozen wooden items, including four complete pointed digging or throwing sticks, three complete and seven fragmentary boomerangs, and three spears. There were also many characteristic Gambieran stone tools (Luebbers 1978). These come from the lowest peat deposits and the shoreline below them, when the original lake was smaller and surrounded by dunes. Edible plants, such as the shoots of water ribbon (*Triglochin procera*) (Gott 1982), and water birds would have made this a good place to camp.

The artefacts can all be dated to between about 12,400 and 8500 years ago. Flint was brought from quarries such as Gran Gran to the site and used there to carve a variety of wooden tools. The straight sticks with one rounded and one pointed end were used to dig up tubers from the soft muds on the shoreline or for throwing at waterbirds. Spears were for hunting or, perhaps, fighting; the best preserved, 120 centimetres long, has both ends sharpened, while two other fragments have delicate barbs carved behind the tip. The boomerangs, probably made of sheoak (Casuarina), may have been returning boomerangs. They were used either to directly strike waterfowl or, perhaps, to disturb them so that they would fly into nets, as was done along the Murray in recent times (Chapter 6).

The boomerangs, now on display in the South Australian Museum, are, naturally, of special interest, demonstrating the great antiquity of this iconic Aboriginal device (Jones 2004). But the wooden tools also provide an immediate reminder of the limited nature of archaeological evidence. Only very rarely indeed can we find even a few of the many things of wood and bark, of hide and hair, of fur and feathers that were made and used by Aboriginal people.

The shores around this lake were visited at intervals over 2000 to 3000 years. It was only one of many such spots. The stone tools Mitchell and other collectors picked up in their thousands from equally old surfaces in the region represent many similar campsites beside the inland swamps and wetlands which lay between the ancient dune ridges.

Figure 4.9 Koongine Cave during excavations in 1986.

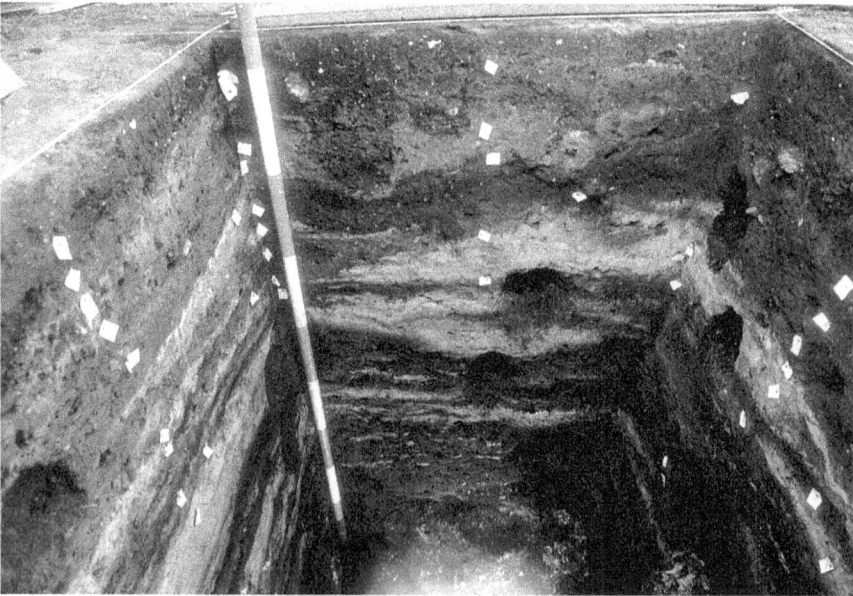

Figure 4.10 Stratigraphy at Koongine Cave. Most of the deposit accumulated soon after 11,000 years ago.

A convenient shelter: Koongine Cave

In the early 1980s, members of the local field naturalists club built a strong mesh fence at Malangine (then known as Noonan's East Cave) in order to protect its rock art from vandalism. To do so they cut a deep trench across the entrance, turning up large numbers of flint pieces. When Roger Luebbers later told me of this, I felt it would be a useful place to begin a program of research in the area. In 1985, I organised a team from La Trobe University, while Ken Mulvaney brought along Aboriginal students from a course he was running for them at the Victoria Archaeological Survey (now Heritage Services, Office of Aboriginal Affairs Victoria) (Frankel 1986).

We opened up our excavations both just within and adjacent to the earlier trench. I sometimes show my students a video of my increasing dismay as over many days I was reluctantly forced to realise that the soft loose fill had been totally turned over by rabbits, who found it ideal for their burrows. The site had no stratigraphic integrity (there was a complete beer bottle more than a metre below the surface) – although we did learn a lot about rabbit warrens. Later analysis of the stone also disappointed, for none of it had any signs of being worked or used (Wilby 2000).

Overcoming our frustrations, we decided to use our remaining time in the field to test Koongine (Noonan's West Cave) 100 metres or so along the same low limestone ridge (Figure 4.9) (Bird and Frankel 2001; Frankel 1991a). Here things proved to be very different. We dug through about 2 metres of more substantial accumulated soils, with easily identifiable alternating layers of charcoal rich or clearer light fill. Of course, rabbits had done some damage here as at so many other sites, but the few burrows could be identified and cleared out. And, again unlike Malangine, there were large quantities of both animal bones and stone tools. Many of the tools – like the one which so excited Ken Mulvaney – are of characteristic Gambieran form, especially in the lower two-thirds of the deposit. This provided for the first time an opportunity to characterise Gambieran tool-making techniques: to see how skilled knappers struck off the large asymmetrical flakes that they preferred and trimmed them to suit; and how their approach to their craft differed from others (Bird and Frankel 2001). But such technical and arcane detail is, understandably, of limited general interest, although it becomes important in defining this regionally and chronologically restricted industry. The tools and the way they were made and used was one element among many through which this society defined itself, marking its relationships with other groups. To what extent this technological, material boundary coincided with other boundaries of language, kinship and social relations remains an unanswered, perhaps unanswerable, question.

Radiocarbon dates show that occupation in the cave was contemporary with the finds from Wyrie Swamp. People first began to use it about 11,000 years ago. After about a thousand years there was a decrease in the rate at which sediment accumulated, so perhaps visits became less frequent. And then, after 8500 years ago it was no longer visited at all. Only 8000 years later, in the very recent past, did people go there again. By that time they no longer made tools in the Gambieran

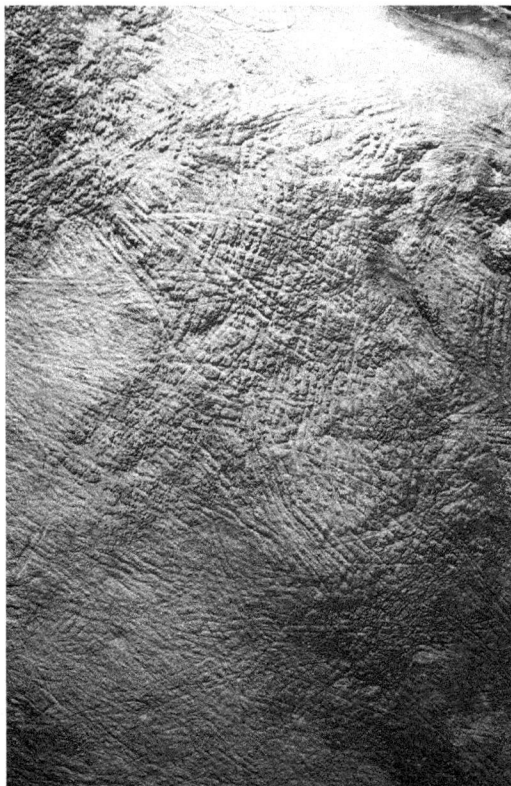

Figure 4.11 Markings on the soft limestone wall of
Koongine Cave.

tradition, for new tool types had replaced the older ones many thousand years
before.

Koongine Cave is in a low limestone ridge which runs parallel to the coast, some
4 kilometres away. Before recent field drainage the land between the ridge and the
present beach dunes and flint pebble beaches was swampy, if not flooded. Today
the cave is 10 metres wide and 25 centimetres deep, and the entrance too low to
walk into with comfort. In earlier times, before the sediments filled the cave, it
would have been wider, more open and with much greater headroom, making it
a sizeable, even attractive place to shelter or to camp. We know from the emu egg
shell found throughout the deposit that people were certainly making use of the
cave in the winter, if not during other seasons. Bones of a wide array of animals,
including kangaroo, wombat, wallaby, pademelon, possum, potoroo, bandicoot,
reptiles and aquatic rats, show that hunters worked across all the different nearby
environments: open grassland, woodland and wetlands. There were also a very few
fragments of marine shell.

These rich archaeological deposits provide insights into what people were
doing at Koongine. But they also throw up two related, more general questions:

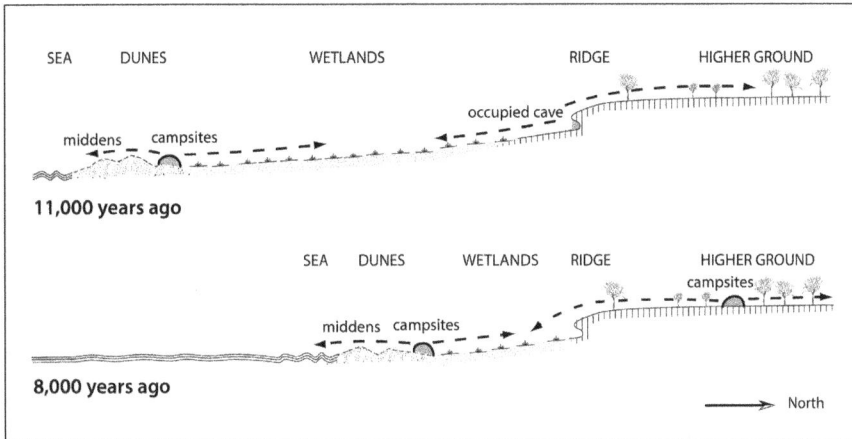

Figure 4.12 Schematic diagram illustrating the changing place of Koongine Cave in relation to the sea and adjacent wetlands.

why was the cave used at all, and why just for this relatively short period, from 11,000 years ago? The answers may lie in seeing the way in which the cave changed its place as the environment changed around it. Location, as the real estate agents say, is everything. But for us it is not a constant.

At the time people began to make use of the cave the sea was about 15 kilometres away, with extensive wetlands in between (Figure 4.12). The marine shells in the lower layers of the site show that the coast formed part of the overall range of those who used the cave, and that there was some direct movement across the intervening wetlands. We may then imagine that people set up home in or behind the coastal dunes, where they could easily access the resources of both sea and the adjacent wetlands. Sometimes, perhaps regularly, perhaps seasonally, people went inland, where different animals and raw material, like flint, were to be found. Koongine, when it was more open and spacious, was a ready-made shelter for occasional use, conveniently situated on the edge of wetlands to the south and woodland and more open country to the north. As the sea level rose and the coast moved northward closer to the cave, the wetlands between contracted so that anyone living behind the dunes could make easy use of its entire extent. When people moved, perhaps seasonally, away from the coast, it would have been more efficient to be based further inland, at locations from which they could easily reach a variety of environments. Koongine was then no longer located in quite so convenient a place and was neglected for many thousands of years.

A local Aboriginal legend, included by Christina Smith in her little book *The Booandik Tribe of South Australian Aborigines*, tells how:

At one time, it is said, the land extended southward as far as the eye could carry from the spot where the township of Port MacDonnell now stands. A splendid forest of evergreen trees, including a wattle out of which grew a profusion of delicious gum, and a rich carpet of grass grew upon it. A man of great height, fearful in his anger and a terror to trespassers on this favoured ground, was the owner. One hot summer's day, whilst taking a walk through his land, he saw at the foot of the wattle-tree a basket of gum. His anger rose, and with a voice like thunder, he cried, 'Who is robbing me of my food?' Looking up he saw a woman concealed among the boughs, and in a loud voice commanded the thief to come down. Trembling, she obeyed, and pleaded for her life. He was relentless, and told her he would drown her for robbing him. Filled with rage he seated himself on the grass, extended his right leg toward Cape Northumberland (Kinneang) and his left toward Green Point, raised his arms above his head, and in a giant voice called on the sea to come and drown the woman. The sea advanced, covering his beautiful land, and destroyed the offending woman. It returned no more to its former bed, and thus formed the present cast of MacDonnell Bay. (Smith 1880: 22–23)

Could this Buandik legend have at its core an ancient oral tradition stretching back 7000 years to the time when these changes were taking place (Nunn and Reid 2015)? Other local legends have also been taken to reflect geological events. The volcanic eruptions of Mount Schank and perhaps Mount Gambier, about 5000 years ago (Smith and Prescott, 1987; Sherwood et al. 2004), may have been incorporated into creation stories as earth ovens used by the ancestral being Craitbul (Smith 1880: 14–15). If so, they demonstrate both the great longevity of traditions over thousands of years and a continuity of culture outlasting innovations in mundane techniques, fashions or local patterns of land use.

Karremarter

By the time that Buandik people saw the volcanic eruptions at Mount Shanck they were no longer making stone tools in the old, Gambieran tradition. There was a new suite of tool types and techniques, with a range of smaller scrapers and backed blades, similar to those described at Billimina (Chapter 2). Such tools were used for a variety of purposes, including spear barbs (Fullagar 2016). Composite spears with stone barbs were different from the early forms found at Wyrie Swamp, which were carved from a single piece of wood. They may have been easier to manufacture and repair, although single-piece spears with carved barbs continued to be used, perhaps for different purposes, until the 19th century. The manufacture of composite spears may have required the use of other new types of stone tools (Luebbers 1978). They were also, in all likelihood, now used with spearthrowers, another innovation which was first seen in northern Australia about 5000 years ago (Allen 1996; Allen and Akerman 2015).

Once again enthusiastic collectors had found and removed large numbers of these small, finely made stone tools from numerous places along the coast. But many still remain on the surface and have been more professionally documented or excavated at several sites. One of these is the site we decided to call Karremarter, 'the banks of the lakes' (Smith 1880: 132), because it overlooks the wetlands of Piccaninnie Ponds, 40 kilometres east of Koongine and just west of Discovery Bay. The Ponds themselves are of international importance and especially enjoyed by divers who explore the clear fresh waters of the limestone sinkhole. They seldom look up to notice the small, low rock-shelter near the top of the adjacent high hill.

It was again the failure of work at Malangine in 1985 that prompted me to ask Wendy Beck to take a few of our team to test the potential of this shelter while we began work at Koongine (Frankel 1986). The deposits were not very deep nor was the stratigraphy clear, largely – yet again! – because of disturbance by rabbits. One find piqued particular interest: the apparent association of a radiocarbon date of about 7000 BP with backed tools, normally thought to be more recent in age. This prompted me to return two years later to carry out a very small additional excavation to clarify the sequence, which showed that the early date was aberrant and has to be set aside. The artefacts from the site provided Nicola Stern, my colleague at La Trobe, with a useful collection for teaching, so that they have probably been studied more often and by more people than any other set of stone tools in the country. They are all now safely stored away from further harassment in the South Australian Museum.

Most of the artefacts were made using flint brought to the site from elsewhere (Frankel and Stern 2011). The best stone came from inland from quarries like Gran Gran. Slightly poorer quality flint was available in enormous quantities from cobble beaches in the area and could be collected with far less effort. Nicola – and, one hopes, her students – could identify subtle differences in the way in which the two types of flint were used. The 'cheaper' local stone from the beaches was brought to the shelter, where it was used to make tools that were immediately discarded after use: an expedient, throw-away industry. It was a little different with the better quality stone, which was carried around as what we can think of as a mobile toolkit. This included cores stripped of unusable cortex or chalky coating, unfinished flakes prepared for making tools and finished tools. Generally, cores from which flakes are struck off are not seen as the most efficient way of transporting raw material over any distance, but bringing them to this site meant that tools could have been made where and when they were needed, ensuring that their working edges were not damaged before use.

A similar array of animals to those recorded at other sites was found at Karremarter, with both woodland and wetland species (Dingli 1995). Not all these bones were left there by people. This and other caves often have scraps dropped by carnivores, owls and other birds. Here the fragmentation and tooth marks on the bones of smaller creatures show they were chewed by Tasmanian devils (*Sarcophilus harrisii*) and tiger quolls (*Dasyurus maculatus*). Bones of both species were found in the site; those of the devils may have been from some of the last of these animals alive on mainland Australia, for devils became locally extinct sometime during the last 5000 years. Many things have been blamed for this, including overall climate change, the extinction of the behaviourally related thylacine and competition from dingoes (or diseases that they may have introduced) (Brown 2006; Fillios et al. 2012).

The shelter was probably used at all times of the year. Emu eggshell indicates regular visits in the winter and it is most likely that the shellfish were collected during the summer. Pipi, so common on other sites near sandy beaches, were in smaller quantities here, with a great concentration on the smaller wedge shell (*Paphies angusta*). Perhaps this was because of a very specific local availability, something seen occasionally elsewhere, as at Cape Bridgewater (Richards and Webber 2004; Richards and Johnston 2004).

Karremarter, as with Koongine, Bridgewater Cave and other occupation sites, has an individual history of use, influenced by changes in the landscape and vegetation. Of no consequence in earlier times, and little enough later, it became one of many convenient places for people to stop and to carry out tasks such as replacing lost or broken spear barbs before moving on along the coast or between it and the forested hinterland – a spot with the added advantage of a fine view out across the coastal plain.

Bridgewater: sites in their context

Bridgewater Cave South, 85 kilometres away at the far eastern end of Discovery Bay, provides a close and contemporary parallel to Koongine. Here, in the mid-1970s, Harry Lourandos excavated one of the limestone rock-shelters on the hill overlooking Bridgewater Lakes (Lourandos 1980a, 1983, 1997). Between about 13,000 and 9300 years ago, the shelter was used by hunters, who, as at Koongine, took a wide variety of species from different environments, including kangaroo, wallaby, potoroo, possum, wombat, bandicoot and rat. The sea was then 3 to 4 kilometres away – it is now less than 2 – and there is some evidence that people occasionally brought shellfish, fish and, perhaps more importantly, seal meat back to the site.

More substantial evidence for use of the coast at this time comes from shell middens at Cape Duquesne, two or three hours' walk east of Bridgewater Cave (Richards 2012). Exposures of shell are visible on old, consolidated soils, spread over a distance of 500 metres along the top of the cliffs, interspersed with dozens of hearth features and innumerable flaked stone tools. Tom Richards carried out small excavations at seven areas of the middens, all of which were created between about 11,500 to 8500 years ago. The sites are now perched on the edge of a sheer cliff 50 metres above the sea. But 11,000 years ago, the sea would have been more than a kilometre away, only rising to its present position over the next few millennia. As it did so, the sandy slope which led down to the shore eroded away, creating the present vertical cliff face. By 8500 years ago, the rock-platforms at the base of the cliff were no longer accessible from what had become an inhospitable, windswept headland.

Turbo account for over half the archaeological sample, with smaller quantities of limpets and top shells – all species which were collected from the rock-platforms below the site. However, the earliest dated shells are oyster, which live in calmer waters or muddy shores. They must have come from short-lived estuaries or closed lagoons in Bridgewater Bay to the east of the headland. Pipi, collected from sandy shores, occur in the latest middens. We have already seen similar varied patterns of shellfish collection along the Victorian coast, changing in detail in response to local conditions of availability and access.

The middens at Cape Duquesne are among the oldest known in southern Australia. Eroded and poorly preserved as they are, we are lucky to have even this evidence of the regular use of the coast at the time the sea began to approach

Figure 4.13 Karremarter Cave at the top of the ridge overlooking the Piccaninnie Ponds and the sea.

Figure 4.14 Wendy Beck excavating at Karremarter, 1985.

its present level. They owe their survival to the steep fall-off of the sea floor, so that the rising waters did not flood over large tracts of land, but rose close to the present day coast. Further west along Discovery Bay there are at least two dozen equally ancient exposures of shells surviving on older consolidated 'terra rossa' soils (Godfrey 1989; see also Frankel 1991b). These, like the earliest dated shells at Cape Duquesne, have oyster and blue mussel – shellfish species which also only inhabit sheltered waters. Their presence at this one time is one indicator of a complex history of lakes, lagoons and wetlands (Head 1983).

A thousand more recent middens have been documented by Michael Godfrey in the more recent mobile foredunes along the shores of Discovery Bay. These show a concentration of pipi, collected from the long sandy beaches during the summer months (Godfrey 1980, 1989, 1994). This was, as he was able to show through analysis of the growth rings of shells, a highly seasonal activity. But people still spent time in the area during the winter, especially in the richer wetland areas towards the northwest of the bay.

Although, as is so often the case, the middens dominate the archaeological record, shellfish were the least important source of food. More foodstuffs were to be found in and beside the freshwater lakes and swamps behind the dunes. The swamps themselves were home to numerous nesting birds, eels and tortoises as well as plant foods. Two staples were *Triglochin procera* (water ribbon) and *Typha* (cumbungi), which grow in open water. In spring, Aboriginal people ate the *Typha* shoots and later in the year their newly grown young flower stems, while the rhizomes could be roasted or pounded to extract the starch. *Triglochin* tubers were harvested either by digging when the water level had dropped or by feeling for them by hand and foot in the mud (Gott 1982a; Gott and Conran 1981). The intensive harvesting thinned out plants, improving their growth and yield (Gott 1982a). In addition to these staples there were many seasonal fruits and berries, such as the native apple *Kunzea pomifera* or 'nurp, a sort of strawberry, which grows in great quantity on … the Glenelg. All the neighbouring tribes had the right to go there, and did so when the fruit was in season' (Lang 1865: 6) – that is, in late January (Gott 1982b). While pipi were mainly collected from the shore in summer, winter use of the wetlands may be inferred from Gideon Lang's description of Aboriginal children at play when they were 'erecting a … perfect imitation of a winter hut' (1865: 27).

After Europeans arrived, the ecology and structure of the wetlands changed and swamps encroached into areas that were previously more open. This may well be because Aboriginal people could no longer continue their traditional systematic swamp management through burning as they had done for many thousands of years (Head 1983, 1987).

Not just more of the same

Westward again, along the coast of the lower southeast of South Australia, the now familiar story repeats itself with local variations. In one of the most detailed studies of coastal sites and their contents, Roger Luebbers explored dozens of middens in his PhD research (1978). Broad shifts from mussels to pipi reflect

Figure 4.15 Bridgewater Caves.

Figure 4.16 A small shell midden in Discovery Bay.

changing landforms and availability at a gross scale. But there are other ways to understand sites in the area. A very fine scale of observation takes us to the limit of archaeological analysis but brings us closer to the people involved.

Noting the distribution of clusters of small heaps of shell in an area at Canunda Rock, and the lack of any later disturbance, Roger looked closely at the exact time of shellfish collection within individual groups. The results were sufficiently clear to allow him to argue that during an Early Occupation Phase (before about 1300 years ago) when pipi were most commonly collected, each heap of shells came from an individual event, discarded during a single meal, and that the cluster as a whole was formed within a fortnight or so during the one season. Each day people returned to their overnight camp, where they would light a new fire for warmth and to cook the day's catch. While there, they also carried out other activities, using a variety of stone tools to make or repair hunting equipment. A further estimate of the amount of food provided by the shellfish suggests that only small groups – perhaps members of an extended family – made use of each campsite.

After about 1300 years ago there are significant changes in the distribution of sites and the quantity and type of shellfish collected, partly enabled by an increased availability with landform changes. There was an associated change in the structure of the sites along the cliff-tops. Turbo were the most common animal remains, along with lobster. Roger Luebbers' analysis suggests that sites of this Late Phase at Abyssinia Bay were the result of only brief visits, possibly by groups of women stopping to have a meal before carrying the rest of the day's catch back to the main camp: the cliff-top middens then represent only the activities of one section of the group, while others were engaged in hunting, gathering and other tasks.

5
Lands of Ngurunderi

[T]he long, long snout of sandhill and scrub that curves away south-eastwards from the Murray Mouth. A wild strip it is, windswept and tussocky, with the flat shallow water of the South Australian Coorong on the one side and the endless slam of the Southern Ocean on the other. (Colin Thiele, *Storm Boy*, 1963)

So Colin Thiele introduces the home of Storm Boy, Hide-Away Tom and Fingerbone to generations of Australians. Like all coasts, it is dynamic, evolving and varied. The sands of the Younghusband Peninsula which block off the long narrow waters of the Coorong from the 'endless slam' of the ocean are the latest in a long succession of ancestral barrier dunes, each left stranded in turn as the land slowly tilted upward, lifting them out of the sea over hundreds of thousands of years.

The lakes at the mouth of the Murray and the Coorong estuary, which extends 100 kilometres southwest, form a complex and rich series of environments, strongly influenced by water flows and tidal conditions. These change with the seasons. But longer-term developments of the entire system over the last 6000 years provide the setting for understanding cultural change. Much of what we know of this comes from the work of Roger Luebbers. Following his work in the lower southeast (Chapter 4), Roger moved his focus northward, with a series of surveys and excavations charting the responses of the Ngarrindjeri to this evolving world (Luebbers 2015a).

Parnka or Hells Gate is the narrowest point between the northern and southern Coorong. In this area Roger found only scattered fragments of shell middens surviving the extensive erosion on the ocean side. The majority of well-preserved cultural sites are on the lee of the peninsula dunes and in the floodplain of the Coorong lagoon. These concentrations of midden refuse form clearly distinct, well-defined mounds, with thick, high deposits in the centre. The separation between the shell heaps suggests long-term use, or regular reuse, of each, as the midden dumps attracted repeated use of the same spot.

Figure 5.1 Looking across the Coorong to the Younghusband Peninsula.

Hells Gate 7 (HG7), the largest of the shell mounds in the area, runs for over 400 metres parallel to the shoreline. Naturally, only a very small amount of so extensive a site could be excavated, but this was sufficient to show that the midden began to form on a low, linear dune, about 1600 years ago. Distinct layers and 'floors' could be identified in the 1.5 metres of accumulation. The earliest layers are more spread out, with traces of individual hearths and clusters of animal remains from single meals. This pattern of occasional, perhaps more casual, use of the place may have been similar to the day-camps suggested for areas further south along the coast (Chapter 4). Later, however, as the piles of shells grew to become a single distinct feature, people used the place in a different way, camping along the top of the mound. Finally, two Ngarrindjeri adults were buried within the last century or two, but their remains and the surrounding deposits were very disturbed by later digging. In 1858, the area of HG7 became part of the first permanent pastoral residence on the Younghusband Peninsula. The Hack family built one structure directly on top of mound HG8, a little over 100 metres from HG7. This brought to an end the direct cultural connection that Tangani people had to this part of their clan estate (Luebbers 2015b).

Almost all the cultural material excavated from mound HG7 was associated with cooking and related activities. Calcrete stones, blackened and cracked by cooking fires, were used to roast fish and to steam reeds for making nets and baskets.

Their method of cooking was either by roasting on the embers, which they do very nicely, and, where they are clean people, very cleanly; and steaming in the native oven. The oven is used in the following manner: A large fire is made, and into it is thrown lumps of stone about three inches in diameter. Then a hole is made in the ground and a fire kindled in it, which is suffered to burn down to glowing embers. Then the pieces of heated stone are placed on the embers in such a way as to secure a pretty level surface. On the top of this green grass is laid, then upon the grass the animal or meat to be cooked, more grass is heaped on the meat, then more hot stones on top of that, and then over all is placed a quantity of earth or sand. As the cooking goes on a smooth pointed stick will be thrust down through to reach the lowest hot stones without touching the food, and then withdrawn; water is then poured into the hole made by the stick to increase the steam below. When the food is supposed to be cooked, the top earth is carefully taken away, then the stones and grass, and there is the meat. I can assure the reader that the savoury smell of meat cooked thus is most appetizing. (Taplin 1879: 42–43)

It is no surprise in a site of this kind that almost all the food remains were pipi, known in this part of Australia as the Goolwa cockle. Although fewer in number, fish – very large Mulloway, up to 50 kilograms in weight, or smaller Black Bream – would have contributed far more to the diet than the shellfish. Using some creative accounting, Roger Luebbers estimated that, if his excavations were representative of the mound as a whole, then some 250 million cockles were eaten and the shells discarded there, along with a million crabs and close to 300,000 fish. These seem like impossibly big numbers, but when spread over, say, one thousand years, or maybe 100,000 meals, they are no longer so incredible at all.

As well as the larger shell mounds like HG7, there are other types of middens. Smaller ridge-top middens are thin, linear-to-oval deposits of cockle shells. They may have been used for special activities, such as ceremonies, or as satellite camps associated with larger central ones. But it is also possible that they represent an earlier form of midden, preceding the development of the midden mounds. And then there were also a few, poorly preserved small surface deposits of estuarine shellfish, including oyster (*Ostrea angazi*) and mussels (*Mytilus edulis*) found throughout the floodplain. These are the remains of small camps, perhaps individual events, on the shores of the lagoon when it was tidal, 5000 to 6000 years ago.

Differences may also be seen between sections of the Coorong. Towards the north the middens are smaller than those in similar locations to the south. The large habitation camps in the southern Coorong are close to traditional crossing points where there was easy access to the peninsula across shallow water. But to the north, in the open conditions at Tauwitchere Channel, seasonal movements must have involved sailing across deep water or by way of long detours to shallower waters. This resulted in a different pattern of collecting and site use, associated with the use of canoes.

Putting together the evidence from his surveys and excavations, Roger was able to develop an overall history of Ngarrindjeri use of the Coorong, which combined social and population change with the opportunities afforded by its development.

About 6000 to 4500 years ago when a chain of inshore islands began to develop, people visited them, in some cases by canoe, for short periods during the summer. These small middens have estuarine species – oyster and mussels.

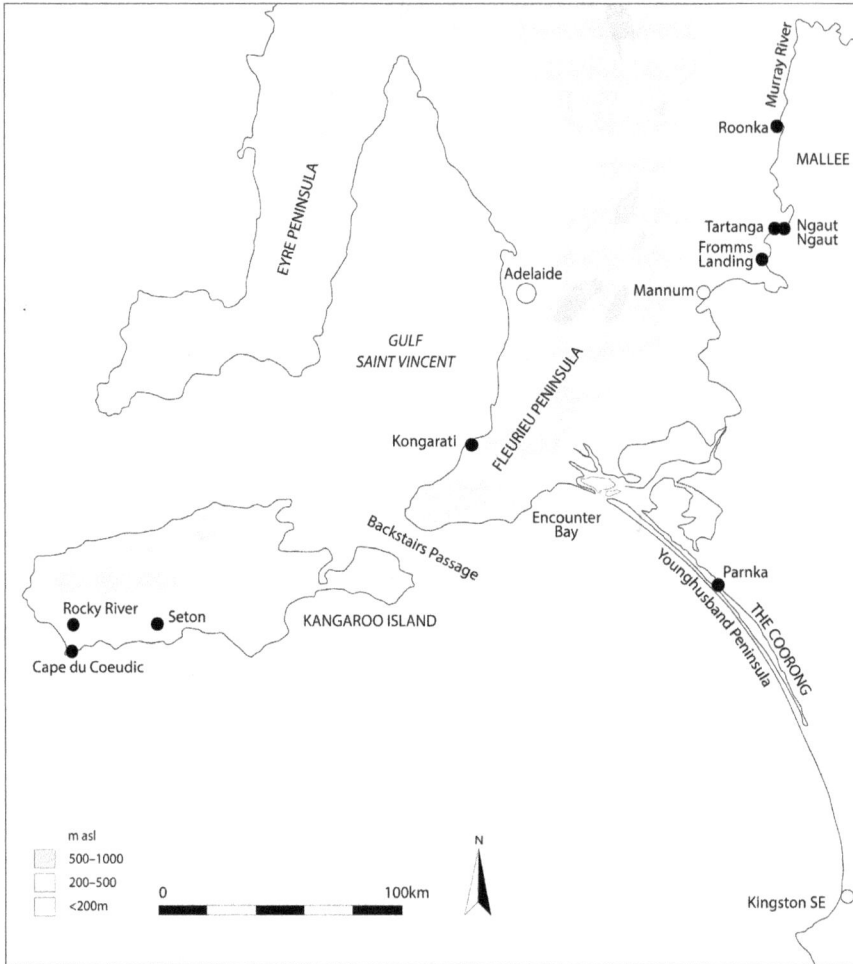

Figure 5.2 The Coorong, Kangaroo Island and the lower Murray.

If people did use the ocean shores of the islands the evidence has not survived. This early Colonisation Phase was followed by what Roger calls an Initial Coastal Settlement Phase. From about 4500 years ago, the peninsula barrier and dunes developed and began to be used increasingly regularly, although still only in the summer and by small numbers of people. At this time the Coorong may have been closed off from the sea, as estuarine shellfish no longer appear in the middens.

After 2000 years ago, when the peninsula and the Coorong were much as they are today, new land-using strategies and landowning systems developed. During this Intensive Settlement Phase, far larger numbers of people now used the Younghusband Peninsula, staying for long periods of time, if not all year round. The stone they needed for their tools was brought from the mainland across to the peninsula. People carried shellfish that they collected on the open ocean beach

Figure 5.3 Large middens in the Coorong.

back over the dunes to the lagoon shores, where the massive shell mounds like HG7 developed through repeated, perhaps even continuous, occupation.

Finally, during what might be termed a Refugee Phase after 1840, some Ngarrindjeri managed to maintain traditional occupation on the ephemeral lakes of the northern Coorong and in association with European pastoral properties in the south. These new camps were located away from the older, traditional ones as a result of social fragmentation and shifts in land-use patterns brought about by European occupation and landscape transformations.

A recent burial and artefacts at Kongarati Cave

Albert Karloan, a senior Ngarrindjeri man, told Norman Tindale a story of the legendary hero Tji:rbuki, how he found and finished the process of smoking the dead body of his sister's son before he carried it away, to several different places. He then came

> to [`Koŋarati`ŋga], where there is a [perki] (i.e. a cave or hole in the hill). About half a mile south, there is a small creek, which is also a camp. Just before Tji:rbuka reached the [perki] [`Koŋarati`ŋga], he sat down and cried: a small spring flowed there. He did not go into the cave but walked south, passing the mouth of the creek, and travelled along the coastal cliffs … to another [perki] … He left the body of his [na:ŋari] outside, and walking into the darkness found a place where there was a suitable ledge of rock. He put sticks up, just as was done

when the body was being smoked, carried the body in, placed it on the platform,
and left it … (Tindale and Mountford 1936: 501)

In 1934, Norman Tindale and Charles Mountford, with a team from the South
Australian Museum, excavated at a small cave on the Fleurieu Peninsula, beside
Saint Vincent Gulf, 60 kilometres west of the Murray mouth. Kongarati Cave is
near the base of a high cliff and only 8 metres above sea level. In it they found the
remains of an elderly Kaurna woman, reverentially placed in a stone-lined burial
pit, packed around with sponges and grass and covered by kangaroo-skin cloaks
and fishing nets. She had been smoke-dried, like Tji:rbuki's nephew, following the
customs of her people. She would not have died so very long ago. One may ask if
this was more of an exhumation than an excavation – it certainly is not something
that would be carried out in the same way today.

The cave had been used both before and after her burial by people hunting
large and small animals and collecting a wide array of rock-platform shellfish. In
the cave there were also many organic artefacts, which may be readily matched
with accounts by several 19th-century European observers. These included
fragments of nets, made

> by roasting the leaves [of a kind of flag] and afterwards chewing them: the leaf
> is then divided longitudinally into four, two of them are twisted together by
> being rolled upon the thigh, and are then twisted together by being rolled in the
> contrary way … In the operation of netting the twine is wound around a short
> stick which answers the purpose of a needle, and the meshes are formed, and the
> knot tied by crossing the string over and beneath the fingers. Thus are made long
> pieces or ribbons of netting twenty or thirty feet long, and about a foot broad,
> which are afterwards put together to make a fishing-net. The net is kept extended
> by pieces of sticks, placed across at the distance of about four feet from each
> other. Some nets are furnished with a bag or pouch. (Meyer 1879: 193)

George Angas described the way in which fishing nets of this kind were used at
Second Valley, a few kilometres from Kongarati Cave. He pictured men with

> a seine about twenty to thirty feet in length, stretched on sticks placed crosswise
> at intervals. A couple of men will drag the nets among the rocks and shallows
> where the fish are most abundant, and gradually getting closer as they reach the
> shore, the fish are secured in the folds of the net. (Angas 1847: plate 21)

Other items in the cave included bone points, perhaps from spears, wooden tongs
used in cooking and fire-making equipment consisting of grasstree (*Xanthorrhoea*)
hearth-boards with holes where hard-wood fire-drills were set, as described by
Heinrich Meyer:

> Nglaiye, s., apparatus for obtaining fire, consisting of two pieces of the flower-stalk
> of the grass-tree. A semi-cylindrical piece is placed with the flat side uppermost,
> and the end of another piece of the same pressed upon it and made to turn rapidly

backwards and forwards by rubbing between the palms of the hands. The friction produces fire in the course of a few minutes. (Meyer 1843: 87)

Understanding change: Ngaut Ngaut and Tartanga

We have just seen Norman Tindale at work at Kongarati cave, a site of very recent activity. He was a polymath whose studies of Aboriginal society and natural history are still fundamental. He also has a special place in the history of Australian archaeology, for his excavations at Ngaut Ngaut (Devon Downs) demonstrated for the first time that a sequence of stone tool types could be defined (Tindale 1982; Smith 2000). It is hard for us now to realise how difficult it was for anyone before the Second World War to appreciate the long history of the Aboriginal past. This was not for want of trying. While everyone knew Aboriginal people had been in Australia long before Europeans arrived, there was no generally accepted evidence or approach to assess just how long this was, or what, if any, changes had taken place in the past. People simply did not have the necessary tools, techniques and concepts. Radiocarbon dating would not become available until the 1950s and there were no other means to work out how old sites or artefacts were. The general opinion was that variations in tools and behaviour were related to local environments, raw materials and customs and not to change through time.

In January 1928, W.R. Roy showed a partial cranium he had found embedded in rock to Edgar Waite, the director of the South Australian Museum. Waite could do little about this as, sadly, he died only a few days later while at the Australian Association for the Advancement of Science Congress in Hobart. But the next year, others from the museum followed up on Roy's discovery, investigating Tartanga Island and Ngaut Ngaut, 60 kilometres up the Murray River from Mannum (Hale and Tindale 1930; Tindale 1957).

Along this stretch of its long journey from the Australian Alps to the sea, the Murray River meanders from one side to the other between the cliffs of the 1.5 kilometre wide trench it has cut into the limestone plain. The depth of the gorge and the reliability of the river means that there is a sharp ecological contrast between the rich woodlands and reed-filled lagoons of the valley and the relatively poor scrub-covered, exposed and semi-arid limestone of the Mallee plains which extend out to the east and west.

Tartanga is a long, low, narrow island where a side branch of the main river forms an open-ended lagoon. In their initial short visit in May 1929, Herbert Hale and Norman Tindale observed abundant evidence of open campsites, and they collected animal bones, stone tools and the rest of the skeleton from which the cranium had been taken. A few weeks later they returned to Tartanga for more extensive fieldwork, digging a long cutting across the island to determine the geological and archaeological sequence and especially the context of the burial. Their understanding of the age of this, and two additional burials, was later framed by the sequence of stone tool types developed on the basis of the excavations at nearby Ngaut Ngaut.

While Tartanga and the potential for finding very old human remains first drew them to the area, Hale and Tindale decided that while they were there they

Figure 5.4 Looking across Tartanga Island from above Ngaut Ngaut.

Figure 5.5 Ngaut Ngaut shelter.

would try additional excavations at Ngaut Ngaut shelter, where Harold Sheard had recently documented rock carvings and noted buried archaeological deposits (Sheard 1927). The shelter was formed by erosion undercutting the base of the 30 metre high limestone cliff that forms the eastern edge of the wide Murray River trench. This created an overhang of varied width along 7 metres or more of the cliff, now about 15 to 20 metres from the water's edge. Although the overhang curves back over the surface to form a sheltered area up to 5 metres deep, this is deceptive. Before sediments built up at the foot of the cliff, the old surfaces would barely have been covered or protected at all. Rock engravings on the soft limestone walls take several forms: some are abstract linear designs, others, possibly earlier, while still schematic, are more naturalistic (Roberts et al. 2014a).

Hale and Tindale initially dug a 50 centimetre wide trench to a depth of 5 metres. One wonders how they managed in so narrow a space – it is certainly not something that anyone would even think of doing in our far more safety-conscious times. As there were deposits at greater depth, a second season of work was organised during the summer. They then excavated far more extensively, with the deepest trench – still only very narrow, and very dangerous – going down some 6 metres below the surface (Hale and Tindale 1930; Smith 1982, 2000). In this unusually deep cutting they were able to observe distinct layers, and to associate these with particular types of stone tools. This was Norman Tindale's key to constructing his innovative 'sequence of cultural phases': 'Pirrian' – 'Mudukian' – 'Murundian', with an earlier 'Tartangan' as found on Tartanga Island. This provided, for the first time, an archaeological basis for understanding Aboriginal history. Operating as he was within the intellectual frameworks of his time (and who cannot?), he linked these 'cultures' to physically different peoples, each bearing their characteristic tools (Tindale 1956). A similar sequence was soon set up in New South Wales and both schemes broadly applied to date sites of all kinds through the types of stone tools in them.

Although they served an important role for many years, Tindale's particular definitions of cultural phases were undermined by the evidence from excavations by John Mulvaney across the Murray at Tungawa, then known as Fromms Landing (Mulvaney et al. 1964). The sequence of stone tools from this riverside shelter showed a basic continuity of technology, although with some variation. Only in the most general way did it match that at Ngaut Ngaut. Tindale's sequence clearly was not universal, and his underlying assumption of a historical succession of cultural groups, each identified by its tools, could no longer be maintained. Neither Tindale's terminology nor his approach to explanation has currency any longer. The development of independent dating using radiocarbon and other techniques and different styles of archaeological analysis and explanation have taken their place. Nevertheless, we must recognise his work as a critical breakthrough in techniques and understanding and in posing a challenge to others.

Apart from the broad implications of the framework Tindale set up, Ngaut Ngaut has its own internal interest. The excavators unearthed the remains of at least two people. The pit in which a small baby was buried was not well defined, but at a greater depth there was the grave of a young child. This was lined with stone slabs in a similar manner to that of the elderly woman exhumed at Kongarati Cave, so this burial custom was used for both young and old, and for at least 1500

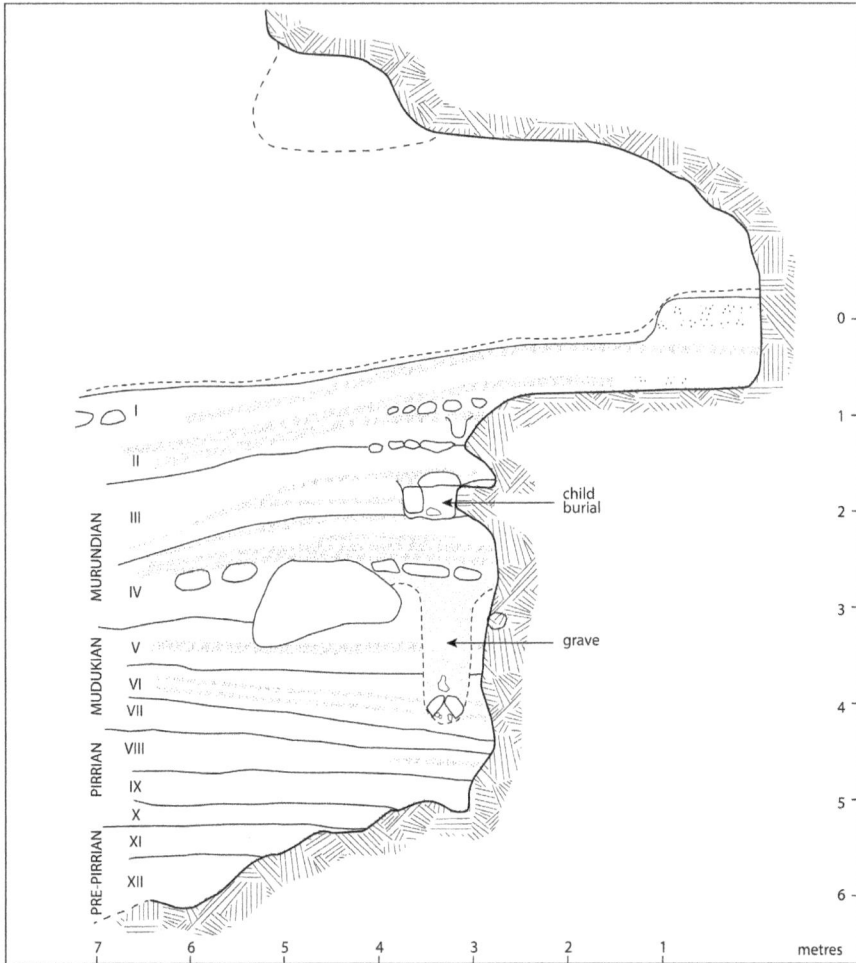

Figure 5.6 Stratigraphic section of the deep excavations at Ngaut Ngaut (after Hale and Tindale 1930: figure 41).

years. At nearby Tungawa, John Mulvaney also found burials, including one small child whose bones were wrapped up in plant material and tied with fibre twine (Mulvaney et al. 1964). We can well imagine a mother finally parting with her child, following the custom along the Murray where:

> Infants not weaned are carried about by the mother for some months, well wrapped up, and when thoroughly dry, are put into nets or bags, and deposited in the hollows of trees, or buried. (Eyre 1845: II, 344)

Among the other aspects of interest from Tungawa is one of the earliest dates for dingoes, which were introduced from Southeast Asia to Australia sometime before 3500 years ago. Dingoes spread rapidly into all parts of Australia, except, of course, Tasmania, and were partly, if not entirely, responsible for the extinction of Tasmanian tigers on the mainland (Fillios 2012). Everywhere they were rapidly incorporated into Aboriginal life, not only functionally but also socially and symbolically. This was certainly the case in Victoria and South Australia (Cahir and Clark 2013).

In the 1970s, Mike Smith re-examined the finds from Ngaut Ngaut. He was able to take advantage of a series of radiocarbon dates to subdivide the 6500 years of occupation into six broad chronological units, each of about a thousand years' duration (Smith 1982; Frankel 1991a). Of course, a thousand years is a very long time indeed, but these units still allow us to trace a history of what people were doing at Ngaut Ngaut. People first camped at the foot of the cliff about 6500 years ago, give or take a few centuries. But it was not always used to the same extent – less frequently at first, then more intensively until 2000 years ago when the number of tools and quantity of bone and shell began to decline markedly. There was a shift in stone tool technology about 4000 years ago as tools became smaller and less uniformly made. Stone points found in lower layers were no longer in evidence during the last two millennia. This may be connected to a roughly contemporary decline in the number of large kangaroo bones, as people relied more heavily on shellfish instead of hunting when camping at this site. Crayfish (available in autumn) began to be eaten in increasing quantities after about 3000 years ago, while there is less emu egg (available in winter or early spring) in the later periods.

What we see at Ngaut Ngaut is complexity and variability: not everything happened in lock-step. We need to disentangle changes which took place at different times and for different reasons. Variations in climate, such as a short but noticeably more arid period for a few centuries about 4000 years ago (Roberts et al. 1999), may account for some of these adjustments – restricting or providing different opportunities which affected the way people moved between the river and the surrounding country. This may explain changes in the types of stone used at different times (Bland et al. 2012). While some different techniques of toolmaking may be linked to broad – even continent-wide – developments, other changes, such as the greater focus on shellfish, may be due to very local events, perhaps as slight as a shift in the river channel. This change may also be connected to the decline in hunting, as people organised themselves and their activities while at the shelter in a different way. The change from winter/spring to autumn occupation must have been part of a new regional pattern of movement and land use as Nganguraku people walked through and across their broader territory, or even represent occasional dry season access to the site by people from the arid mallee scrublands (Chapter 8).

Before we leave Ngaut Ngaut it is important to recognise that it, like other Aboriginal places, has another set of values, quite apart from the archaeology – best explained by Isobelle Campbell, chairperson of the Mannum Aboriginal Community Association Inc. We may leave the last word on the site to her:

Ngaut Ngaut is one of Australia's very special places. The Aboriginal people of the Mid Murray, Riverland and Mallee value Ngaut Ngaut as a place of great cultural significance. It is a place intimately tied to our Dreaming, a place where the 'old people' lived and a place that preserves the environment. It is also a place that demonstrates our ongoing connection to our country and provides us with a sense of belonging. Our community values Ngaut Ngaut as a place where we can teach our children about their culture. (Campbell in Roberts et al. 2014b: 7)

Kangaroo Island riddles, mysteries and enigmas

Ngurunderi … could see the two women walking along the coast, so he followed them to Newland's Head or the Edge. Standing on the point he could see them once more. At some distance the wives turned and saw him afar off. They began to hurry, anxious to get to Kangaroo Island. So Ngurunderi walked slowly on … and entered Kaurna tribal country. The two women hurriedly walked down Tankilla beach to Tjirbuk (Blowhole Creek). From there they could see Kangaroo Island, the spirit land. At that time Kangaroo Island was almost connected with the mainland, and it was possible for people to walk across. Picking up all their belongings, consisting of mats (for fish) and nets (to carry food in), they began to walk across. In the meantime Ngurunderi hurried up to Tjirbuk and could see them going across. When they had reached the centre, Ngurunderi called out in a voice of thunder, saying '*Pink'ul'ug'urn'praŋukurn*' (Fall waters-you). Immediately the waters (sea) began to come in from the west, wave upon wave, driving the two women from their course. So rough, so strong were the tempestuous waves that the women tried to turn their faces toward the mainland. At last, fighting against the waves no more, they were carried into the open sea, taking with them their net baskets. But again, as the sea grew calmer, they tried to swim to Tankallila beach, but could not and were at last drowned. They were, however, metamorphosed into Meralang (the Pages, or the Two Sisters, opposite Tankilla beach on the mainland, or the north east of Cape Willoughby on Kangaroo Island). (Berndt 1940: 180–181)

So Albert Karloan, a senior man of the Manaŋi clan, and Thralrum, of the Lewurindjerar clan, told the long story of the ancestral hero Ngurunderi travelling down the Murray, forming the land as he went (Berndt 1940; see also Berndt and Berndt 1993; Clarke 1995). Albert Karoan called Kangaroo Island Nguruŋaui, where the spirits of the dead go for a short while, following the track of Nurunderi. Others call the island Karta.

The European story of the island begins with Matthew Flinders and Nicholas Baudin. Shortly before their famous meeting in Encounter Bay on 8 April 1802, both had landed on Kangaroo Island. Neither saw any evidence of Aboriginal people there, Flinders noting that 'the extraordinary tameness of the kangaroos and the presence of seals upon the shore concurred with the absence of all traces of men to show that it was not inhabited' (quoted in Tindale and Maegraith 1931: 275). This set up a theme running through much of the archaeological research on the island.

Kangaroo Island was cut off from the mainland by rising seas a little over 10,000 years ago (Lampert 1981; Nunn and Reid 2015). Although only 14.5 kilometres wide, the treacherous waters of Backstairs Passage meant that sailing across from the mainland would never have been easy. At first this provided an obvious reason

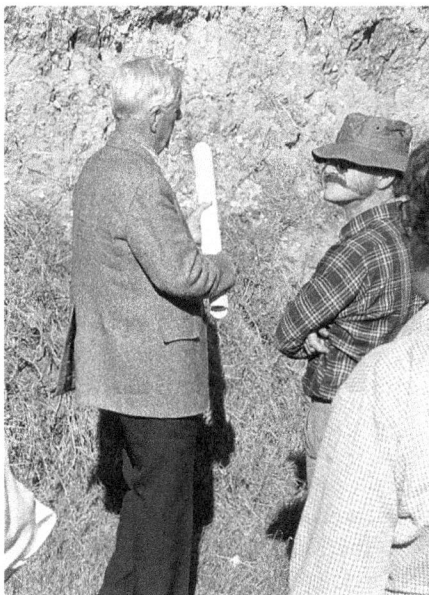

Figure 5.7 Norman Tindale and Ron
Lampert, South Australia, 1980.

why Aboriginal people did not use the island. But then stone tools were found there and documented by Norman Tindale. These were generally very large core tools – where, rather than using large or small flakes struck off a cobble or block of stone (or core), the cores themselves were shaped to make tools. Both their form and presence on the uninhabited island suggested to him that they must date from a time before the island was cut off, and that they were earlier than any of the types in the sequence of cultural phases he had defined at Ngaut Ngaut and Tartanga. When Tindale and his colleagues found similar tools on the mainland this reinforced the notion of an early, widespread culture, which, by 1941, he began to call the 'Kartan' (Tindale 1957).

There was, it seemed, a simple solution to the riddle of the large stone tools: Kangaroo Island was abandoned when it was cut off from the mainland as it was not big enough to support a viable population. But then further mysteries and enigmas appeared. These were largely of archaeologists' own making.

In the 1970s, Ron Lampert turned his attention to the Kartan and Kangaroo Island (Lampert 1982). During his research he was shown a small cave in a limestone ridge about 6 kilometres from the south coast of the island, its shape and aspect providing excellent shelter from even the worst winter weather. He called the site 'Seton' after the owner of the property, and excavated part of it in 1971 and 1973. It proved to have been first used nearly 20,000 years ago, with evidence of occupation for the next 7000 years – that is, until about two millennia before the island was cut off. But other sites he excavated gave a range of dates showing people were on the island for 5000 years after that time, immediately raising a new puzzle: when and why did this population die out?

More recently, Neale Draper carried out rescue work at an inland site at Rocky River. Despite the difficulties of dating open sites of this kind, which are always subject to disturbance, the dates from his test excavations show that people were camping on the shore of an intermittent swamp or lagoon at intervals from 7000 to 1000 and perhaps even as recently as 400 years ago (Draper 1992, 2006).

If Mathew Flinders and Nicholas Baudin were correct in their belief that Kangaroo Island was uninhabited in 1803, we are left with several major questions. Did people live continuously on Kangaroo Island for at least eight or nine millennia and then suddenly disappear so very recently? If so, why did this happen? Was there really no contact with the mainland for all that time? Or could we use the idea of 'abandonment' to suggest a series of alternating episodes of occupation (or at least visitation) and abandonment from the time the island was cut off?

And, just to confuse the issue further, none of the early sites Ron Lampert excavated had tools of the classic 'Kartan' form, but contained only smaller tools. What did this mean? Was the Kartan even earlier than had been thought? Were some tool types characteristic of the Kartan really core tools, or were they just cores? Were there two periods of occupation or were there differences in the activities taking place at different sites?

One series of answers to questions about differences in the sets of stone tools is presented by Neale Draper (1987, 1992, 2006). The presence of flakes at some sites and core tools at others is not because of changes from one technology to the other but more to do with the local availability of stone, so that tools of quartzite are larger than those of quartz. In addition, different tools were needed and used on the coast and further inland. Once again it is better to disentangle different variables and to look at the artefacts outside of a framework of defined types, cultures or phases and to identify local patterns of function, access to raw materials and availability of other resources. Sites on Kangaroo Island, as elsewhere, were used at different times and in different ways. Nowhere is this more clearly seen than at Cape du Coeudic on the southwest coast of the island.

At Cape du Coeudic, Neale Draper excavated a spacious limestone rockshelter set in a limestone ridge near the top of the cliffs overlooking a small bay (Figure 5.8). The shallow deposit and radiocarbon dates of between 8000 and 7500 years ago show it was used for only a short time. Most of the animal bones were those of sea lion. Kangaroo Island was, of course, already an island, but the sea had continued to rise, approaching close to the present coastline just about the time the rockshelter was used. The sandy beach near the rockshelter was then much bigger than it is today, and ideal for sea lions to haul out. But as the sea rose higher, the beach disappeared and with it the sea lions, avoiding the now rocky coast. For that one short time Cape du Coeudic was a desirable place for sea lions; the nearby shelter was an equally convenient place for people to camp and hunt them.

As well as sea lion, both kangaroo and wallaby were hunted. As usual, larger animals such as these were normally butchered, if not eaten, where they were killed. But some bones were carried home. Cut marks on many of these indicate that skins were removed, quite possibly to make cloaks similar to those seen on

Figure 5.8 Cape du Coeudic shelter (photo: Neale Draper).

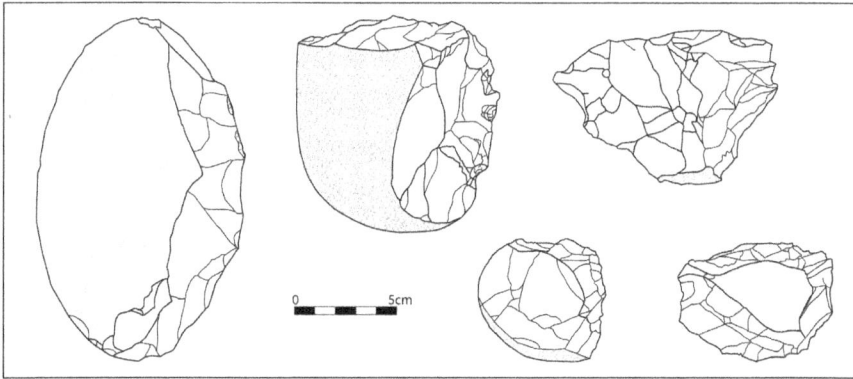

Figure 5.9 Quartzite tools from Cape du Coeudic (after Draper 1987: figure 4).

the mainland in recent times and which were placed within the burial at Kongarati Cave.

The body parts of the sea lions and the other large animals that were brought back to the shelter have another story to tell. Most are those with a high meat or marrow content: all the kangaroo and wallaby long bones were smashed open to extract the rich marrow. Heads of both kangaroo and sea lion were also brought home even though they have little or no meat. Neale Draper's suggestion is that this was because the brains were extracted – providing nutritious, easily chewed and digested food, especially suitable for pregnant women, nursing mothers, young children being weaned and elderly folk. If this was the case, then we can envisage occupation of the shelter by family groups, including those least mobile or able to take on the more strenuous tasks. The wide range of other animals, including small mammals, birds, reptiles and rocky shore shellfish, adds to the picture of both men and women of varied ages using the shelter and going out from it to hunt or collect in different ways and at different places in the vicinity.

We still have no final answers to the long history of Aboriginal use of Kangaroo Island in the more distant past. A final chapter to the archaeological story brings us into the 19th century. Gangs of sealers – as rough a bunch of men as there ever was – came to hunt fur seals for their skins and sea lions for their oil. Some came seasonally, others chose to stay more permanently on the island. Some brought with them Aboriginal women from Tasmania, and later they were joined by – or captured – Ngarrindjeri women from the local region. Their descendants live on the island today. Tindale identified some collections of stone tools as typically 'Tasmanian', arguing that they were produced by some of these women (Tindale 1937). But a more complex story can be told if we do not assume that techniques of making chipped stone or similar tools made of bottle glass – or indeed any other activities – are essentially ethnic markers or symbols of resistance and maintenance of traditional practices. Lynette Russell has argued that the material culture of sealers' camps should instead be seen as the product of cross-cultural entanglements, where the interactions between people from very different backgrounds created a new, independent, hybridised way of life (Russell 2005, 2012).

Maru ancestors at Roonka

Individual burials were found at several of the South Australian sites we have looked at so far. It was very different at Roonka Flat, where an extensive burial ground was excavated over many years by Graeme Pretty and hundreds of volunteers between 1968 and 1977 (Pretty 1977; Walshe 2009). Excavating burials and studying ancestral remains has often been, and often still is, a contentious issue. Many First Peoples find this offensive, especially when they have not been consulted or appropriately involved, as was certainly the case until the last few decades. We will return to this issue in the next chapter (Chapter 6). Graeme Pretty was fortunate to have the support of a senior Maru man, Colin Cook, and other members of the Gerard Aboriginal community. More recent researchers have had similar support from the local Aboriginal communities as work continues on the people buried at Roonka Flat.

Roonka is a little north of Blanchetown, about 50 kilometres up the Murray River from Ngaut Ngaut. In this area the old western cliff of the Murray trench had collapsed, opening up access to the river. The valley was once a rich area of open woodland and wetland, but much of it is now desolate and barren, the result of a sad, and unfortunately not unique, history of events. Starting in the 1840s, box gums along the flats were ring-barked as pastoralists believed this would improve pasture; but any added value – if there was any - was undermined by overstocking. More drastic clearance of whole forests of native pines followed; the trees felled

Figure 5.10 Looking across the Murray to Roonka.

fuelled river steamers during the second half of the 19th century. Overgrazing, drought, floods, rabbits and goats all contributed to further degradation, with additional collateral damage from the construction of locks and weirs as water backed up, flooding and killing surviving red gums.

Roonka Flat itself is a raised sand ridge of about 350 hectares, rising about 5 metres above the river. In 1961, a flash flood exposed several burials. Further damage was caused by casual collectors visiting the site over the next few years. Graeme Pretty's excavations began in order to salvage what he could; neither he nor anyone else realised the complexity of the task (Pretty 1977; Tochler 2009; Pate 2006). By the end of the fieldwork, the team had excavated in several places; the largest, Trench A, was some 450 square metres in area. They found the remains of over 200 people buried at the site.

These burials were not all of the same age: the earliest took place 10,000 years ago, the most recent at the time of the European invasion. Graeme Pretty defined three broad, pre-European periods, despite the complexities caused by both ancient and modern landscape changes. The earliest (Roonka I) is quite unrelated to the very much later burials. Four hearths and associated stone tools and mussel shells in Pretty's main Trench A are evidence of people living near the river some 20,000 years ago during the arid phase at the height of the last Ice Age. There are other equally ancient remains in the vicinity as well as numerous open sites – scatters of tools and hearths – spread out across the river flats. But here we will focus on the burials of the last 10,000 years, for these have many stories to tell, about individuals as well as broader customs, lifeways and relationships.

Roonka II, the period from about 10,000 to 7000 years ago, has numerous graves, including some vertical shaft tombs. The funeral customs associated with these are particularly complex. The corpse was first placed fully erect into the shafts. The shafts must have been left open for a time as the bodies were later rearranged. Some graves have traces of red ochre and burnt wood, and a few other items, such as a fossil shell pendant or a bone point. The other burials, where the body was laid out flat, do not have associated artefacts. Two infants were placed alongside adults in their shaft tombs, but otherwise there are only the remains of adults – almost all men, buried in an area away from everyday campsites. The bodies of women must have been treated differently or buried in a separate location.

Roonka III refers to the last 4000 years, right up until the 1850s. The original land surface, where it survived at all, was badly disturbed in the recent past. But sufficient good evidence survived of hearths with numerous oven stones, isolated patches of mussel shell and scatters of stone tools. The most common and best-preserved features were the six dozen burials found in the same areas where people were living. While it is possible that people moved camps away from where they had recently buried a relative, it is no surprise that over several thousand years repeated use was made of the same ground. Even so, it may be that people did not always maintain a reverence for – or had a different way of connecting to – ancestral burials, as John Eyre once observed that:

> The natives have not much dread of going near to graves, and care little for keeping them in order, or preventing the bones of their friends from being scattered on the surface of the earth. I have frequently seen them handling them, or kicking them with the foot with great indifference. (Eyre 1845: I, 350)

Most burials during the 4000 years of Roonka III were in shallow rectangular graves or oval pits. Unlike in earlier times, both men and women were buried in the area. Young children were often placed in graves together with adults – more often than not, with men. Bodies were laid out in different ways. Earlier burials were placed in a contracted or crouching position on their backs. Some later bodies were also contracted, but now were lying on their side. Others were laid out flat on their backs with the feet extended, often with the feet bound together and the head more or less oriented to the west. John Eyre again gives a description allowing us to envisage the drama of the funerals, where

> The grave being dug the body was laid out near it, on a triangular bier (birri), stretched straight on the back, enveloped in cloths and skins, rolled round and corded close, and with the head to the eastward; around the bier were many women, relations of the deceased, wailing and lamenting bitterly … Two men now got into the grave, spread a cloth in the bottom, and over that green boughs. Other natives turned the bier round, and lifting up the body, gave it to the two in the grave to lay in its proper position, which was quite horizontal, and with the head to the west, the grave being dug east and west: green boughs were now thrown thickly into it, and earth was pushed in by the bystanders with their feet, until a mound had been raised some height above the ground. All was now over,

and the natives began to disperse, upon which the wild and piercing wail of the mourners became redoubled. (Eyre 1845: I, 349)

The status of the deceased may have dictated the choice of burial type and the range or quantity of accompanying grave-goods. The bodies of women and children were often placed on woven mats, while stone tools, bone points and ochre were seen as more appropriate for men. Older men, of high status, seniority and authority, tended to be buried with more items than younger ones. Grave 109 was one of these richer burials. One man, presumably a very well-regarded man, was buried in a deep oval pit with a small child resting on his left arm. A headband of two strands of matched pairs of wallaby incisors was on his head and a series of bone pins along his body. Other pins and animal ankle bones were also found, suggesting he was buried with a skin cloak fixed in place with bone pins, with the animal paws handing over the shoulder. Other bits and pieces may have come from a second headband and a variety of other items.

Among the more regular burials, some more unusual cases stand out, such as the unfortunate man buried in Grave 45 who was killed by a bone-tipped spear which shattered and displaced his ribs as it penetrated his body.

Other customs, apart from burial, can also be seen. In several parts of Australia, one stage in young men's initiation was marked by knocking out one or two teeth: not a pleasant process. This was the practice at Roonka. There was, however, a change in detail. Tooth avulsion, to use the technical term, was more common in the earlier Rooka II period. At that time both of the central incisors in the upper jaw – the most visible of all teeth – were removed, or, if only one tooth was taken out, this would normally be on the left side. Later, tooth avulsion was less common, and normally only one incisor on the right was removed (Durband et al. 2014). Whether this practice should be seen as indicating two groups of people, each with its own tradition, or as a change in local custom over these many millennia, is an open question. But there is little other reason at present to suggest a change in population.

People at Roonka were relatively healthy, at least as far as can be seen from their skeletons: only about one-third had signs of diseases, or traumatic damage affecting their bones (Pretty and Krucin 1989). If children survived the first three years of life they had a good chance of living into their late teens and adulthood. But very few people lived to the age of 50. About half died in their 20s and 30s.

As might be expected among people living an active and strenuous life, there is evidence of broken bones, all of which had healed successfully. Some fractures were the result of accidents, but others, especially broken arms, could well have been caused during violent fights. People also developed osteoarthritis, especially with increased age. Some of these conditions were the result of repetitive actions: osteoarthritis of the elbow joint probably developed because of the frequent and repetitive actions of throwing boomerangs or spears.

Another line of analysis makes use of the way in which bone chemistry reflects the sources of food eaten. Much of this work has been carried out over the last 25 years by Donald Pate (1997, 1998, 2000, 2006). He has been able to show that men and women had somewhat different diets. Men ate greater quantities of land animals; women and children ate more fish, vegetable foods and shellfish.

Overall, however, most protein in the diet came from local land animals and to a lesser extent freshwater fish and shellfish from the river. Food from elsewhere – whether marine food from the coast or animals from arid areas away from the river corridor – was not significant. The people of Roonka seldom moved either far down the Murray to the coast or away from the river out into the dry Mallee country.

6

The central Murray

As we move further up the Murray from Roonka, the course of the river becomes the boundary between New South Wales and Victoria. Its character is different. The central Murray is still, as it always has been, a narrow, winding ribbon, rich in plants and animals, between the arid and semi-arid plains to either side (Figure 6.1). Here the river is not set down in a defined trench, for the land is flat, as most of Australia is flat. But it still comes as a surprise to my students when they realise that their classrooms in the northern suburbs of Melbourne are higher above sea level than the Murray, several hundred kilometres inland. There are still subtle differences: low ridges, dunes and shallow depressions that assume local significance. Before modern water controls, the river flows were extremely variable, with occasional excessive floods or prolonged droughts, even to the point where the river dried up completely. The waters peak in spring, when the river spills out, filling numerous meandering anabranches, ancient stream channels and billabongs before gradually draining away and drying out over the long, hot summer.

Despite seasonal and other less regular variability, the riverlands were one of the richest areas of temperate Australia, well endowed with plentiful water, fish, plants, animals and waterbirds:

> They catch vast numbers of ducks in an ingenious manner. The lagoons run for some length, narrowing at the end, where the trees close in; two or three blacks plant themselves near this narrow pass, having extended a large net from tree to tree; the others then proceed to the top of the lagoon, driving the ducks before them. As they fly by the ambuscade, they throw their boomerangs whizzing over the heads of the birds, which, dreading that their enemy, the hawk, is sweeping at them, make a dash under the trees, strike the net, and fall as if shot, when the natives dash in after them. I imagine it is the panic that seizes the birds, for I have seen a hundred caught by such means. (Stuart 1853, in Bride 1898: 371)

> The tribes along the Murray made splendid nets, which they used most successfully. The Billybongs which run inland for miles, and served as reservoirs to hold the waters which were brought down by the floods, had weirs placed carefully across their mouths in summer, when the water was very low; and these weirs,

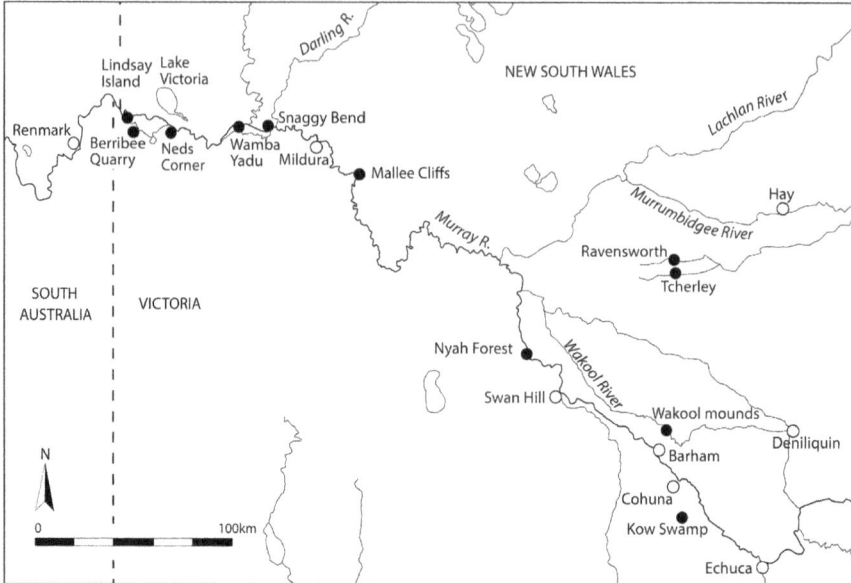

Figure 6.1 The central Murray region.

which were formed of stakes interlaced between little twigs, served most effectually to retain the fish which had passed over them during the floods, and which, when the water got low, were secured with ease. (Davis in Smyth 1878, 2: 324)

Probably at all times in the past canoes were to be found along the river; there is a strong possibility that during a short, unusually wet period 24,000 years ago, people used them to reach an island in the Willandra Lakes system, only 100 kilometres north of the Murray (Fitzsimmons et al. 2015). But, whatever their antiquity, canoes were certainly a key to life along the river in the recent past (Edwards 1972). As described by the explorer John Eyre,

[a] large canoe will hold seven or eight people easily; it is often twenty feet [6 metres] long. The following is a description of an ordinary one for fishing: length fifteen feet [4.5 metres], width three feet [1 metre], depth eight inches [20 centimetres], formed out of a single sheet of bark, with one end a little narrower than the other and pointing upward. This end is paddled first; the bottom is nearly flat, and the canoe is so firm, that a person can take hold of one side, and climb into it from the water without upsetting it. It is paddled along with the long pine-spear *moo-aroo*, described as being used in fishing at night by fire-light. In propelling it the native stands near the centre, pushing his *moo-aroo* against the water, first on one side and then on the other; in shallow water one end of Canoes do not, of course, survive for long, although there are now modern re-creations where Aboriginal communities have fashioned both canoes and the tools to make them (Chapter 3; Griffen et al.

2013). What do survive for longer are the trees from which the bark for canoes was taken (Figure 6.2).

Over 7000 of these scarred trees have been documented in Victoria alone, but, while recognising their heritage value, they seldom excite archaeologists, for their nature is obvious, they are all relatively recent and there seems little more to learn from them. Nevertheless, they can still show patterns of bark removal in relation to campsites and availability, as, for example, in the southwestern Wimmera, where bark was taken wherever it was convenient (Chapter 8, see also Chapter 11). In the different environment along the Murray, where there were other demands and the constant need to replace old canoes every few years, any Aboriginal man, as Peter Beveridge noted, 'in his rambles keeps his eyes about him, with the view of discovering a suitable tree from which he can take a canoe, wherewith to replace his now frail craft' (Beveridge 1889: 69): the *moo-aroo* is placed on the bottom, and the canoe pushed along. (Eyre 1845: 264-65)

canoes are made from the bark of the redgum tree; bark of other trees is also used, but merely for temporary use, as none but the former will stand the weather without curling or splitting. They are made in all cases from a single sheet, without tie or join. In making these vessels, trees with natural bends are chosen, as curves so obtained preclude the necessity of having to use fire to give the required rise, stem and stern.

When the bark for a canoe is cut, stretchers are placed across it at intervals of three to five feet to prevent it from curling up. Short props are also placed under the bows and stern to keep them from becoming depressed by reason of their own weight. If at this stage the canoe should not have the exact shape desired by the maker, he places heavy billets of wood inside at those parts which require pressing outwards, and the bark, being green, the pressure effects the end aimed at. After this, and whilst the weights are still in the canoe, and the props outside, a coat of well-puddled clay is spread over the interior, which effectually hinders sun cracks. In this condition, they are left in the sun to season. After ten to fifteen days' exposure, the bark has become so hard as to be able to retain the shape ever after, no matter how roughly it is handled. It is therefore launched without ceremony upon the water, where it is destined to float for the few brief years of its existence. (Beveridge 1889: 64–65)

The size of pieces of bark removed was related to both the type of tree and the intended function. In the Barmah Forest, bark was cut from many more yellow and black box trees than river red gums, but mainly for smaller dishes, shields or other utensils (Figure 6.3) (Bonhomme 1991). When people took bark from the red gums it was more often as larger slabs, most suitable for canoes.

Mounds on the Murray

Blackfellows' ovens are not by any means misnomers, as the mounds so called are essentially 'cooking places', and they are formed in the following manner: A family, or (as the case may be) several families, who have taken up their quarters

Figure 6.2 A scarred tree near the Wakool River.

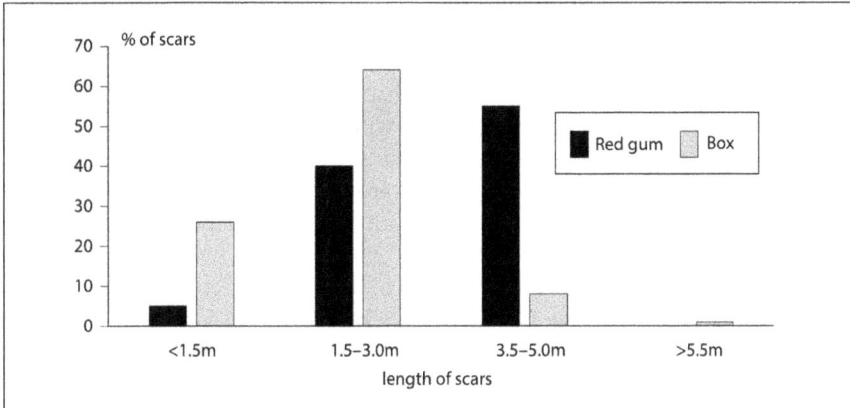

Figure 6.3 Size of scars on river red gum and box trees in the Barmah Forest (data from Bonhomme 1990: table 6).

where food chances to be plentiful, have something to cook – for example, I will say an emu; a hole is therefore dug, about three feet in diameter, and about eight or ten inches in depth; this work is always performed by 'Lubras', and their only implements are 'yam-sticks'. If there are not any stones in the vicinity, the most tenacious pieces of earth found during the excavation are carefully put aside. When the hole has attained the desired depth, it is filled with firewood, upon which the selected pieces of earth are placed, the wood is then ignited, and, by the time it is all consumed, the earth nodules have become baked into the consistency of brick, and as a matter of course are red hot. When this result has been achieved, the hot clay is removed by a pair of 'aboriginal tongs', after which the hole is carefully swept out, and a layer of damp grass placed over the bottom and round the sides; the dismembered emu is then packed carefully on the grass, when it is covered over with more moist grass; the red hot clay is then spread equally over the grass, and the whole is then covered over with the finer earth that had been taken from the hole; but should the earth covering be too thin to keep the steam from escaping, it is supplemented by earth dug in close proximity. Ashes are never used as an oven-lid, because, being fine, they would run through the interstices of the red-hot clay, and grass as well, and so spoil the food. Before the caloric has time to become exhausted from the clay nodules and the hole itself, the food is as perfectly cooked as if it had been done in the most improved kitchen range. When the cooking has been completed, the covering is scraped off, and this *debris* (calcined clay, ashes, and earth) becomes the nucleus of a blackfellow's oven. This process being continually repeated for many years, perhaps centuries, results in the heaps which are actually blackfellows' ovens, although often improperly designated tumuli.

As a general rule, the blacks do not use their cooking mounds to build their camps upon; an exception to this exists, however, on the large inundated reedy plains of the lower Murray, where blackfellows' ovens are more numerous and larger than any I have seen in any other portion of Australia. (Beveridge 1869: 186–87; see also 1883: 37–39)

This description by Peter Beveridge, a keen observer who was closely involved with Aboriginal people in the area, provides us with a clear image of the formation and use of a characteristic type of site: the mounds most commonly found in the floodplain of the Murray and in similar areas around. The earliest known examples formed some 4000 to 5000 years ago, a little to the north on the riverine plains off the Lower Murrumbidgee River (Martin 2011).

In the 1970s, Peter Coutts organised one of his annual Victoria Archaeological Survey summer schools in the Nyah Forest, a little north of Swan Hill (Coutts et al. 1979). Stands of river red gum line the main river bank and spread across either side of the Parne Milloo Creek, an anabranch of the Murray, which meanders across the clay floodplain. Although still periodically flooded, for most of the year the creek dries up, leaving isolated, shallow, reed-filled billabongs. Peter and his students located 122 mounds in the 10-hectare area they studied. Most of them were less than 20 metres in diameter, but some were far bigger, up to 50 metres across and rising 1 metre above the plain. A similar range in size is seen elsewhere, as in the Barmah Forest, always related to their location (Figure 6.4).

Three mounds were excavated in the Nyah Forest, including the largest, Dry Plains 1 (mound DP/1). This mound had clearly been recently disturbed. Soil had been illegally carted away for market gardens; rabbits had burrowed into the looser soils on the mound, for they naturally preferred these to the surrounding alluvial clay, baked hard in the hot dry summer months; and then rabbit-trappers had followed, ripping open the warrens. The excavation trench stretched out from the centre of the mound onto the surrounding floodplain (Figure 6.5). There was no neat layering of deposits from discrete episodes of site use or formation, nor could this be expected. Not only was this due to the recent disturbance, but also because of the way in which a big mound like this built up over generations of digging, re-digging, and raking out the contents of ovens. Much of the mound was made up of fragments of the baked clay heat-retainers used in the earth ovens where both the animal and plant food had been cooked. But there was little evidence of what people ate. Of course, as this was primarily an area for cooking and not necessarily for eating, food would have been distributed around a more dispersed camp, and the refuse discarded away from the oven. Although few in number, the scraps that survived came from a wide range of animals, birds, fish, crayfish and shellfish, suggesting a diverse and varied diet.

Only a handful of artefacts were found in DP/1, despite the large area excavated – none at all were found in the other two, smaller, excavations. There were only nine small stone tools made of quartz, flint and chert; the latter, at least, must have been carried in from at least 100 kilometres away. Four mussel shells may have been used for scraping flax, to make twine for nets or other items. A similar number of small, broken bone tools, pointed at both ends, could have been used for many purposes – as ornaments, fish-spear points or awls.

Mound DP/1 began to form about 1200 years ago. It is big, with a total volume of some 600 cubic metres. How did mounds become so large? Peter Beveridge provides some of the answer, noting that:

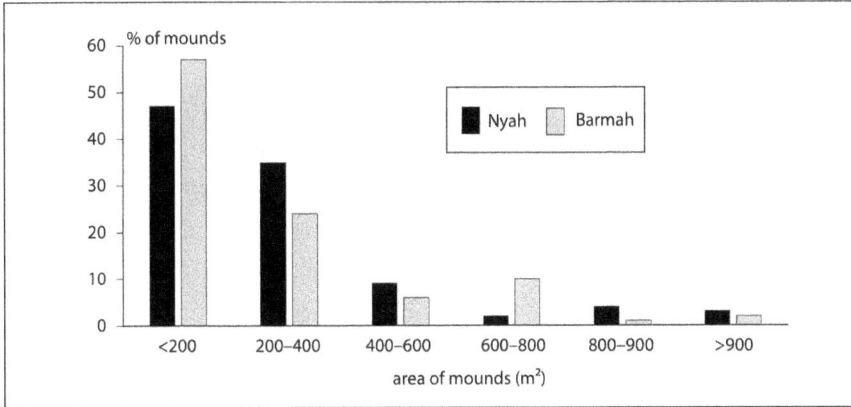

Figure 6.4 Relative sizes of mounds in the Nyah and Barmah Forests (data from Bonhomme 1990: table 4).

As long as the camp remains in one place, the same hole is used for baking their food in, and when it is understood that at least a barrowful of fresh clay is required every time the oven is heated to replace the unavoidable waste, in consequence of the clay being used in an unwrought state, it will readily be seen how these mounds gradually, but surely develop. Bones, too, of the animals which they use for food, beside charcoal, tend materially to hasten their growth. (Beveridge 1898: 34)

Even if only half the volume of DP/1 was made up of clay from heat-retainers, many hundreds of meals must have been cooked there. In addition, once mounds reached a certain size they also became convenient places in other ways, when

the snow-waters cover the plains for miles on each side of the river, the ovens stand up out of the flood, perfect little islands, looking green and refreshing to the eye, because of the great growth of the succulent saltbush with which their crests are clothed. These island-mounds the blacks, during flood-time, make their camps upon, conveying their firewood in canoes, oftentimes a distance of four or five miles. Sometimes the blacks will remain as long as a month at a time on one of these tiny islands, living upon the enormous and oily Murray cod, supplemented by eggs of nearly every kind of aquatic bird, and the birds themselves; besides they have the young and succulent kumpung (broad-leaved flag), which shoots up through the water, by way of vegetable. Thus, every article of consumption, even to the material for constructing their camps, has to be brought to the spot, and, of course, the daily refuse adds materially to the growth of the mound. (Beveridge 1869: 187; see also 1889: 35) (Figure 6.6)

The fragmentary remains of three people were found within mound DP/1, but they and their graves had been very badly disturbed when rabbiters ripped up the surface. It seems that their bones were initially dried, some were stained with ochre

Figure 6.5 Victoria Archaeological Survey excavations at mound DP/1 (photo: Aboriginal Victoria).

Figure 6.6 A mound rising above Murray River floodwaters.

Figure 6.7 Measuring a low mound in 1983.

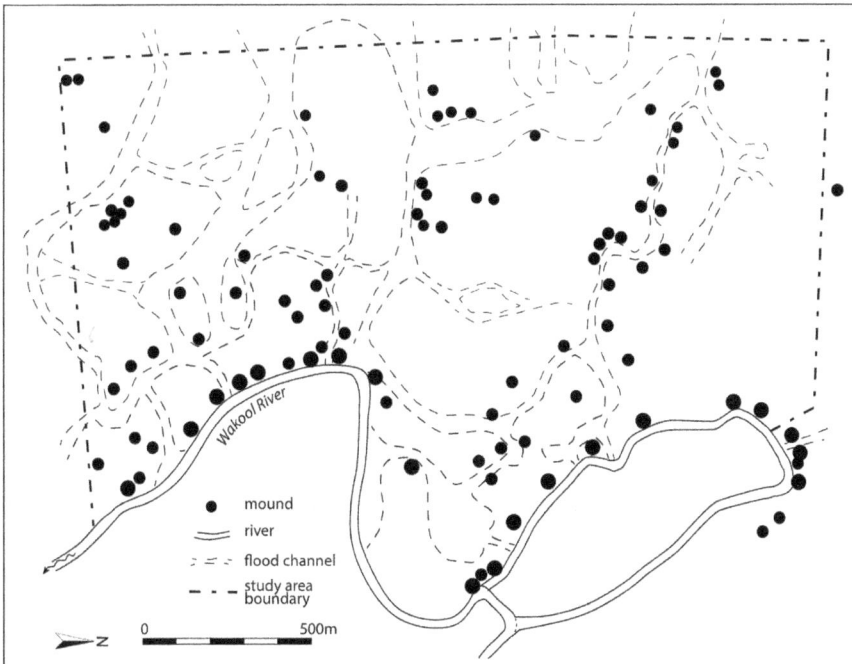

Figure 6.8 Distribution of mounds near the Wakool River.

and then the remains were cremated. Although quite common, burial in an oven mound was not the usual custom along the river corridor, even during the most recent periods. Most burials took place in sand dunes beside the river or lakes, but perhaps DP/1 and other mounds were used at times when people were living close by or when other places were inaccessible.

In his Nyah Forest study, Peter Coutts noted a relationship between the size of mounds and the way the local area was seasonally flooded. A similar pattern can be seen 100 kilometres upstream where the Wakool, a major side branch of the Edwards River – itself an anabranch of the Murray – meanders off to the north before rejoining the main river well downstream of the Nyah Forest. In 1982, Annette Berryman was interested in following up on Peter Coutts' work and carrying out her postgraduate research somewhere near Deniliquin. So we started looking around for a suitable area. At that time my office at La Trobe University happened to be beside the university dentists (in those days universities had such support services for their students) and in casually passing the time of day I mentioned this to one of them. 'Ah,' said Rhys Lewis, 'why not come out to my block on the Wakool where there are lots of mounds?' We did not need a second invitation, and after a preliminary exploration were able to set up camp beside one of the largest mounds in an idyllic spot beside the Wakool River. Big old river red gums stood at intervals along the bank, with scattered stands of younger black box regrowth further afield. It was Easter, and it had recently rained enough to start new growth after the long hot summer, so that the looser, richer soils of the mounds stood out green against the dry clay floodplain.

During our initial survey season in April 1983 we walked over every inch of our friendly dentist's 250 hectare property, locating, measuring and describing 95 mounds and 11 scarred trees and plotting their location in relation to the subtle changes in topography (Berryman and Frankel 1984; Frankel 1991a) (Figure 6.7). As everywhere in the floodplains, water initially overflowed from the main river into the adjacent wider and deeper channels before progressively filling the smaller and shallower hollows further away. After the flood season the process was reversed as the water slowly drained back, leaving a few small pools to slowly dry out completely. We found that the largest mounds were spaced out along the bank of the Wakool itself, and those further out were smaller and lower (Figure 6.8). This makes perfect sense: people spent far more time close to the main watercourses, and far less near the short-lived ponds. There is a further intriguing, still unanswered question regarding the spacing of the larger mounds along the bank of the Wakool. Did particular groups – families perhaps – regularly return to exactly the same mound-site and keep as far as possible from other mounds? Did they assume some special significance marking a persistent relationship between families and place?

Later in 1983 we returned to the area and excavated small sections of three of the mounds. While generally similar in their makeup to those excavated in the Nyah Forest, none had any artefacts or traces of food refuse. They are slightly older, but still relatively recent, all having been formed within the last 3000 years. Associated with one mound we came across a heap of clay heat-retainers, still in the position where they had been raked out of the earth-oven when it was last used by someone 2700 years before (Figure 6.9) (Downey and Frankel 1992).

Figure 6.9 Clay heat-retainers raked out of an oven 2700 years ago.

Figure 6.10 Surveying sites at Neds Corner, 2012.

What were people cooking in these ovens? Sarah Martin provides some clear answers from her excavations at two mounds (Ravensworth 3 and Tchelery 1.1) near the Murrumbidgee River, both of which were used at some time between 5000 and 4000 years ago (Martin 2011). In her fine mesh sieves Sarah was able to collect small fragments of charcoal, bone and shell. Microscopic study of 19 charcoal samples confirmed a menu featuring bulrush (*Typha*) rhizomes – the 'compung' of the Wemba Wemba or 'balyan' of the Wiradjuri – and other wetland plants (*Triglochin* and *Bolboschoenus*). All of these were also seen in pollen samples from the sites and as leaf impressions on some clay heat-retainers. There were also bones of small, medium and large birds – ducks, waterhens and swans – along with fragments of their eggs. The larger fish bones in the sites were very broken up, so only a few could be identified as sizeable Murray cod or golden perch. Most of the fish bones were the vertebrae of tiny little fingerlings:

> They have a net also nearly as fine as the mesh of a coarse cheese cloth, with which during the spawning season they take millions of young fish, many of which are less than an inch in length. Besides these, at the same time they catch immense numbers of young lobsters and shrimps, or prawns, all of which are mixed up and cooked in the same condition as they are taken from the water. This dish is deemed a luxury of the highest order by the aboriginal epicure. The cooking of these small fry consists merely of boiling them very slowly until the shrimps become red, when the dish is ready. The aboriginal pot made for this sole purpose is an elbow or knot of a tree scooped out until it becomes a mere shell of wood. This vessel is set upon cold ashes, which have been placed to the thickness of two inches above red-hot coals, so prepared for this purpose. (Beveridge 1889: 84)

Neds Corner: surveys and shellfish

Mounds are the most visible archaeological features on the floodplains. But there are many other less assertive sites: the scatters of stone tools, shells or clay heat-retainers that represent less focused activity or repeated returns to particular spots. In 2002, the Trust for Nature took over Neds Corner, a 30,000 hectare pastoral station, with a view to its rehabilitation and long-term conservation. The station is just south of the main river, with a low-lying floodplain similar to those on the Wakool and the Nyah Forest. Once up on the low bank it is a different world – a seemingly featureless open saltbush plain. But there are subtle variations: old eroded dunes border a few shallow hollows, some of which fill with water after rain, when all the clay surface around becomes heavy, sticky and difficult to walk across. This we often have to do. But on sunny, crisp mornings there is nowhere better to work.

Since 2008, Neds Corner has provided a regular site for field training by La Trobe University, for both archaeology honours students and Aboriginal students studying for a TAFE Certificate IV in Aboriginal cultural heritage management (Cosgrove et al. 2013; Garvey 2013). Each year cohorts of students spend a week or more at Neds; the accumulating evidence from their surveys contributes to a more

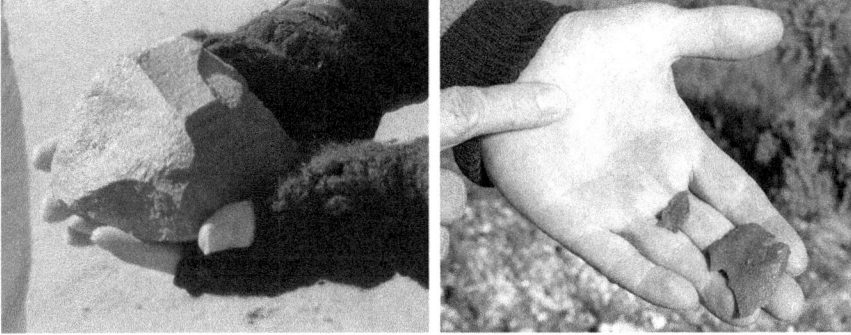

Figure 6.11 A large core and small stone artefacts at Neds Corner.

Figure 6.12 The stone quarry at Berribee.

complete view of the area and provides the basis for a management plan which will be useful for both the Trust for Nature and the Traditional Owners – Ngintait, Latji Latji, and Nyeri Nyeri.

The most common evidence of past activity that they come across as they trudge further away from the river are scatters of clay heat-retainers. While there are small, low mounds near the river, out on the plains it seems that people did not return to and repeatedly reuse older sites, so no mounds formed. They find few stone tools. These are, for the most part, small well-worked pieces, but there are rare examples of larger blocks from which sharp flakes could be struck off

Figure 6.13 A shell midden on the bank of the Murray near Swan Hill.

when needed (Figure 6.11). These would have been carried in from nearby sources, most probably those beside the Lindsay River, about 25 kilometres to the west. The Berribee quarry is an impressive area of spoil dumps and hollows spreading over at least 500 metres along a ridge, where people dug out silcrete and other stone (Figure 6.12) (Grist 1995; see also Hill 2006). Generally, suitable stone was not readily available along most of the central Murray floodplain east of Neds Corner, so quarries like this must have had a particular importance and the stone been more highly valued, and used more carefully, the further people were from the source. Stone was also carried south from the quarries near the river into the Mallee, the artefacts gradually declining in quantity and size with distance.

There are also shell middens (Figure 6.13). As she developed her research at Neds, Jillian Garvey excavated two of these in 2014 (Garvey 2015; Garvey and Perry 2015). One (the Homestead midden) can be traced over about 400 metres along the low dune that had developed by 15,000 years ago when the river system was significantly different (Figure 6.14). Radiocarbon dates from Jillian's small excavation match this early date. The second, similarly long, thin and narrow (the Murray River midden), formed on the more recent dunes bordering the modern river channel. Here she excavated a 500- to 600-year-old partly eroded hearth with clay heat-retainers.

Both dune systems and the shell deposits on them are now much worn down and eroded, especially close to the river's edge. Among the scattered and broken shells are occasional small fragments of bone. Jillian's interests are, however, more on the shellfish collected and consumed. At both sites there were river mussels

Figure 6.14 David Clark and Jillian Garvey excavating a hearth in the Murray River midden, 2014 (photo: Anthony Dall'Oste).

(*Alathyria jacksoni*) and river snails (*Notopala sublineata*). Jillian was able to compare the sizes of river mussels from the two middens with some she collected from the river. The three sets are different – shells from the 15,000-year-old Homestead midden would have had, on average, about twice as much meat as those of the more recent Murray River midden. The modern samples are twice as big again. The opposite is seen with the river snails, where modern examples are generally smaller than the ancient ones. But to what extent this is due to changes in the shellfish populations, season of collection or simply sampling remains an open question. As Jillian has shown, the river mussels have a high level of valuable saturated fat (particularly palmetic acid) and of polyunsaturated fatty acids, which are beneficial for cognitive processes. Other trace elements (iron, magnesium, sodium and zinc) would also have been of dietary importance. While providing a good source of protein and these other elements, the small size of shellfish means that people would have had to eat very many animals to meet what is now considered the minimum nutritional requirements. Shellfish would have been a valuable, fairly easily collected supplement to a more broadly based diet, perhaps especially, for some people, as noted by Hawdon in 1838, where 'the food of their women and children consists chiefly of roots of different kinds, wild yams, freshwater muscles and the Tortoise' (Hawdon 1952: 41).

Burials: from collection to repatriation

The particular circumstances of geography and customs and archaeology have resulted in an unusual concentration of burials in the central Murray; we have already seen this downstream at Roonka. Research on these sites provides intimate details of individuals, communities, health and traditions. But it also demonstrates the changing nature and social context of archaeology (Donlon 1994).

In Chapter 4 we saw something of the effects of amateur enthusiasts who collected thousands of stone tools. Something similar, although more bizarre and of greater general concern, happened with Aboriginal ancestral remains. Nineteenth-century anatomists in Australia and Europe were avid collectors, who gave little thought – if the truth be told, none at all – to the feelings of relatives and descendants. The most prolific collector of all was George Murray Black, who from 1929 to 1950 worked his way up and down the Murray River between Echuca and the South Australian border. While he was more interested in those he thought were old, he did not scruple to dig up the most recent graves, including those of smallpox victims who would have died in the 19th century. Generally, little is known of the contexts from which he excavated the hundreds of Aboriginal skeletons that he sent to the Australian Institute of Anatomy in Canberra and later to the University of Melbourne (Robertson 2007).

Valuable as these extremely large numbers of remains have been to researchers, social change caught up with these and other collections. In 1984, Jim Berg, then the director of the Victorian Aboriginal Legal Service, took legal action regarding the Murray Black collections in Melbourne, setting in train a process which led to the eventual return of all those Aboriginal ancestral remains whose origin could be established (Griffiths 1996). The remaining 38 people whose provenance remained unknown were ceremonially buried in the Kings Domain Gardens in the centre of Melbourne (Figure 6.15). An equivalent process of repatriation was initiated by the National Museum of Australia, which had inherited the larger collections from the old Institute of Anatomy. Over the last 30 years many other ancestral remains, both from Australia and abroad, have also been brought home. These include significant ancient individuals, such as the 40,000-year-old woman and man from Lake Mungo, whose remains are now stored in a secure 'Keeping Place' controlled by the local Traditional Owners.

In 1967, Alan Thorne was cataloguing the old collections of ancestral remains in the dark, depressing vaults of the National Museum of Victoria. In one box he came upon about 150 small fragments of bone including pieces of a skull which appeared to be very old as they were heavily mineralised and encrusted. They reminded him of one of the first 'ancient' skulls to come to the attention of researchers, the so-called Cohuna cranium, collected in 1925. The prospect of locating more very old remains that would contribute directly to answering some of the major questions of the origin and source of Aboriginal people was intriguing. But no one knew where these bones had come from. It was far from easy for Alan West, the curator of anthropology, to trace their source: the only clue was a single police label, itself taken from an older container (West 1977). Eventually, more detective work among old police records led Alan West and Alan Thorne to the precise location beside Kow Swamp and even to the rest of the

Figure 6.15 Memorial marking the burial site of 38 Aboriginal people in the Kings Domain Gardens, Melbourne.

same skeleton. Alan Thorne later began excavations at the site, which continued for several years, while at the same time the construction of an irrigation channel disturbed many more burials (Thorne and Macumber 1972).

Graves were found in two main areas at Kow Swamp, one associated with an ancient shoreline and others on a nearby former creek which once flowed past the northern edge of the lake where the Cohuna cranium and two other burials had previously been found. Most of the burials were dug into the sandy dunes which had formed on the eastern shore of Kow Swamp between 26,000 and 19,000 years ago (Stone and Cupper 2003). In all, remains of at least 40 people were excavated: men, women and children. Few were at all complete. Only three have been directly dated. They are very widely spaced in time, and it is likely that the burials took place at long intervals over many thousands of years, between at least 15,000 and 9000 years ago, at a time when the lake held fresh water. The people were all placed in shallow graves. Some were stretched out on their left side; others were more tightly crouched with the knees drawn up towards the chin and the hands in front of the face; at least one was cremated. Stone tools, ochre, shells and marsupial teeth accompanied some burials. Unusually in an Australian context, people at Kow Swamp and some of their neighbours enhanced their looks by binding the heads of children so that they grew in a flatter or more elongated shape than normal (Durband 2014).

Despite their scientific importance, all the ancestral remains and associated artefacts from Kow Swamp were handed over to the Echuca Aboriginal Cooperative in 1990. This was not universally welcomed by archaeologists, no matter how supportive they were of Aboriginal rights in other respects. Many would have preferred the creation of secure 'Keeping Places', like that set up for the Mungo remains. This, while giving control to Aboriginal communities, would allow the possibility of further research in the future (Mulvaney 1991). At the heart of the vigorous debates of the 1980s was whether the information that could be obtained from ancestral remains was more important than the beliefs or attitudes of Aboriginal people today; equivalent debates continue to take place all around the world, and in many different circumstances. Aboriginal voices find an echo in the words of the late Chief Rabbi Immanuel Jakobovits on medieval Jewish burials excavated in York in the early 1980s:

> Whatever the scientific and historical loss, I hope you and the general public will appreciate our paramount concern for the reverence due to the mortal remains which once bore the incomparable hallmark of the Divine image and which, we believe, have an inalienable right to rest undisturbed. We are convinced that the dignity shown to humans even centuries after their death can contribute more than any scientific enquiry to the advancement of human civilisation and the enhancement of the respect in which human beings hold each other. (Quoted in Lilley et al. 1994: 300)

In many other circumstances, quite different relationships have developed between researchers and Traditional Owners, who take their role as custodians and managers of heritage very seriously. Where burials are exposed either by nature or through development, specialist documentation precedes reburial or whatever other mitigation work is needed. Lindsay Island is one such case. This is a large tract of land between the Lindsay River and the Murray in the far northwestern corner of Victoria. As elsewhere in the region, a maze of small creeks and channels carry floodwaters from the Murray River into swamps, billabongs and floodplains. Numerous sites have been recorded on the island, including many scarred trees, a few mounds and a very small number of stone tools. But it is also well known for burials, which have been observed and excavated over many years, notably by Robert Blackwood and Kenneth Simpson in the 1960s (Blackwood and Simpson 1973).

Early in 1989, Colin Pardoe undertook a project for the Victoria Archaeological Survey to document sites – and in particular burials – which were exposed on a large area of sand dune (or meander scroll) formed on the inner curve of the Lindsay River (Pardoe 1989). He was able to document 65 burials in one discrete section of the dune and another 79 more widely spread across the area. Without excavation, and carrying out all his observations in the field, Colin's ability to analyse the burials in forensic detail was naturally limited, although he could collect enough information to compare the burials on the 'Cemetery Dune' with the more dispersed individuals. In both sets about two-thirds were men. The men were more consistently oriented west-southwest, but there was greater variation among the women. Even though they are quite concentrated, only one burial on the Cemetery Dune cut across an earlier grave, suggesting that the burials may have been marked in some way and that they were probably all relatively recent, perhaps all from the last few hundred years.

The site of Wamba Yadu is on an old sand dune only 50 metres from the Murray. It may once have been about 2 metres high, but the sand has now almost entirely disappeared from much of the area, exposing the remains of 47 burials as scattered bones or more complete skeletons on the clay surface below. With the permission and support of the Mildura Aboriginal Corporation, Colin Pardoe was able to document the site and the ancestral remains (Pardoe 1993a) but, as on Lindsay Island, closer, more forensic study was not possible. Hearths, shells and stone tools show that the place was used at some earlier time for general camping, but this ceased once it began to be used as a burial ground, during the last few thousand years. There was an unusually high proportion of women: normally two-thirds of burials are men, but here the situation was reversed. The relatively low number of children (11 per cent) is not unusual, reflecting a combination of custom and preservation. Men were generally placed stretched out on their backs, and all were oriented in a similar direction. The women's burials were less uniform, including crouched and lying on either the left or right side. One small woman was cremated.

And finally, briefly, a fourth example: Snaggy Bend, where Peter Clark and Jeanette Hope carried out a survey in response to local Aboriginal concerns (Clark and Hope 1985). They documented 150 (of a total of perhaps 200) burials which were exposed by wind erosion on the crest of a low dune. Most people were placed either fully stretched out or crouched, more often than not with the heads to the west. But there were also cremations, including some where the bones had been broken up, or covered with red ochre, and 'bundle' burials, which must have taken place after prolonged and complex ceremonies. While some of the burials were clearly of considerable age, others were very recent indeed, to judge from the presence of glass beads, cloth and fragments of knives. There are also half-a-dozen 19th-century European graves in the same area of the dune. People from the local station must have known of – or perhaps even seen – Aboriginal funerals on the dune and felt that this was therefore an appropriate place for their own.

Persistent places: burial grounds and cemeteries

Although quite common, burials in mounds such as those at DP/1 were not the most usual custom along the river corridor, even during more recent times. As our four examples illustrate, most burials took place on well-defined areas of slightly higher ground beside the rivers or lakes (Littleton 2007b). Sometimes they are isolated from others or widely spread out, but in some places they are fairly tightly clustered. Where there were many burials close together within a small area that was not used in other ways, Colin Pardoe argues that this should be regarded as a 'cemetery', somewhere deliberately set aside and used by a particular group over several, perhaps many, generations. In such cases, these places came to have a special symbolic value and served as deliberate signals of a strong association between particular people and place (Pardoe 1988).

In some areas (especially near where the Darling joins the Murray) there do seem to be some defined cemeteries, although none – so far as we know – were used for more than a few hundred burials at most. Further up the river, east of the junction with the Murrumbidgee, there is less structure of this kind (Littleton 2007b). This difference may be related to the density of population, for areas such as Lake Victoria could have supported relatively large numbers – but just how many people was that? Colin Pardoe once estimated that over the last 6000 years there may well have been as many as 10,000 burials around Lake Victoria alone. This seems an incredible figure until you realise it means, on average, two deaths per year. You do not need to be an actuary to do some rough sums with a pencil on the back of an old envelope (should you still have, and know how to use, such primitive equipment) to work out that this would not need a local population of more than, say, 150 people – a figure in keeping with the numbers estimated by the first European observers (Kefous 1983, 1988).

Concentrations of people led to the material demonstration of territory through regular burials in recognised cemeteries. But, as so often, time becomes an issue, for the graves we know of were generally dug at rare intervals over many thousands of years, making this type of connection less clear. It may be that the apparent clustering of burials was due to the local coincidence of mundane, practical factors of topography and environment. The greater availability of food in some areas encouraged people to use them more often and for longer; the more people there were in a particular place the more likely it would have been for some to die nearby; adjacent sand dunes and ridges were the easiest or generally preferred places to dig graves; and so on.

We can equally well see burial grounds as 'persistent places' in another way. People may come and go but such places retain a significance. Once an area began to be used for burials, it might continue to serve for centuries, although only intermittently and at long intervals, and even where there were few or no direct links between people at very different times, or even, as we have seen at Snaggy Bend, of entirely different backgrounds (Littleton 2007b; Littleton and Allen 2007b). But within such a long-lasting tradition there are many variations. More often than not, consistency of layout and orientation was limited to a relatively small number of burials made over only one or two generations. Local practices, as at Roonka, changed through time. Sometimes, however, the discovery of earlier graves influenced later practices. One clear example where grave-diggers must have hit upon and then copied a previous burial is at Katarapko, where the new grave was placed beside and exactly parallel to one dug 3000 years before. In other cases more recent burials cut through older ones as a different custom was followed.

Despite these short-lived and local differences there are some broad and long-lasting trends all along much of the central Murray corridor. Most burials were simple inhumations in what may have been quite shallow graves. Cremation was not common, and seems to have been used only for some young women. With no evidence of burning nearby it is likely that the cremation itself was carried out elsewhere, and the burnt and smashed bones were carried to the grave site. Children were never buried alone, but are found either with other children or with an adult.

Health, wealth and relationships

The undulating sandy plains and linear dunes of western New South Wales end in the low, red sandstone Murray Cliffs, overlooking the floodplain of the Murray River. Aboriginal burials are often exposed along the cliff-tops, and in 1986 reports of vandalism and amateur souveniring worried the Aboriginal communities at Mildura and Dareton. Colin Pardoe was asked to investigate (Pardoe 1988). By the time he visited the site there was no longer any trace of the graves, and the bones were broken and in a confused jumble; in fact, there were parts of three people mixed together from burials that must have taken place near one another but at very different times. At least one of the people – whose skeleton was the most complete of the three – died about 6600 years ago. He was a fairly large man of between 40 and 50 years of age. His teeth were quite worn, as might be expected from someone of his age, especially when there was a good deal of grit in the food and where teeth were used when making tools or chewing flax to make twine; but no other dental problems could be seen on those that were still available. From a depression fracture on the top of his skull it is clear he had suffered a severe head wound, although it was not quite severe enough to kill him. Despite later infection it had healed well. The direction and shape of the fracture indicates that it was probably caused by a blow received during face-to-face combat, his enemy striking him with a club held in his right hand – a not uncommon event if historical records are to be believed. Similar depression fractures have been found on a significant number of men's skulls elsewhere along the Murray, showing a consistent, if low, level of violence.

This kind of biographical detail, providing an insight into an individual life, could be deduced from the close study of any ancient skeleton. Put together with many others, some general patterns emerge. Particular characteristics of life along the Murray are highlighted when compared with other parts of Australia (Webb 1989, 1995).

Although our understanding must be tempered by biases in the samples available for study, (Robertson 2007), Steve Webb argues that the more recent Aboriginal populations of the Central Murray region were, somewhat surprisingly, the least healthy of all, with high frequencies of malnutrition, parasitism and non-specific infections (people in the arid interior were generally the healthiest). Adults were more likely to die before their mid-30s than people in other areas. This seems counter-intuitive. If the Murray River corridor was so rich in plant and animal resources, one might expect better health. But, instead, measures of anaemia (seen in bone pathology), and signals of interrupted growth in teeth and long bones, show that people in this area were subject to chronic stress, much of which can be attributed to the relatively high population density. One effect of this was a greater reliance on a high, but not really the most nutritious, carbohydrate diet (seen in the build-up of calculus on their teeth). But the Murray corridor also became a less healthy environment, with parasites and infection affecting people as much as any seasonal or more unpredictable food shortages (and we also remember the presence of debilitating mosquito-borne diseases such as Murray Valley encephalitis and the Barmah Forest virus). It was this same density of population that made the Murray River people so susceptible to the

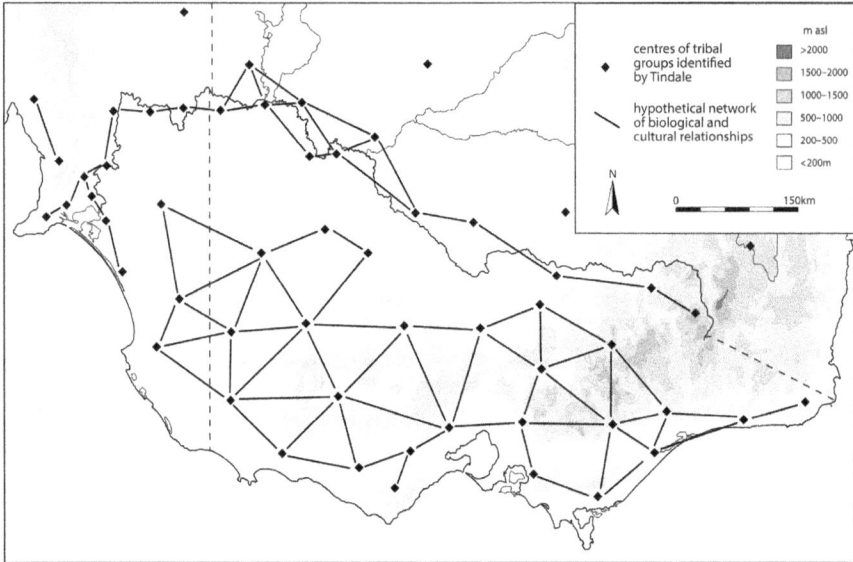

Figure 6.16 Schematic diagram of different forms of relationships: exclusive systems along the Murray and more inclusive connections in other areas (after Pardoe 1990: figure 4).

highly contagious smallpox which had so devastating an impact in the late eighteenth and early nineteenth centuries:

> I once had occasion to remove the whole of a blackfellows' oven to make a road way; it contained 8700 cubic feet [246 cubic metres]. During its removal, I found twenty-eight human skeletons. This great number surprised me, but upon making inquiry, I found that they were the remains of those who had fallen victims to the smallpox whilst that epidemic ravaged the aboriginal tribes; but notwithstanding the friable nature of the chosen burial-ground, the deaths were so frequent that many of the bodies were left unburied. (Beveridge 1869, see also 1883: 30, 1889: 37)

There is now no way of knowing whether this was indeed a burial site of smallpox victims: certainly Beveridge and his informants believed it was. Smallpox ravaged Aboriginal populations along the Murray and elsewhere even before the first European explorers reached the area. Although often thought to have spread from Port Jackson, its introduction to Australia by Maccassans from Suluwesi who regularly visited the north coast to collect trepang (sea cucumber) is perhaps more likely (Dowling 1997; Campbell 2002). Whatever the sources of this and other new diseases, a very high proportion – at least a third, perhaps much more – of the population died as a result (Chapter 11).

In more normal circumstances, Steve Webb has shown that women were more prone to anaemia than men, as is normal across all populations. Older people along the Murray were more likely to develop osteoarthritis through heavy work, such as digging for tubers, than those in other regions, while the effects of chewing fibrous bulrushes to make twine for nets used for hunting and fishing can also be seen in damage to both teeth and jaws. As again might be expected among people leading an active life, many had, at some time in their lives, broken arms. Broken legs, especially common in arid areas, are not a feature of life on the river. We have already seen evidence of conflict on the skull of the man from Mallee Cliffs, and also of violence at Roonka. But this was less common along the Murray than in other areas; perhaps alternative forms of conflict resolution were in force.

So much for aspects of daily life. Bones also have stories to tell about genetic – and hence social – relationships. Colin Pardoe's examination of large numbers of ancestral remains provides a basis for assessing these relationships between people along the Murray and in other areas of southwestern Australia (Pardoe 1998, 1990, 1994, 2006). While noticeably distinct in some respects from people elsewhere, there is great diversity along the river corridor, with those in each region showing the closest similarity to their nearest neighbours up- or downstream. In contrast, people living in the less predictable, more arid areas – such as the Mallee and Wimmera to the south – have greater physical similarity to others in all directions and across long distances. How should we understand this difference?

Colin Pardoe's explanation links genetic affinities with ecology, population density and social behaviour. As we have seen, the richer resources of the Murray corridor allowed a relatively high density of occupation, with each group focused on a particular local area, sometimes signalling control of their territory by repeated-use burial grounds or cemeteries. The local availability of marriage partners and of adequate food meant that there was no need, and perhaps little desire, to forge alliances with people from more distant areas: keeping, as it were, river frontage properties in the family. As a result, social links to people away from the river or from more distant areas along it would have been limited, leading naturally to the distinctive genetic patterns observed. Riverine people had, in effect, an *exclusive* (or closed) approach to social and genetic sharing or relationships (Figure 6.16).

It was different elsewhere. In areas where their world was less reliable and resources more dispersed, people needed to be more mobile, to move more frequently and over longer distances. It was also very helpful to maintain kinship connections with as many people as possible in all directions, to ensure rights to different territory and the ability to call on relatives in other areas when need arose. An *inclusive* (or open) system was therefore advantageous. The resulting social ties led, equally inevitably, to more widespread, more homogeneous genetic distribution.

7

Dry country and wet

The water-yielding Malleè, called the Weir Malleè, was known to the natives long before the arrival of the whites … During a recent visit … my friend, Mr Peter Beveridge, rode with me into the Malleè, accompanied by one of his native stockmen, who, on our approaching the edge of one of the plains, at once pointed out the tree. It grows upwards of twenty feet high, and scarcely differs in appearance from those around to the eye of a stranger, but easily to be detected on the brownish tinge of its leaves being pointed out. Our black immediately proceeded to cut a yam stick about five or six feet long, which he pointed with his tomahawk, and then, tracing the roots by a slight crack discernible on the surface of the ground, he dug underneath it till obtaining space enough for the point of his stick, he pushed it under and then prized up the root as far as he could. Going further from the tree he repeated the operation until he had, perhaps, fifteen or twenty feet of the root laid bare. He now broke up the roots into lengths of three to four feet, and, stripping off the bark from the lower end of each piece, he reared them against the tree, leaving their liquid contents to drop into a pannikin. On holding a piece of root horizontally no water is to be seen, but the moment it is placed in an upright position a moisture comes over the peeled part, until the pores fill with water which drops rapidly.

The natives when travelling in search of water, on finding the tree, usually cut off a large piece of the bark to serve as a dish, which they place at the foot of the tree, leaving the broken roots to drain into it, whilst they smoke a pipe or light a fire. The root, on being broken, presents to view innumerable minute pores, through which the water exudes most copiously; from a pint to a quart of pure water being procurable from a root of twenty to thirty feet long. (Cairns 1858: 32–33)

Easily dismissed as arid and desert lands, the Mallee and Wimmera are in reality diverse. Some parts are indeed desert, though covered with saltbush, but there are many far more hospitable patches, especially towards the south. But still, you don't have to move very far from the Murray to find yourself in the Mallee, uninviting and dry, in sharp contrast to the river corridor (Figure 7.1). As you drive south from Mildura towards the Wimmera, you pass over the low linear

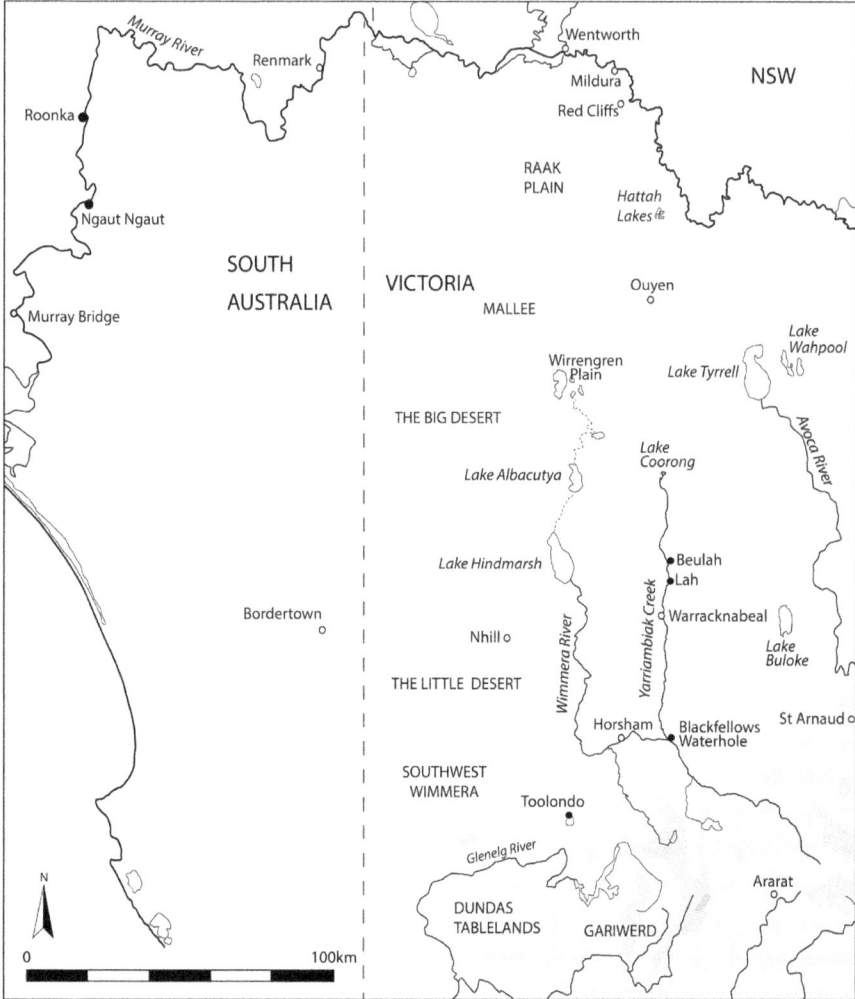

Figure 7.1 The Mallee and Wimmera.

dunes before the land becomes flatter, a seemingly endless plain with few clear landmarks apart from the occasional sets of grain silos – many now decorated with impressive giant paintings – beside the railway tracks. The winter rainfall is low and long hot summers often turn to drought. Travelling further south is to move towards grasslands, wetlands and the wooded areas of the higher ground closer to the Grampians/Gariwerd and Pyrenees, where the rainfall is more than three times that of the northern plains. Although the only permanent surface water is Lake Hindmarsh, the major rivers that flow slowly north from the divide – the Wimmera, Yariambiack and Avoca – structure the country and support Lake Albucutya and other heritage-listed wetlands. None of the rivers ever reached as far north as the Murray. Beyond the overflow lakes there are smaller, far less reliable soaks and small lakes, which only rarely hold any water at all and then never for long.

In the recent past, Aboriginal people would venture from the Murray into the Mallee to collect *taarp* (a sugary excretion from insect larvae), of which they were fond (Beveridge 1889: 127), or set out on expeditions in search of raw materials such as ochre for decoration and ceremony:

> In the very barrenest portion of the barren Mallee Scrub there is a considerable depression or dry lake, distant from the Murray River about eight miles. The bottom of this lake is composed of bright red ochre, which the natives use in large quantities in the ornamentation of their own bodies, and in decorating their opossum cloaks as well. To procure this paint the tribes nearest thereto make yearly journeys to the lake, and in doing so frequently undergo serious privations by reason of the scarcity of food and water on the way. They take a supply of water with them in bags formed of wallaby skins, but as it takes them ten days or more to make the journey both ways and prepare the paint, their water usually runs short long before they return to their starting points. (Beveridge 1889: 27)

Nevertheless, others did call the Mallee home, although their country could never have supported more than a small number of people (Ross 1985). Like other hunter-gatherers in arid areas, their 'main strategy was to be highly mobile and opportunistic, as resources ebb and flow over time and space, using pulses of rainfall to disperse across foraging territories and falling back on small wells and waterholes as the country dries out' (Smith 2013: 11). Robert McKinley and other Aboriginal men explained to Norman Tindale (1974: 134, 215) how the Ngarkat of the South Australian Mallee lived in this way and had different skills and customs from those who lived along the river. Their relationships with these more settled people was often awkward, for they needed to keep on good terms with them by not trespassing into their territories in normal times so that they could, when essential, approach to camp at appropriate places beside the river. They made use of designated pathways at such times. One led down the cliffs to the Murray at Ngaut Ngaut, where Ngarkat people could spend time during the hot summer days, retreating to their own country in the scrub at night.

During the wetter climate of 30,000 years ago, people could make more use of the area, as seen at Box Gully on the eastern shore of Lake Tyrrell (Chapter 1), but the more arid conditions which followed led to a retreat to better watered places. This may not have been a total abandonment, for elsewhere in Australia people managed to adjust to a different way of life when the deserts came to them. Several thousand years of increased water availability after 14,000 years ago meant that lakes on the Pine Plains, which now very rarely receive water from the Wimmera–Outlet Creek system, would then have been filled, creating a longer riverine corridor from the south through the dunes. Further north, other lakes or soaks fed by groundwater would also have held water, providing habitat for shellfish and a focus for other animals – and for people.

One date of 8500 years ago obtained from shell associated with stone tools and hearths on the Raak Plains shows that people did make use of that area during

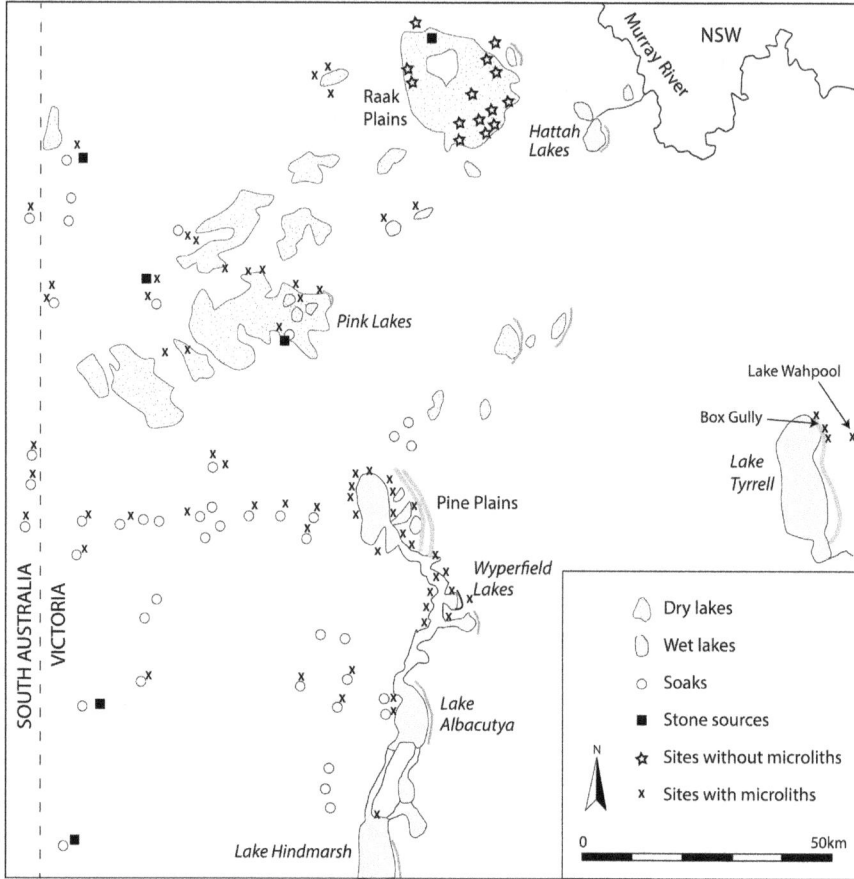

Figure 7.2 Distribution of sites in the Mallee (after Ross 1981: figures 4 and 5).

these better times. The only stone tools documented there by Annie Ross during her extensive surveys of the region are cores, large flake scrapers and large utilised flakes (Ross 1981, 1982; see also Kefous 1982) (Figure 7.2). There were none of the characteristic later types of microlithic small tools, which suggests that the area was not occupied – perhaps barely even visited – once conditions changed for the worse after 8000 years ago, when the Mallee once more became as dry as it is today. Elsewhere there are numerous sites with microliths, evidence that people were using other parts of the Mallee within the last 5000 years or so (Figure 7.3). By and large, the more recent archaeology of the Mallee lands reflects a patchy and fluid level of activity. There are few substantial sites and what we know of them comes not from excavations but from surface surveys, such as those carried out by Annie Ross, with the attendant problems of determining their extent or age, especially where artefact collectors had, once again, been busy:

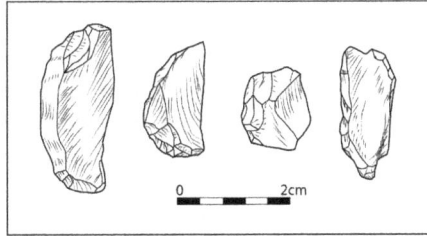

Figure 7.3 Microlithic stone tools from Lake
Wahpool (after Bell et al. 1981: figure 10).

Excellent sites for collecting artefacts of several types are the camping places
situated in sheltered bends of the Yarriambiac at LAH and BEULAH.

Lah, unfortunately, is as popular with amateur collectors as it is extensive!
It is combed regularly, and many fine specimens gathered there join the legion
of unclassified collections lost to science. A once well-sheltered sandy rise (now
subject to wind and water erosion), snug in the crook of an arm of the
Yarriambiac – open to the east, and protected from the south, west and north – is
the site of LAH No. 1 camp. Some twenty acres are worth prospecting here, four
close to the creek being littered with an astonishing quantity of chips, flakes and
stone debris. Much of the material is 'foreign' to the area, and I am of the opinion
that the stone was obtained by the natives from sources at least fifty miles away
(and worked into implements at this and similar camps at intervals in the Mallee
where rocks and outcrops of stone suitable for implements are rare). (Hofmaier
1957: 68)

Yariambiack Creek

Forty years after Keith Hofmaier described the sites on and near his property,
Johan Kamminga and Mark Grist carried out an extensive survey along the
Yariambiack Creek (Kamminga and Grist 2000). They were able to add 28 open
sites with scatters of stone tools to those few already known; none of them of
any size or particular quality. Typically for broad-scale surveys of this kind, only
scatters exposed on sandy dunes or sand sheets or where there was some local
soil disturbance can readily be found. Other stone tools may well be more deeply
buried. Much more common were scarred trees, mostly grey box. None of these
were very old, many showing signs of having been cut with steel axes, and so not
all need have been cut by Aboriginal people. One scar was large enough to have
provided bark for a canoe, but otherwise it was not possible to tell what the bark
was used for. Larger slabs may have been used for buildings, smaller ones for dishes
or shields. Five trees had other sets of holes. While it is tempting to see these as
made by Aboriginal hunters in search of possums and the like, the fact that they
were cut with steel axes leaves the identity of the people who cut them uncertain.
Finally, one particular place can be linked, albeit indirectly, to specific Aboriginal

activities: an otherwise unmarked old river red gum in Warracknabeal believed to be where Aboriginal corroborees or ceremonies took place.

This seems very little to show for millennia of activity in the area, but closer consideration of the stone tools does provide some further insights. Although the most common stone used was the widely available quartz, other types were, as Hofmaier suggested, 'foreign' to the area. Some came from sources not too distant, including quartzite from Gariwerd, but other stone had its origin more than 200 kilometres away: greenstone hatchet heads from Mount William in central Victoria and flint from the coast. These would have been some of the many items exchanged at large gatherings (Chapter 10). Historical accounts note one meeting place on the Wirrengren Plain in Wyperfield National Park (Massola 1969b; McBryde 1984a). People came there from all directions. The Wergaia of the southern Mallee came with spear shafts, nets, baskets, white pigments, possum skin armlets and rugs; people from the Murray with mussel shells; those from Chinkapook with red ochre.

Aldo Massola (1973; Kamminga and Grist 2000) made up one hypothetical route along which people travelled from east of Lake Boloke to Lake Hindmarsh, based on his knowledge of archaeological sites mixed with a good many assumptions (Figure 7.4). While speculative at best, this still gives an impression of the long distances covered and of strategies needed to cross sometimes inhospitable areas to participate in important events.

Journeys and meetings were never simply about exchanges and access to utilitarian items or goods that were not locally available. There was always also a social dimension in cementing relationships and connections, especially in the unreliable areas of the Mallee and northern Wimmera. Here, open (or inclusive) social strategies which provided the framework to keep up good relationships with neighbours were especially advantageous, in contrast to the more closed (exclusive) behaviour in more fertile, richer or reliable environments such as those to the south or along the Murray River.

Blackfellows Waterhole

One of the more favoured places along the Yariambiack and Wimmera is in the Berrabool Reserve, where several ponds lie along Corkers Creek. Blackfellows Waterhole is one of the largest of these. As the name implies, it was known to 19th-century Europeans as an Aboriginal place (see Chapter 11) but it also has evidence of far older use. It did not escape the attentions of artefact collectors: 'the sandy rises bordering this swamp must have been much camped upon by the Aborigines, because large numbers of stone implements, mostly microliths, can still be found there' (Massola 1969: 111; see also Mitchell 1949).

Despite the collectors' efforts, there were still many stone tools exposed in the low dunes in the 1980s when Anne McConnell surveyed the site (McConnell 1985). On the basis of her observations of the geomorphological history of the area and the artefacts, she suggested that the area around Blackfellows Waterhole was used for at least the last 5000 years. We now know that people were there considerably earlier.

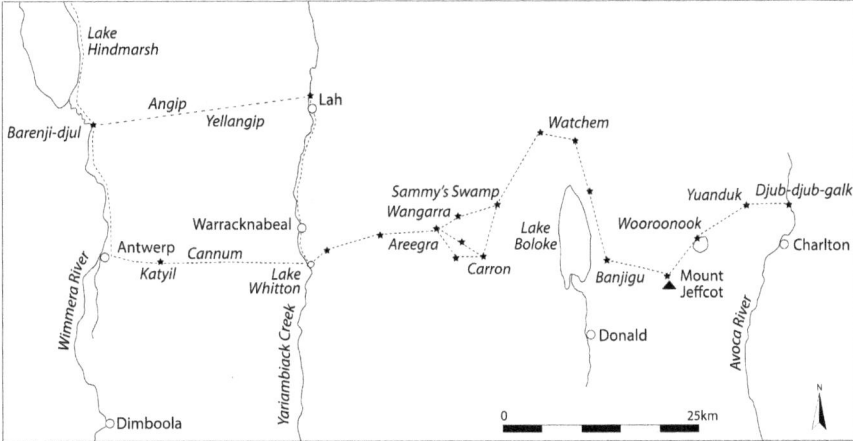

Figure 7.4 Hypothetical trade route between the Avoca River and Lake Hindmarsh (after Massola 1973: figure 1).

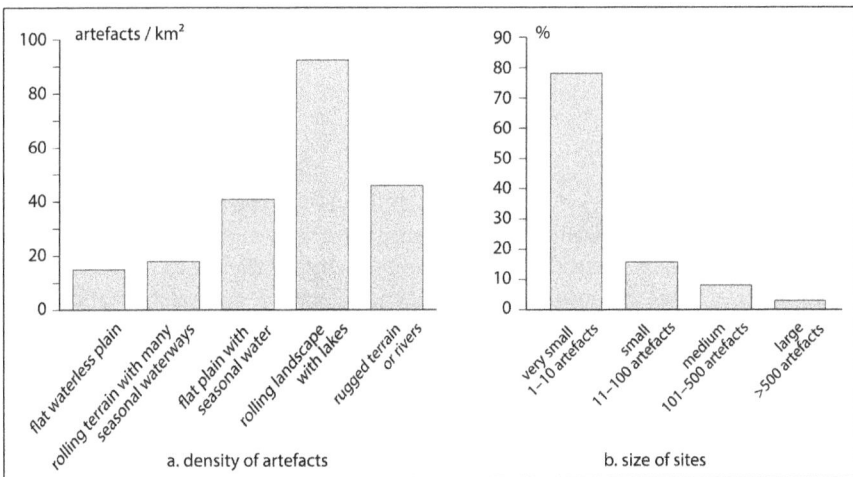

Figure 7.5 Sites in the southwest Wimmera. a. Density of artefacts at very small and small sites, b. Relative numbers of sites of different sizes (data from Bird and Rhoads 2011: tables 4 and 6).

In 2002, Aboriginal Affairs Victoria arranged a field school in collaboration with the Goolum Goolum Aboriginal Cooperative and Wotjobaluk Traditional Land Council (Webber and Richards 2004). As part of the training program they excavated in two places. Square 2, with 19th- and 20th-century artefacts, will be discussed in Chapter 11. While there were also similarly recent items in the uppermost layer of the 1x2 metre Square 1 (Figure 11.19), lower down there were only stone tools. Some of these were relatively recent, perhaps only 500 years old at most. Others were perhaps a thousand years older, but few, if any, had been deposited in that particular place for many thousands of years before that. However, towards the bottom of the excavated square, artefacts were found with fragments of charcoal dated to 9000 years ago. The excavators were not able to dig deeper than that, so there may well be older material still. Of course, it is hard to generalise to a whole site, let alone a broader area, from one small excavation, but perhaps Blackfellows Waterhole was regularly visited during the same wetter phase that saw people out on the Raak Plains far to the north.

While only a very small amount of stone was found in Square 1 – barely a half a cupful – the tools previously observed and collected on the surface include many different types. Locally available quartz was, as so often, the most common. In addition, like the sites recorded along the Yariambiack Creek, other types of stone came from both near and further afield, including silcrete, fine-grained basalt, rhyolite, tachylite and coastal flint. Different materials were favoured for particular types of tools: quartz for nosed and small thumbnail scrapers; coastal flint for other, steep-edge scrapers; and silcrete for small geometric microliths.

Southwest Wimmera

The extensive, undulating sand plains west and north of the Glenelg River provide a contrast to the corridors along the Yariambiack Creek and the Wimmera River. There is little permanent surface water, although winter rains fill the shallow swales where chains of lakes and swamps lie between the ancient compacted sand ridges. Caroline Bird and Jim Rhoads looked at the relationship between landform and scatters of stone tools (Bird and Rhoads 2011). It is no surprise to find that there is a greater density of artefacts where water is more readily available or in the most diverse environments (Figure 7.5). Permanent lakes and swamps were therefore the focus of occupation, at least during the drier months. At other times, people could disperse across their country, splitting up into smaller groups to make the best use of scattered, short-lived seasonal ponds.

Three-quarters of all these sites documented, however, are very small indeed, with fewer than ten artefacts visible on the ground, and more than half of the rest have less than 100 artefacts. Only a handful are large or very large scatters of stone tools. As might be expected, these are near water; but they are not just anywhere near water. Along watercourses, most sites are still relatively small, for people did not prefer any one section of the bank over others. It is only where some particular local feature led to repeated use of a specific spot – a pond or perhaps a sheltered area – that there are denser clusters of artefacts. Such places were used more often,

Figure 7.6 Sketch plan by G.A. Robinson of a maze of
channels near Mount William (State Library of NSW).

but perhaps still in a way similar to all the other areas when there were no reasons
to favour one locality over another.

Scarred trees are, as so often, common. Jim Rhoads (1992) pointed out two
advantages in studying these artefacts (for we must think of these trees as artefacts,
even if they are alive and a by-product of manufacture): they remain where they
were made and must all be from the same short period of time. Neither of these
limits is true of the stone tools which litter the land and are a more constant focus
of attention. By plotting the details and distribution of more than 200 scarred trees,
Jim was able to show that bark of red gum and grey box trees was removed in a
different way and for different purposes, but this was not, as one might expect,
related to the size or girth of the tree. In the area he looked at, the selection of trees
was unconnected to the availability of water or other particular features, but was
broadly the same as other archaeological evidence of general campsites – so people
did not go out of their way to search for particular trees, but took bark where it was
most convenient, close to home.

Quartz was generally the only type of stone at the smaller sites as it was
widespread and easily picked up for immediate use. This type of stone forms a
uniform background distribution of artefacts representing what we might think of
as off-site activities in contrast to more specific, regularly occupied places where
people camped for longer and undertook a wider variety of tasks. While quartz was
always the most common raw material at these larger sites, they contain a wider
array of different types of stone, including quartzite and silcrete, which came from
nearby sources in Burrunj (the Black Range), Gariwerd or at Mount Arapiles. One
of these areas is near Clear Lake, where there are more large sites than elsewhere.

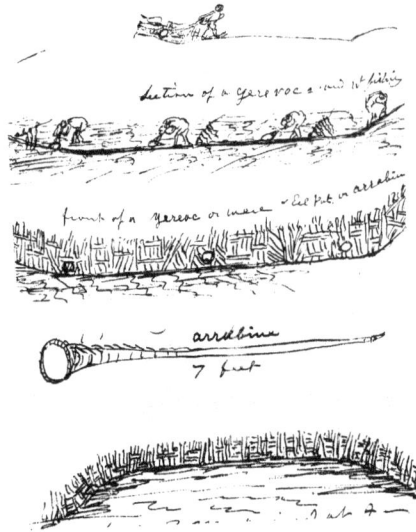

Figure 7.7 Notes and sketches by G.A.
Robinson of wickerwork weirs and an
arrabine or basketry funnel for catching eels
(State Library of NSW).

Eels in the Wimmera wetlands

Gariwerd, Mount Talbot and Burrunj form the last outliers of the Great Dividing
Range. While the Wimmera River and Yariambiack Creek flow north towards the
Mallee, another series of rivers drains southward towards the coast. Near their
headwaters, lakes and ponds beside the Glenelg and Mount Talbot Creek created
one particularly, perhaps unusually, favourable area, archaeologically seen both in
the size of artefact scatters and in the variety of the stone found near Clear Lake. A
major attraction was provided by eels.

Eels are still common south of the Dividing Range from the lower southeast
of South Australia, across Victoria and up the east coast of Australia. The adult
fish spawn in the Coral Sea, far to the north. The larvae then drift south on ocean
currents, eventually washing up on the shores of Australia and New Zealand.
Sensing freshwater, the larvae turn into tiny elvers which make their way into
rivers, swimming upstream and, if necessary, moving across damp land to settle in
large numbers in the still waters of swamps, ponds and dams. It may be a decade or
two, if not more, before a mature eel, prompted by a springtime rush of water, will
join others swimming downstream in a massive run, the start of their long journey
to the sea and then on to their breeding grounds. With lower sea levels exposing
the Bassian Plain, the currents that now wash larvae onto the western Victorian
coast would have been blocked, so that there were no eels in the area until well

Figure 7.8 Part of the Toolondo fish-trap (photo: Aldo Massola, 1962).

after the Last Glacial Maximum. But since that time they have become especially significant to Gunditjmara and other peoples of southwestern Victoria.

At Toolondo, a few kilometres south of Clear Lake, there are – or were until recently – the remnants of a series of earthworks, similar to those on the eastern side of Gariwerd described by Charles Hall (Chapter 2) and by George Augustus Robinson, who noted on 9 July 1841:

> an immense piece of ground trenched and banked, resembling the work of civilized man but on inspection I found it to be the work of the Aboriginal natives, and constructed for the purpose of catching eels. A specimen of the art I had not seen before of the same extent and therefore required some time to inspect it ... These trenches are hundreds of yards in length. I measured at one place in one continuous triple line for the distance of 500 yards. These triple water courses led to other ramified and extensive trenches of a most tortuous form. An area of 15 acres was thus turned over ... these works must have been executed at great cost of labour to these rude people the only means of artificial power being the lever, the application and incentive of force being necessity. The lever is a stick chisel, sharpened at one end by which force they throw up clods of soil and this formed the trenches, smoothing the water channel with their hands. The soil displaced went to form the embankment.

The plan and design of these ramifications was extremely perplexing and I found it difficult to commit it to paper in the way I could have wished. All its varied form and curious curvilinear windings and angles of every size and shape and parallels, etc; at intervals small apertures left where they placed their *arabines* or eel pots. These gaps were supported by pieces of the bark of trees and sticks. In single measurement there must have been some thousands of yards of this trenching and banking. The whole of the water from the mountain rivulet is made to pass through this trenching ere it reaches the marsh; it is hardly possible for a single fish to escape. (Presland 1980: 91–92; see also Clark 1990: 113)

When Aldo Massola visited Mount Talbot Station in 1962 he recognised how lucky it was that cultivation had only recently begun in the area, so that some of the ditches still survived (Massola 1962). He was able to follow these for several hundred metres (Figure 7.8). He was told that odd stakes from the weirs could once also be seen in the trenches, and some claimed, or at least had heard older folk claim, to have seen the fish traps being used: rare physical evidence of what we would otherwise only know from the 19th-century European observations and Aboriginal oral traditions.

Fourteen years later, Harry Lourandos followed up on Massola's brief account and investigated the Toolondo system in greater detail (Lourandos 1980a, 1980b, 1987, 1997). Harry was able to trace one interconnected line of channels for nearly 4 kilometres, from south of Budgengutte Swamp northward across the intervening seasonally marshy land to Clear Swamp (Figure 7.9). In places, other parallel ditches, side-branches and inter-connecting channels could also be identified, sufficient to give some impression of the original complexity of the system, which may have rivalled the one described by Robinson. The channels themselves varied in width and depth. At their widest they were up to 2.5 metres across and some as much as 1 metre deep, dug down through the looser softer topsoils into the hard clay beneath. It would never have been easy work to dig and lever out clods of earth using 'stick chisels', or perhaps small wooden shovels (Massola 1957).

One radiocarbon date from fill within a ditch is essentially modern, which we can take as confirming the local stories that the complex was used well into the 19th century. But it is impossible to say when the work first began, or to trace its history. For the complex was not designed as a whole. Rather, it developed piecemeal over long periods of time – for all we know over hundreds, if not thousands, of years. Each generation in turn cleaned out, recut, modified and maintained older channels or, when appropriate, dug new ones to enhance or direct the flow of water from the swamps and lakes. Although the earthworks could not increase the numbers of eels – that was dependent on random effects of sea currents and tides – they provided additional nooks and crannies in which they could live. Here, individual fish could be speared at any time. More importantly, it encouraged seasonally migrating eels to swim where they could most easily be harvested in very large quantities, attracting large congregations of people to enjoy this seasonal abundance.

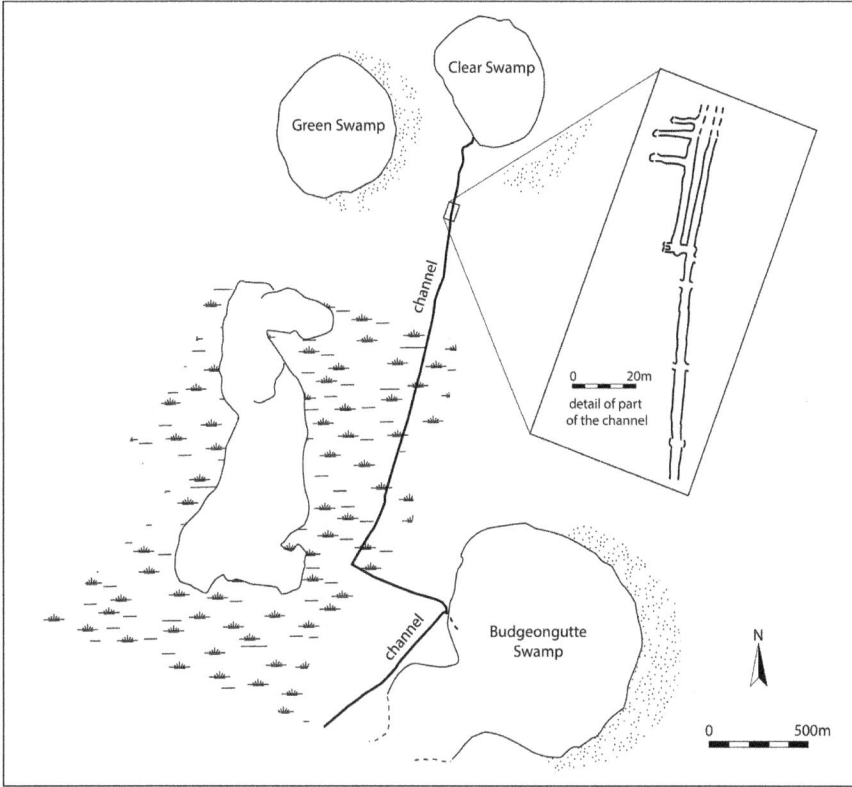

Figure 7.9 Plan of the Toolondo fish-traps (after Lourandos 1980b: figures 3 and 4).

8
About Budj Bim

Western Victoria 30,000 years ago. Budj Bim erupts. Lava flows from Mount Eccles down the valleys south towards the sea at Tyrendarra. Landscapes are transformed into rough, rocky jumbles of basalt boulders; rivers and creeks are blocked or forced into new channels. Small swamps and ponds form in depressions in and around the lava, while Darlot Creek establishes a new course along its western edge. These new basalt flows added to the extensive fields of stony rises created by Mount Rouse, Mount Napier and other lesser volcanoes, providing local challenges and opportunities for people living in the complex and rich lands that lie between Gariwerd and the coast (Figure 8.1).

Catching eels at Condah

There are barely any physical traces of the once-extensive earthworks dug to channel and trap eels, such as those at Toolondo (Chapter 7). But similar facilities – infrastructure as we might now call them – are preserved in stone across rivers and among the lava fields at Lake Condah.

The area around Condah Swamp and Lake Condah itself has a rugged beauty, admired by early Europeans no less than by Aboriginal people, as

> [a] splendid fresh water lake … about a mile and a half long and three quarters of a mile wide, and contains almost every variety of fish in abundance, with swans, ducks &c. It is of considerable depth, and receives a river about fifty yards broad; one side is bold and rocky and contains a number of small coves into one of which a beautiful stream empties itself, and the other side is a gently sloping shore surrounded by a fine tract of country. (David Edgar in the *Portland Mercury*, 11 January 1843)

But this beauty was insufficient to prevent plans for major projects in the late 19th century to drain the Condah swampland by improving the flow of water south through the lake and into Darlot Creek in order to open up farmland. Alexander Ingram was one of those involved. As a surveyor and engineer he

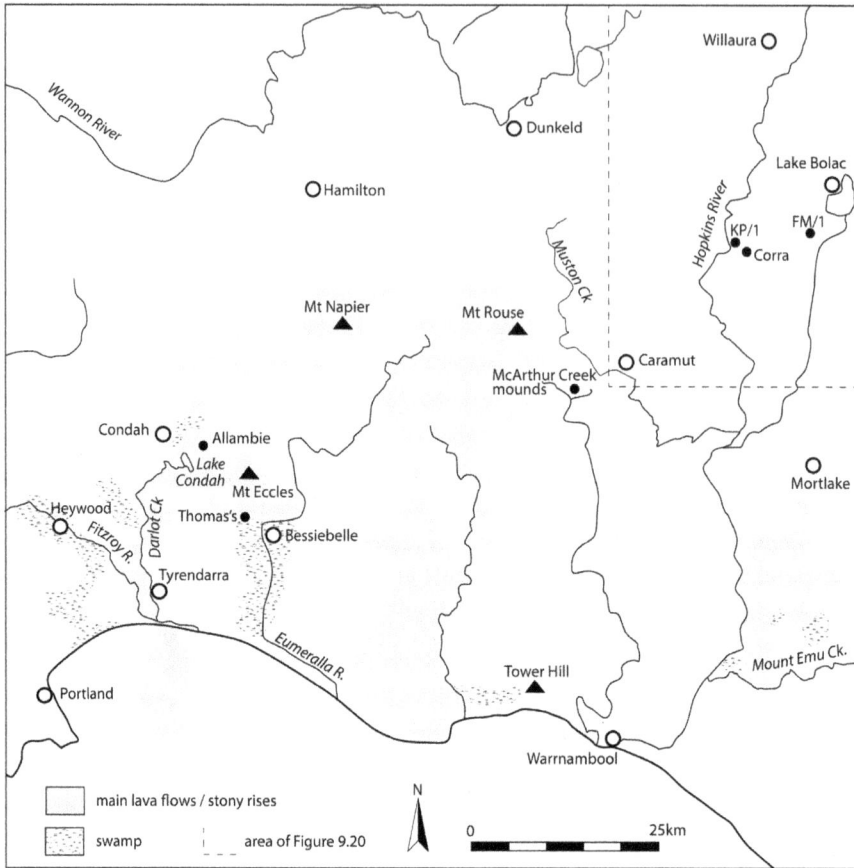

Figure 8.1 Southwestern Victoria.

became fascinated – perhaps even obsessed – by the scale and complexity of the Aboriginal structures that he observed (Richards 2011):

> At the south-western point of Lake Condah, near where it overflows the valley of Darlot's Creek, along the margin of the rough stony ground until it joins the permanent stream of the Condah Mission Station is situated one of the largest and most remarkable aboriginal fisheries in the western district of Victoria. The position has been very well chosen, as the small bay is the lowest point on the western side of the lake. Owing to the peculiar formation (open trap scoriae) along the eastern, southern, and part of the western sides of the lake, the water sinks very rapidly and becomes very low during the summer months, but as it receives the drainage of a large extent of country the water rises very quickly during the winter, and first flows into the scoriae at the point named, which has been facilitated to some extent by the channels formed by the aborigines for trapping eels, trout, &c. These channels have been made by removing loose

stones and portions of the more solid rocks between the ridges and lowest places, also by constructing low wing walls to concentrate the streams. At suitable places are erected stone barricades with timber built in so as to form openings of from 1ft to 2ft wide; behind these openings were secured long narrow bag nets made of strong rushes. The mouths of the nets were from 2ft to 3ft wide secured to a hoop. They were of various lengths, some 10ft long, the principal portion being about 4in. or 5in. in diameter. The smallest ends were made to open so that the eels, &c. could be easily extracted.

There are numerous small fisheries constructed in suitable places in small bays and outlets where the water sinks into the trap scoriae down along the margin of the valley of Darlot's Creek. Across the valley at suitable places were erected large barricades constructed with strong forked stakes, horizontal spars, and vertical stakes strengthened with piles of stones. Openings were also left in these. Many of the aboriginals residing at the Mission Station still construct similar barricades for trapping purposes, and large quantities of fish are secured during winter, more particularly since an outlet drain has been made in connexion with the drainage of Condah Swamp. (Ingram in Worsnop 1897: 104–5; Kenyon 1912: 119–10)

Alexander Ingram was right to be so taken with these complex systems, foreshadowing their broader recognition as one of the first places included on the Australian National Heritage List, following decades of research by archaeologists and local Aboriginal communities (Massola 1969a; Coutts et al. 1978; Head 1989; A. Clarke 1991, 1994; Builth 2002, 2004, 2014; Lane 2009; McNiven and Bell 2010; Gunditjmara People and Wettenhall 2010). It has been no easy task to identify, trace and document the many, often convoluted and extensive, features among the confusing fields of stone, and then to relate them to patterns of water flow and changes in lake levels (Figure 8.2).

Before the modern drains were cut, Lake Condah flooded seasonally, one rocky hollow filling after another, with occasional floods reaching unusually high levels. When the waters subsided during the summer, pools would progressively empty as the lake reverted to swampy marsh. This was not always the case. For about 20,000 years a ridge of lava prevented water flowing south out of Condah Swamp into the lake. Eventually, accumulating sediments in the swamp slowly raised its bed, and with it the water level, until about 8000 years ago it was high enough to spill over into the lake (Head 1989). While some of the stone structures visible today could have been used at that time, this would only have been possible during exceptional floods, and until about 4000 years ago even the lowest known traps within the lake basin were above normal water depth. Once again, as sedimentation raised the level of the lake bed these could have been used more often, but only in the last one or two thousand years were they in regular use. Whether there are older, buried structures is anyone's guess.

Much of the detailed archaeological recording at Lake Condah was completed at the cost of much stumbling and scrambling over the uneven, rocky ground during two major seasons of surveys as part of Victoria Archaeological Survey summer schools in 1977 and 1981, directed by Peter Coutts. Carefully prepared detailed plans of many structures of different kinds, some hundreds of metres in

Figure 8.2 Stony rises at Lake Condah.

Figure 8.3 A channel cleared of stones at Lake Condah.

length, still provide the basis for our knowledge of what Peter and his colleagues, and more recently others, began to refer to as Aboriginal engineering works (Gunditjmara People and Wettenhall 2011; Jordan et al. 2011). Gunditjmara people took advantage of natural drainage lines and depressions in among the heaps of basalt blocks and boulders in and around the lake. Water flows were improved by clearing away stones and accumulated earth to create long, narrow channels, providing easier and predictable routes for eels and other fish (Figure 8.3). In some cases, the basalt blocks were used to line the channels, sometimes stacked or built up into low walls (Figures 8.4, 8.5). At appropriate places, often on very slightly higher ground, stone traps or weirs were built across depressions and channels or beside hollows. It was at gaps left in the trap walls that people could fix in place their long, conical baskets, funnelling in the eels so that they could be readily harvested as they emerged from the narrower end, as described above by Ingram, using the same techniques seen in other areas where wooden and wickerwork weirs were built across rivers or earth-cut channels (Figure 8.7):

> at Kilgower … He … took me to a very fine and large weir and went through, with several other of the natives, the process of taking eels and the particular spot where he himself stood and took them. I measured this weir with a tape, 200 feet; five feet high. It was turned back at each end. The eel pots are placed over the holes and the fisher stands behind the *yere.roc* or weir and lays hold of the small end of the *arrabine* or eel pot. And when the eel makes its appearance he bites it on the head and puts it on the *lingeer* or small stick with a knob at the end, or if near the bank, he throws them out. The fishing is carried on in the rainy season. *Arrabine* or eel pot made of bark or plaited rushes with a … round mouth and having a small end to prevent the eel from rapidly getting away.
>
> These *yere.roc* or weirs are built with some attention to the principles of mechanics. Those erected on a rocky bottom have the sticks inserted in a groove made by removing the small stones so as to form a groove. The wier [sic] is kept in a straightline. The small stones are laid against the bottom of the stick. The upright sticks are supported by transverse sticks, resting on forked sticks … These sticks are three, four or five inches in diameter. Some of the smaller wiers are in the form of a segment or circle. The convex side against the current. (G.A. Robinson, 30 April, 1841, in Clark 1998: 163; Presland 1977: 65)

The channels, ponds and weirs that at Lake Condah were thousands of years in the making, with small, individual and incremental changes as different parts were modified, expanded and adjusted. When lake levels fluctuated as slight climatic variations increased or reduced rainfall, lower-lying sections might become inaccessible, or those higher up left stranded and useless. Old structures could be improved and new ones developed. And, like any facility, each new season would bring with it the need for repairs and general maintenance: cleaning out silts left by the previous floods and replacing stones knocked or fallen off barriers and channel sides.

Something of this process has been revealed by recent fieldwork at the Muldoons trap complex at the southwestern end of Lake Condah, where the water flows out of the lake into Darlot Creek. Ian McNiven and his students

Figure 8.4 Water flowing through a gap in a stone barrier at Lake Condah.

Figure 8.5 Stone weir built across a drainage line at Lake Condah.

Figure 8.6 Muldoons trap complex, with funnel entry leading to an excavation trench across the channel (arrowed) (photo: Ian McNiven).

from Monash University have spent several years working together with the Gunditjmara community exploring this area (McNiven et al. 2012, 2015) (Figures 8.6, 8.7).

One of their particular interests was in the age and development of channels and barriers. By carefully excavating within one channel between built stone walls they were able to find charcoal in the lowest sediments, which showed that an initial phase of construction took place at least 6600 years ago, a time of higher rainfall and full lakes and rivers. In their excavations they could see that basalt blocks had been removed from either side of a solid central ridge, leaving two parallel channels. As soil filled in the lower sections, the bedrock kerb was eventually buried and the channel became much shallower – perhaps it was entirely neglected and not used at all for many thousands of years when a drier climate meant that normal floodwaters did not reach the site. Within the last 800 years, however, the channel was once again in action, with water now running between side walls built by stacking blocks up to four courses high. Even more recently, about 350 years ago, a barrier two to four courses high was constructed using blocks levered up out of the surrounding lava field and loosely piled up to form a wall about 1 metre wide. The last phase of renovation and use probably took place in the 19th century, perhaps in an attempt to maintain traditional practices when the lake began to be drained by Alexander Ingram and his co-workers.

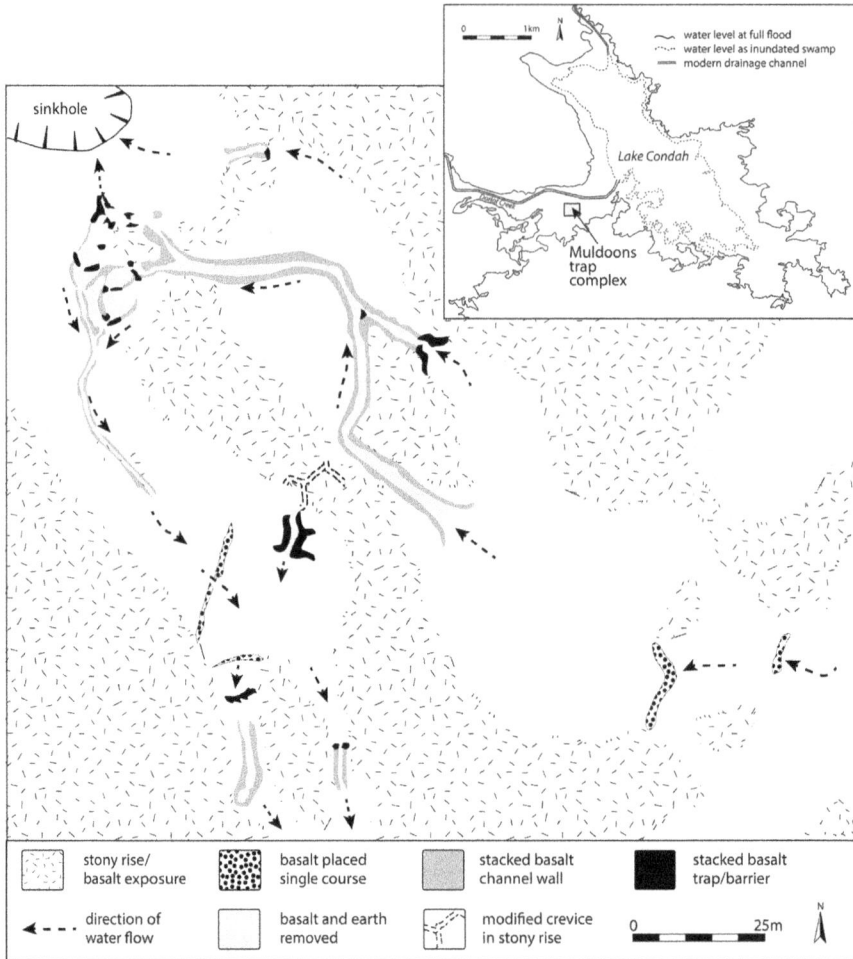

Figure 8.7 Plan of Lake Condah and detail of Muldoons trap complex (after McNiven et al. 2015: figures 2 and 3).

Ian and his students also found many very tiny chips of stone: the 147 pieces weighed only 9.7 grams, hardly more than a teaspoon of sugar. These are the fine fragments that fly off when stone is knapped, something like sawdust. There were none of the larger flakes or the cores from which they were struck, and the sharp edges of some fragments had been worn smooth by water action. These minute artefacts, by-products of toolmaking, had been washed downstream along with other sediments and trapped by the built walls. Trivial and displaced though they are, they do have another story to tell. Almost all are coastal flint collected from beaches 20-odd kilometres to the south – a reminder that the lake was only one part of Gunditjmara people's broader territory, for they made use of many different environments, including those along the coast (Chapter 3).

Life in the stony rises

The natives formed these wind-breaks of stone, placed on edge in a circular form, some of them very perfect, leaving the entrance generally toward the east, the prevailing winds coming from the north-west and south-west. These circles are common on the plains or eastern parts of this property [Purrumbete], where the branches of trees could not be procured for giving shelter. When we first occupied this country it was quite common for the natives to use these circles as camping places, always having the fires in the centre. The fires were very small, as they had frequently to carry the wood long distances. The circles were generally formed of large stones on their edges, and bedded in the ground close together, without any other stones on the top, thus forming good protection from the wind as they lay around the fire. The stones are of the common basalt, there being no other in the district. The situation selected was generally where water was convenient, or in some favourable place for game. The circles were about the size of ordinary mia-mys, that is from ten to twenty feet in diameter. (Peter Manifold in Smyth 1887: II, 235)

[N]ear a large waterhole in a fine permanent stream known as 'The River' are the remains of an old aboriginal camping-place, the name of which is Narrarrabeen, consisting of about twenty stone foundations, of horseshoe form, from 4ft to 7ft in diameter, and opening towards the east, a point from which the wind rarely blows. They are built among the loose blocks of cellular basalt, and appear to have been made by piling the stones removed to level the floor into a dry-stone wall about 1ft high on the western or windward side. On this foundation – Mr Ingram learned from Tommy White … the ordinary mia mia of bark was erected … Similar stone foundations are found among the rough basalt around Mount Eccles and Lake Gorrie. (Reynell Eveleigh Johns quoted in Worsnop 1897: 105–6)

These slightly differing accounts by European observers have their counterparts in the archaeological record. People needed some shelter, whether well constructed or just simple windbreaks, when spending time in the stony rises, which at first sight appear both uncomfortable and unproductive. However, not only was there the seasonal superabundance of eels to be harvested using the weirs, races and channels, but there were other fish to be caught and wetland plants available for collection.

During their fieldwork in the 1970s, Victoria Archaeological Survey staff and volunteers began mapping the small, rough stone circles in several areas (Coutts et al. 1977) (Figure 8.8). Perhaps somewhat over-enthusiastically, they identified 128 structures in one 10 hectare paddock at Allambie (Wesson 1991) (Figure 8.9). Follow-up studies by Annie Clarke reassessed the evidence. She was able to show that many of these features were not made by human hand, but were instead the result of geological processes or where rocks lifted up by the roots of collapsing trees mimicked built structures (Clarke 1991, 1994). Nevertheless, there are still a good many real stone circles, or, rather, horse-shoe-shaped arrangements,

Figure 8.8 A stone circle at Allambie.

generally with the opening to the east, as described in the written accounts. Most have a floor area of between 4 and 7 square metres, but some are a good deal larger. These structures are not difficult to make, and it would not take long to quickly clear a space and arrange the stones around it into a low wall only one or two courses high as the footing for a superstructure of branches and bark. Later the stones would remain more or less in place, eventually giving the misleading archaeological appearance of a dense settlement. But it is of course impossible to say how many – or indeed if any – of the circles were in use at one and the same time, although, as discussed elsewhere, several shelters or huts may have been needed for members of the one family, keeping an appropriate distance from one another.

The hut foundations excavated by the Archaeological Survey all proved to have very shallow deposits within and beside them, for little soil development is possible in these exposed rocky fields. In 1981, Jane Wesson cleared 18 square metres within and beside one of the Allambie sites, PAL 20 (Wesson 1981) (Figures 8.10, 8.11). Little sediment had accumulated on the bedrock in or around the walls and it seems that it was not repeatedly rebuilt and may have been used only for a short time, perhaps only once. The radiocarbon dates are all indistinguishable from modern samples, so it was not very old. It was built and used not very long before, if not at the time of, the arrival of Europeans.

There was a central hearth within PAL 20, as well as other fireplaces outside. Whoever sat and kept warm at this shelter cooked and ate there; made, used and repaired tools; and, doubtless, gossiped with the neighbours. Six hundred and eighty fragments of bone from small and larger marsupials were left lying about;

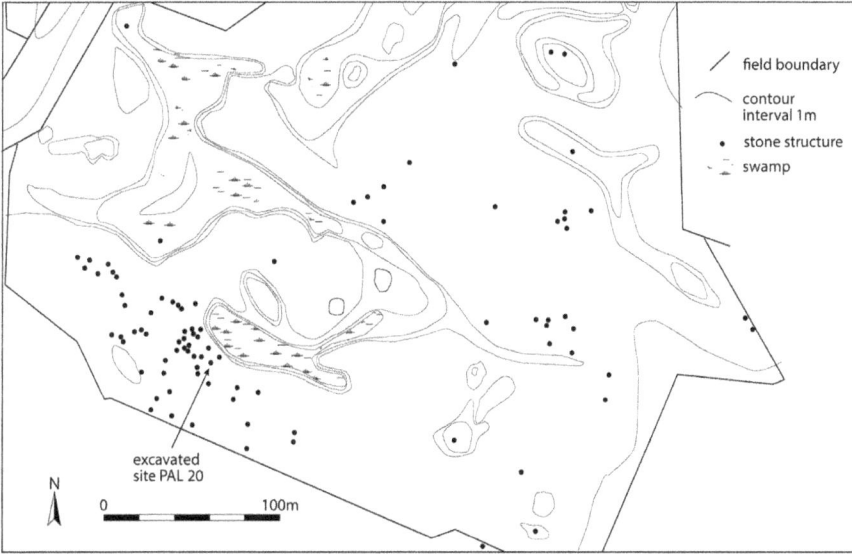

Figure 8.9 Plan of stone structures at Allambie (after Wesson 1982: figure 7, revised following Clarke 1991).

Figure 8.10 Excavations in and beside stone structure, PAL 20, 1981.

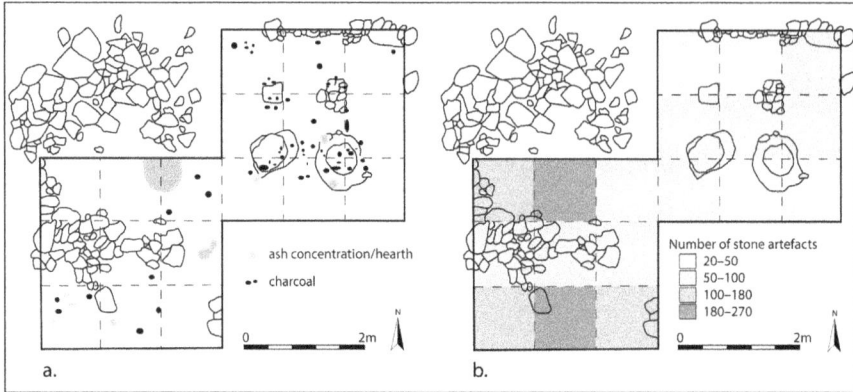

Figure 8.11 The excavated area of PAL 20. a. distribution of ash and charcoal, b. density of stone artefacts in each square (after Wesson 1981: figures 15 and 20).

many of them were burnt, either from the original cooking or when later dropped into the fire. The lack of larger pieces may be because they were tossed further away, or perhaps they were fed to dingoes. The animals were hunted using spears, perhaps barbed with small backed points, 16 of which were found in the site. Often broken in use, these were extracted from the spear to make way for newly knapped replacements. There were two dozen less distinctive tools, several cores and over 1000 of the flakes which had been struck off them and discarded unused. Entirely unnoticed would have been the thousands of tiny chips which flew off the cores as they were struck – akin to those washed down into the Muldoons fish trap. Like them, almost all the PAL 20 stone was coastal flint, brought to this campsite from the beaches 25 kilometres to the south.

The difficulties of investigating structures in the stony rises have continued to challenge archaeologists (Williams 1988; Lane 2009). In 2002, Sharon Lane spent four weeks alone with her tape, compass and the newly available convenience of a hand-held GPS exploring an area of the Thomas property near Bessiebelle, where the lava flows ended along seasonally swampy land, once a 'great resort of the Aborigines' (Lane 2008). Here, snake-infested woodland and scrub made the task of finding sites on the rugged ridges even more difficult than usual, as if identifying the scrappy evidence of rough semi-circular arrangements of stone in the confusion of fragmented lava was not hard enough already. Later, she dug small test pits at a dozen of the possible sites. At all but one, artefacts came to light, providing a degree of certainty to her identification, as well as helping her to select places where more extensive excavations would be worthwhile (Figure 8.12).

At Sites 7721-882 and 7721-883, Sharon had the help of many student volunteers to clear a broad area, taking in both structures and a large area around, recognising that the spaces outside of individual circles are as important as those inside (Figure 8.13). For these were not houses such as we have, where activities take place indoors. Rather, we should think of them more like the tent we would put up when

Figure 8.12 Excavations on the Thomas property in the stony rises: Structure 883 on the right and 882 partly covered by the white tarp in the background (photo: Sharon Lane).

camping: convenient for sleeping and to escape the rain, while normally we prefer to sit around outside, enjoying the campfire.

As at PAL 20, the open side of Structure 882 was on the east, away from the prevailing weather. Stones had been removed to clear a space beside a natural flat area of jointed basalt, and used to build the rough surrounding wall, perhaps two, or at most three, courses high, designed to provide protection and the footing for a wooden framework and bark covering. The messy later history of the site, which included effects of tree-roots, erosion and bushfires, made it impossible to be certain about the duration of original use, but it is likely that it was made and used on only one occasion. This could have been at any time during the last few thousand years.

Five thousand one hundred and fifty small pieces of stone – a total weight of less than 1 kilogram – were found strewn around both inside and around the stone circles, although they were more concentrated within Structure 882. The range of artefacts is broadly similar to that at PAL 20 – mainly small unusable flakes with a few small cores from which they had been struck. Identifiable tools included similar geometric microliths and asymmetric backed points, as well as scrapers and at least one woodworking adze. Did someone sit within the hut during poor weather, taking the opportunity to make or repair tools and equipment?

Almost all the stone, again as at PAL 20, was flint brought from the nearby beaches, half a day's walk away. Probably only two or three nodules of flint would

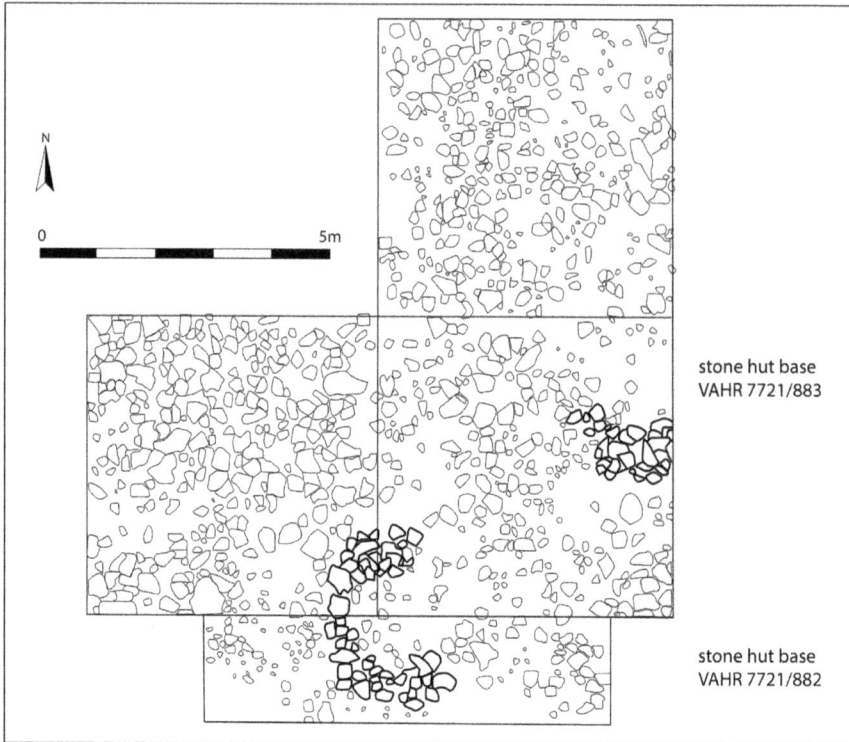

Figure 8.13 Structures 882 and 883 among stones (after Lane 2008: figure 8.2).

have been sufficient to account for all the pieces found. Few flakes still had any of the chalky outer cortex or skin that covers beach-washed nodules of flint; this had been knocked off before the lumps of stone were carried inland – or, perhaps, the flint came by way of other places where whoever it was who stayed at the site also had access to bits of quartz, quartzite, basalt and chert.

In the lower layers of soil in nearby Structure 883, Sharon found similar flint artefacts, but in the uppermost layers there were also fragments of flaked bottle glass, which could all have been discarded at the same time. Perhaps Structure 883, like 882, was first used before – maybe even well before – the 19th century. And then again briefly at some time after the European invasion. Perhaps it was then one of the places where Gunditjmara people took refuge and from which they waged the 'Eumeralla War' of the 1840s (Critchett 1990; Gunditjmara People and Wettenhall 2010) (Chapter 11).

Huts or houses?

Mia-mia, wuurn, willam, loondthal, wurley: some of the many words for shelters, dwellings, huts or houses in Aboriginal languages of Victoria and South Australia which were taken over into English in the 19th century. They are seldom heard today, perhaps because, like the more general *humpy* and *gunyah*, they may sound either patronising or derogatory. What should we use in their place? In this book, I have here normally used 'hut', for the word carries the appropriate connotation of a temporary or short-lived and simple structure. But others prefer 'house'. Indeed, elsewhere so have I, referring to the sites in the stony rises as 'stone houses', as do others. 'Stone-walled huts' or 'stone huts' have also been used, as well as the more neutral 'stone circles', which emphasises their archaeological appearance over their original purpose. 'Stone-based huts' is perhaps more technically correct, avoiding any implication that they were built entirely of stone.

Huts into mounds

Intriguing as the stony rises are, they cover only a small part of the Western District. Much of the surrounding country is more comfortable and includes some of the best grazing lands in Australia. In the past it would have been no less productive. Here people

> were always mindful of the seasons in selecting the localities in which to spend their time, taking into account not only the natural features of the ground, but the facilities for obtaining food. They constructed tolerably good bark willams in the winter, while in the summer they were content with such shelter as a few broken branches afforded. They were rarely without good fires. (Smyth 1878, I: 141).

Most of the sites we find today are, as everywhere, scatters of stone tools – once again, severely diminished by many artefact collectors (Warren 1985). But in southwest Victoria there are also mounds (Figures 8.14, 8.15). These are best thought of as the remains of the more substantial winter huts.

In 1975, the Victoria Archaeological Survey excavated several mounds. Just below the surface of one of them, Corra 3, a series of post holes were found (Figure 8.16). With a little imagination one can see many of these forming a roughly circular shape about 2 metres in diameter, with some additional holes just to the west, and one in the centre. These must have been where sizeable branches were set into the ground to form the framework of what was once

> [a] strongly built hut ... shaped somewhat like a bee-hive, was about ten feet in diameter, and more than six feet in height. There was an opening about three feet six inches in height, which was generally closed at night with a sheet of bark. There was also an aperture at the top about nine inches in diameter, through which the smoke of fire escaped. In wet weather this aperture was covered with a sod. These buildings were firmly built, and plastered with mud, and were strong enough to bear the weight of a man. (Smyth 1878, I: 126)

The area of Corra 3 began to be used about 1300 years ago, but the hut itself was probably built about 600 years later. A sizeable area of dark soil with many burnt

Figure 8.14 A mound in the Western District.

stones and pieces of charcoal just to the north is where the people cooked and kept warm, matching James Dawson's description of ovens

> made outside the dwellings by digging holes in the ground, plastering them with mud, and keeping a fire in them till quite hot, then withdrawing the embers and lining the holes with wet grass. The flesh, fish or roots are put into baskets, which are placed in the oven and covered with more wet grass, gravel, hot stones, and earth, and kept covered until they are cooked. (Dawson 1881: 17)

However, things are never quite so simple. Even during the 19th century, those few Europeans who interested themselves in Aboriginal sites, if not in the people themselves, debated the significance of mounds. Many asserted that mounds were primarily ovens for cooking *myrrnong*, the yam daisy, a staple root vegetable (see Chapter 10). Others, like James Dawson, perhaps better informed, saw them differently:

> Native mounds, so common all over the country … formed homes for many generations. The great size of some of them, and the vast accumulation of burnt earth, charcoal and ashes which is found in and around them is accounted for by the long continuance of the domestic hearth, the decomposition of the building materials and the debris arising from their frequent destruction by bush fires. They never were ovens or original places of interment, as is generally supposed, and were only used for the purposes of burial after certain events occurred while they were occupied as sites for residences – such as the death of more than one

Figure 8.15 Sketch of a hut by George Augustus Robinson (State Library of NSW).

occupant of the dwelling at the same time, or the family becoming extinct; in which instance they were called 'muuru kowuutung' by the Chaa wuuring tribe and 'muuruup kaakee' by the Kuurn kopan nuoot tribe, meaning ghostly place and were never afterwards used as sites for residences, and only as places for burial. (Dawson 1881: 103)

Perhaps Dawson was influenced in his opinion by the excavations he carried out in 1869, at a time when archaeology was in its infancy, the word itself only just taking on its modern meaning. In the trenches he dug across several mounds he saw 'a complete history of the growth of these mounds … where the marks of old fires or hearths are directly traceable by saucer shaped streaks and layers of wood ashes intermixed with pieces of charcoal' (quoted in Williams 1988: 16).

His comments could well describe some of the confused complexity seen in modern excavations. For we need to understand the dynamic history of site formation and changes that took place once a substantial hut was abandoned. The roof would have gradually collapsed, the thick layers of earth, sods and thatch falling into a low uneven heap as the wood and bark rotted away. This, in turn, could attract reconstruction, or an entirely new building where people could take advantage of the old remains, perhaps even by the same family returning to a favourite spot. Or perhaps their descendants chose the same place for similar reasons many, many generations later. And so a mound might gradually build up

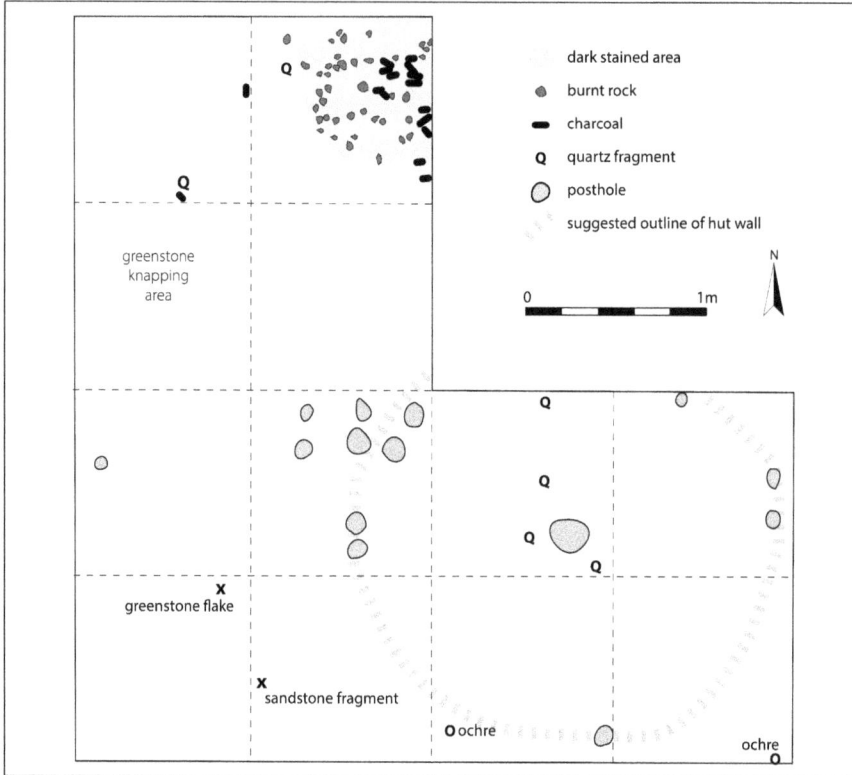

Figure 8.16 Plan of the upper layer of Corra 3 Mound.

in a somewhat higgledy-piggledy fashion, with older layers scuffed up or trampled down during later episodes of construction and occupation. Although oven pits occur in mounds, they might well have been outdoor areas at the time when they were used for cooking by people living close by. And then, to complicate an archaeologist's life further, mounds were also used for burials, whether as described by Dawson or following some other custom. Finally, there is the added nuisance of rabbits and the impact of vigorous attempts to get rid of them.

The life histories of several mounds excavated by the Victoria Archaeological Survey in the 1970s may well have followed such a path. Some of these sites must have been used at different times, and in different ways, before, during and after their incarnation as a substantial hut. We can see this at Mound KP/1 (Figure 8.17). Radiocarbon dates from a charcoal feature on the natural soils below the mound show that people were there about 9000 years ago (Coutts et al. 1976; Coutts and Witter 1977). It is possible that this gives us an exceptionally early date for the type of hut that could form a mound if these artefacts were discarded within and then covered by the collapsing roof. But it may rather be a fortuitous use of exactly the same spot 7000 years later, when a substantial hut happened to be built there. Despite the disturbances and confusing stratigraphy, the excavators felt that

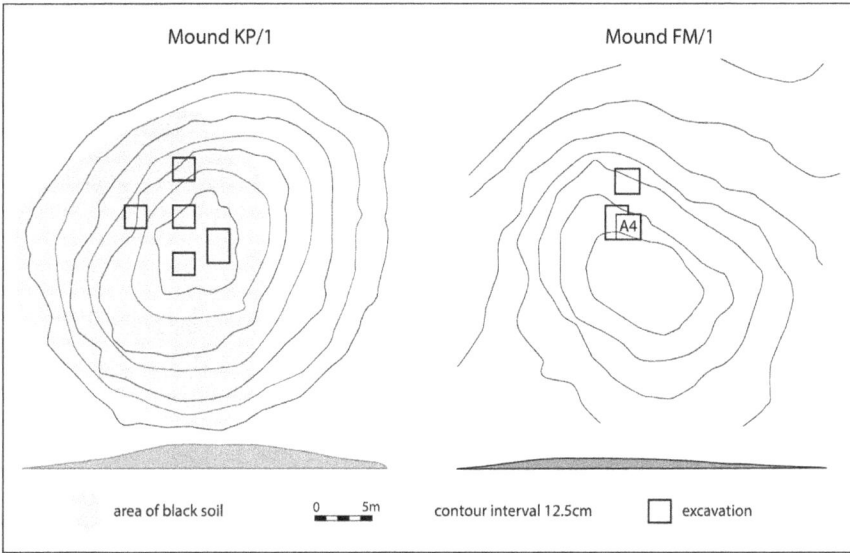

Figure 8.17 Contour plans and profiles of mounds KP/1 and FM/1 showing the location of excavated areas (adapted from Coutts et al. 1976: figure 7).

Figure 8.18 Victoria Archaeological Survey excavations at a mound in the Western District, 1975 (photo: Aboriginal Victoria).

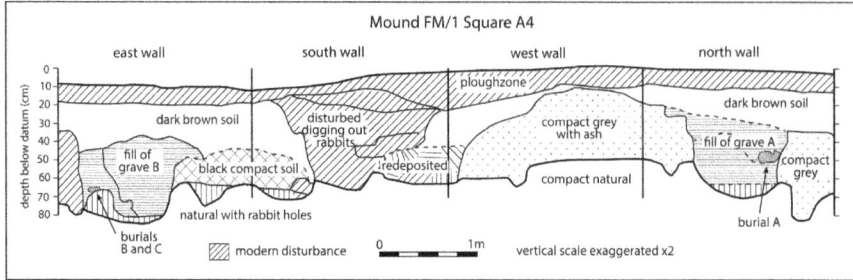

Figure 8.19 Simplified stratigraphic section drawing of the four sides of the 2x2m Square A4, Mound FM/1 (after Coutts et al. 1976: figure 9).

the places where some specific activities took place could be identified, including flaking floors where quartz tools were made and fireplaces or ovens with stone heat-retainers. Several centuries after that, a small child was buried in a pit dug into the mound, followed, again after many years, by the burial of a mature woman and the charred remains of a little girl.

Mound FM/1 has an equally confusing stratigraphy, with much ancient and modern disturbance of the original collapsed structure and discarded artefacts (Lewis 2000) (Figures 8.18, 8.19). The hut, or series of huts, built there about 2700 years ago, may not have lasted very long before falling out of use and decaying into a low mound. A few centuries later, the old mound was used again on at least three occasions as a burial place. Two of the excavated burials were disturbed by later activities, including burrowing rabbits. A third man, about 25 years of age, was placed on his side in a large oval pit about 40 centimetres deep. He had once broken his left forearm and – was it in the same accident? – two of the bones of his left hand, one of which healed unevenly, and may well have caused him some inconvenience and discomfort (Jurisich and Davies 1976). Just beside his body was a collection of lower jaws of at least 25 bandicoots: were these from an ornament or had they once decorated a cloak? Near him were a few scattered bones of a child, who must have died some time earlier.

A variety of stone tools was found at FM/1, broadly similar to those found in other mounds. They include scrapers of different types for making and repairing wooden tools, preparing food or working skins, as well as geometric microliths and backed points. Quartz pebbles and cobbles from nearby creek beds provided most of the raw material, but a wide variety of other types of stone was also present, including small amounts of porcellanite from Mount Stavely and flint from the coast. The exact sources of most stone are less certain, but it may have come from up to 100 kilometres away, a reminder of the extent of connections or distances travelled. This diversity contrasts sharply with the almost complete monopoly of coastal flint in the stony rises. Could this be because the stony rises were used for shorter periods and for special purposes and at a time when people's immediate links were to the nearby coast?

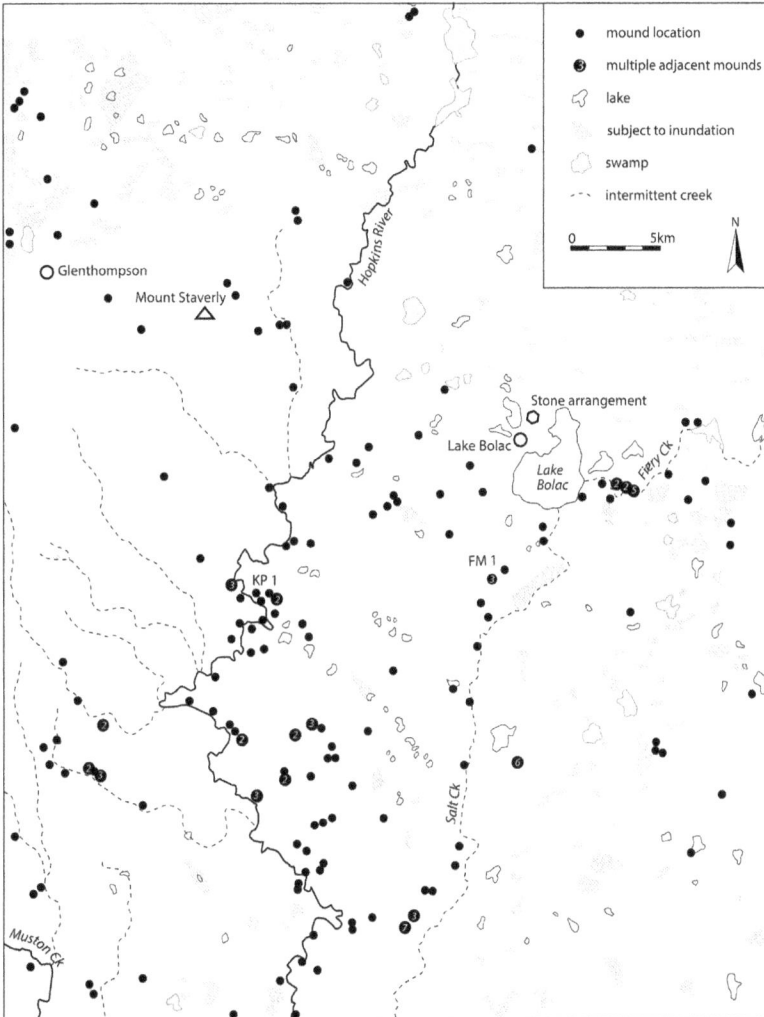

Figure 8.20 Location of mounds recorded on the 1:100,000 Willaura Map Sheet by the Victoria Archaeological Survey (after Coutts et al. 1976: figure 2).

KP/1 and FM/1 were only two of several mounds excavated by the Victoria Archaeological Survey in the 1970s and by others since. These all need to be seen in their broader, landscape context. Alongside their excavations, Peter Coutts and his teams also engaged in an ambitious attempt to locate all the sites in the 2470 square kilometres of the 1:100,000 Willaura Map Sheet (Victoria Archaeological Survey, no date). Despite the ravages of time, erosion, rabbits, rabbit-eradication and land improvement, 207 mounds were found and described by following up on older reports and by talking to landowners, who always have an intimate knowledge of their properties (Coutts et al. 1976) (Figure 8.20).

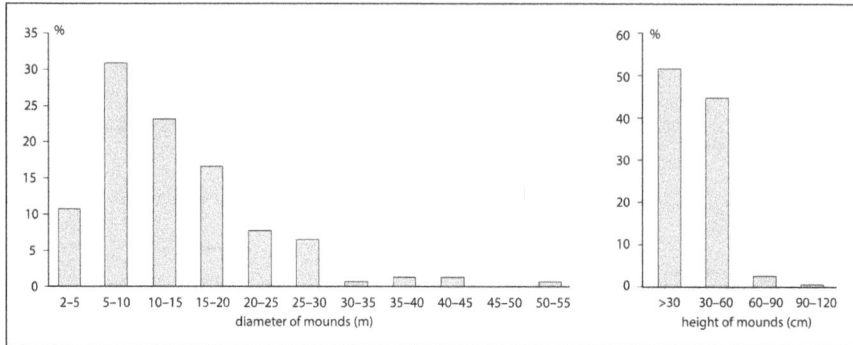

Figure 8.21 Dimensions of mounds in the Willaura area (data from Coutts et al. 1976: figure 3).

Many of the mounds now appear only as softer black, charcoal-rich patches against the brown soils of newly ploughed paddocks. But others, like KP/1 and FM/1, still rise as much as 60 centimetres above the surrounding land. Most are between 5 metres and 15 metres in diameter (Figure 8.21). But it is hard to say whether any were originally very much bigger, for their soils are likely to have been spread more widely both through natural deflation and the effects of ploughing. Mounds are often found in clusters, largely because people preferred to build their huts in similar locations, often choosing higher ground beside rivers, creeks or low-lying swamps and wetlands. Although close to one another, and seemingly parts of a single community, individual huts may well have been built and used on widely separated occasions - years, decades or even centuries apart. At McArthur Creek, a set of seven mounds is spread out over 100 metres along the flat top of a rise overlooking a large waterhole (Williams 1984, 1988) (Figure 8.22). McArthur Creek Mound 6 was formed about 1000 years after its near neighbour, Mound 5. People, 30 or 40 generations apart, were using the same locality in much the same way. But many mounds were indeed parts of larger encampments, such as one near Mount Napier at a place which

previous to its occupation by white men, was a favourite resort and as this was the only permanent supply of water, a village had been formed. I counted 13 large huts built in the form of a cupola. When seen at a distance they have the appearance of mounds of earth. They are built of large sticks closely packed together and covered with turf, grass side inwards. There are several variations. Those like a cupola are sometimes double and have two entrances; others again are like a niech. Then there are some made of boughs and grass. And last are common screens. The permanent huts are those in form of a cupola. Three of these huts had been occupied a day or two previous to my visit. A shield, or in the language of the natives, por.ral, as also a bucket or po.pare.re, and a shield of boughs for catching birds were left at the huts. (G.A. Robinson, 10 May 1841, Presland 1977: 85–86; Clark 1998a: 196)

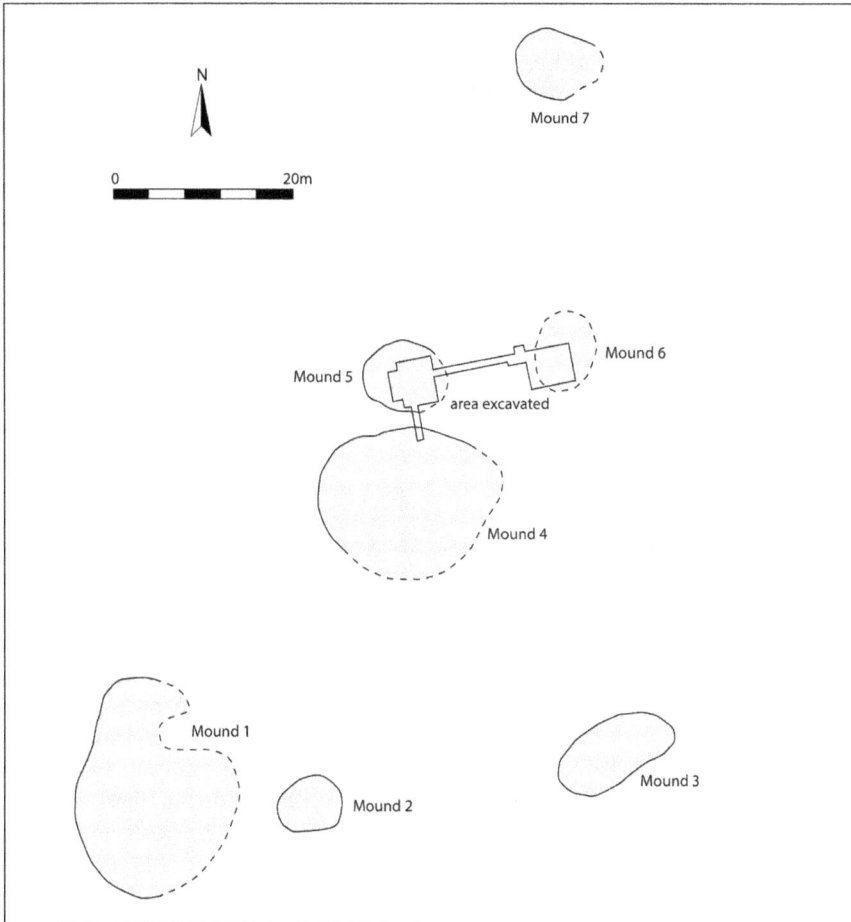

Figure 8.22 McArthur mound cluster. Mound 6 is about 1000 years older than Mound 5 (after Williams 1988: figure 6.4).

There are other reports of even larger groups of huts, but, as with those in the 'village' described by Robinson, it is not always clear whether they all were in use at one and the same time, and we have to beware of confusing the permanency, and perhaps longevity, of huts and permanency of occupation. Estimating the size of everyday camps and how long people stayed in them is far from easy, making it even more difficult to calculate local or regional populations (Williams 1985). While there is little doubt that several thousand Dhauwurd wurrung (Gunditdjmara), Girai Wurrung, Djab Wurrung, Djargurd wurrung and Jardwadjali people lived in southwestern Victoria at the time of the European invasion, estimates based on documents rather than archaeological evidence vary considerably – and all report on communities already drastically affected by European settlement and introduced diseases. Jan Crichett (1990), for example, suggests that there were about 3500 people in the area in 1841; Harry Lourandos (1980b) argues for twice that population density.

Finally, we have yet another set of questions. None of the mounds that have been excavated are older than about 3000 years (Bird and Frankel 1991a; Godfrey et al. 1996). So, while we know something of where mounds are located and how they were formed, we need to ask how or why this new form of building became fashionable in this part of Victoria in the relatively recent past. Does it mean people were spending more time at these camps and investing more energy in their construction? If so, was this because greater rainfall and the expansion of wetlands and swamps provided more food, or could this have been linked to increasing numbers of people, reducing the size of social territories? Do we need to explain the invention and adoption of substantial huts in terms of such social, economic or environmental factors, or could it just be for comfort and convenience?

Seasons at the lakes

Lakes seem obvious focal places, with water, birds, fish and associated plants and animals. But we have little evidence of lakeside occupation in Victoria. Lake Bolac provides one glimpse of a single episode of activity about 14,000 or 15,000 years ago as the climate began to improve after the cold and dry conditions at the height of the last Ice Age (Coutts 1982; Bird and Frankel 1998). Here, on the lakeside dune, Peter Coutts excavated a few quartz artefacts beside a small fireplace together with the bones of *Megaleia rufa*, the red kangaroo. There are none of these exceptionally big kangaroos there now, but the more arid environment at that time suited this species (Crowley and Kershaw 1994; Horton 1984). Later, its range contracted northward as wetter conditions prevailed in western Victoria. Lake Bolac, along with associated rivers and wetlands, was not colonised by eels until considerably later. Once established, these fish attracted large numbers of people for short periods during the autumn (Chapter 10).

At the end of March 1841, George Augustus Robinson passed nearby. He noted many abandoned campsites and other evidence of recent occupation, doubtless left by the hundreds of Aboriginal people who had gathered there to harvest eels from the lake and nearby creeks. There were also massive quantities of rotting dead eels heaped about – he could smell them from more than 3 kilometres away (Clark 1998: 115–20). The lake was nearly dry, so these eels may well have died naturally, perhaps because of increased salinity of the remaining water. Something similar happened in 2007 when thousands upon thousands of eels died in western Victorian lakes (Environment Protection Authority 2007). Although rare natural events such as this would have had an immediate local impact, broader patterns of life, the distribution of populations and the development of cultural and economic systems need not have been affected. These dependl on longer-term environmental circumstances and established traditions.

The Corangamite Basin lies to the southeast of Lake Bolac (Figure 8.23). Millennia of volcanic lava flows, which only ended 8000 years ago, shaped this landscape. Numerous smaller lakes surround Lake Corangamite, which, with an area of 230 square kilometres, is the largest perennial inland lake in Australia. At

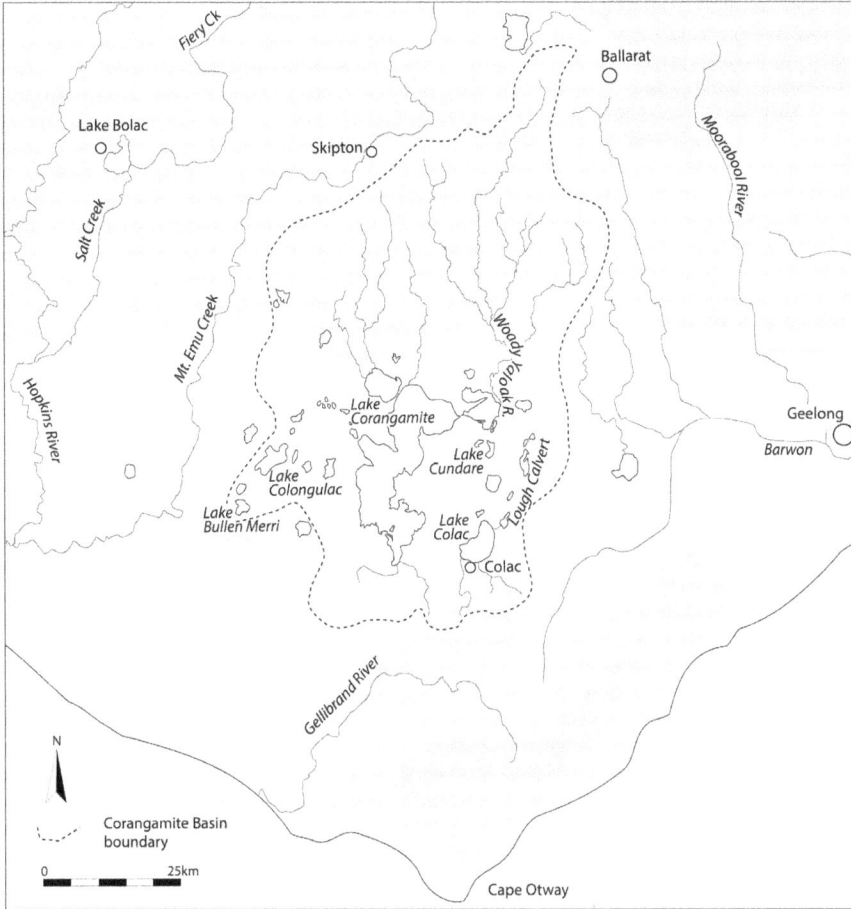

Figure 8.23 The Corangamite Basin.

first sight this seems a well-watered and rich environment, but closer inspection shows it to have severe limitations and constraints. Unlike other areas of southern Victoria, the rivers of the basin do not flow to the sea, but drain into the landlocked Lake Corangamite. Eels, so abundant and important at Lake Bolac and elsewhere, were not to be found in this closed drainage basin. With no outlets, most of the lakes are brackish, if not extremely salty. Many are quite unsuitable for human use. Some of the others only have drinkable water when flushed by winter rains. It was a patchy environment with seasonal variations, as noted, for example, by George Armitage:

> Their chief support was fish, caught in the river in the summer and autumn seasons, and in the winter and spring they depended on their success in hunting, together with the root called the 'murnong'. (Bride 1898: 175)

Through assessing environmental and historical evidence such as this, Ian McNiven suggests that people within the Corangamite Basin arranged themselves in different ways throughout the year, with seasonal patterns similar to those known in other parts of Australia (Pickering 1994; Dortch 2002). During the wetter months of winter and spring, when water was more readily available, people split up into smaller groups, spread out across wider areas, where they could collect a variety of plants and animals on dry land and in the creeks and lakes, hunting birds, collecting eggs and fishing, as described by Thomas Learmonth in 1837. After scaring away a large group of Aboriginal people, he

> found a fishing weir of the natives, in which were small conical nets of good workmanship. Nearly a bushel of delicious little fish like white-bait were in the nets ... (Bride 1898: 96)

During the summer, when smaller creeks died up and lakes were more brackish, people would group nearer to reliable and fresh water, such as Lake Colac and the Woady Yaloak River, perhaps remaining there for longer periods. In the recent past, the topographic boundary of the Corangamite Basin did not define any one specific group's territory. Djargurd wurrung, Gulidjan and Wada wurrung people all made use of different parts of it and doubtless also moved further afield into the surrounding country (McNiven 1998: figure 8). But it is still likely that the pattern of seasonal aggregation and dispersal was here, as elsewhere, a long-lasting tradition, connecting people and country in different ways.

Water quality naturally affected where people of the area set up camp. In 1994, Ian McNiven undertook a detailed survey of the area (McNiven 1998). He found – not surprisingly – most sites and isolated artefacts along the shores of lakes and within 100 metres of rivers (Figure 8.24). 'Inland' areas away from water had little to show for millennia of activity. There was also a clear correlation between the density of sites and the degree of salinity in the lakes (Figure 8.25). Lake Colac stands out as having the largest and most numerous sites, fitting well with the suggested pattern of concentrated summer use. This was perhaps the season when ceremonies were also held nearby, for a ceremonial site similar to those at Sunbury (Chapter 10) could still be seen close to the southern shore 50 years ago, although I looked in vain for it in 1980 (Massola 1966; Frankel 1982a). Several nearby mounds were also destroyed by the mid-1960s, through road widening, drainage schemes and other construction, including the Colac drive-in theatre, now itself an archaeological relic of the late 20th century.

Alongside his extensive survey, Ian also carried out a small excavation on the northeastern shore of the lake. Although people used this particular place some 7000 years ago, he found that there was a far greater density of stone tools during last two millennia. Perhaps the basin was barely used, if used at all, during more arid periods, or when the red kangaroo was hunted at Lake Bolac, and only became home to larger numbers of people very much more recently.

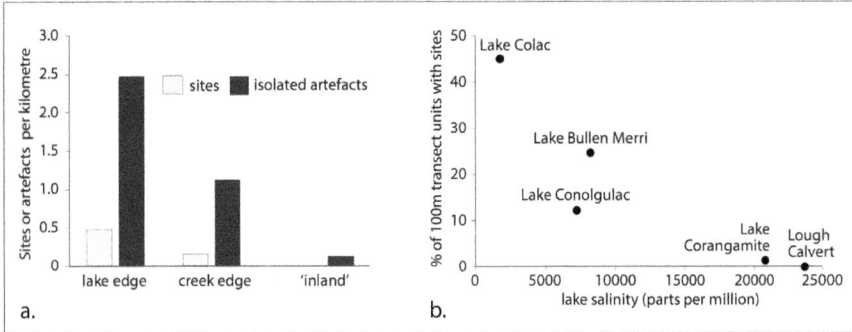

Figure 8.24 Location of sites in the Corangamite Basin. a. Relative density of sites (artefact scatters) and isolated artefacts in relation to main sources of water (data from McNiven 1998: table 2); b. Relationship between density of sites and water quality of several lakes (after McNiven 1998: figure 10).

9

Into the high country

On 8 January 2003, as in 1968, there was yet another reminder of

> what Victorian gum species
> do at least one time in
> each human generation
> (Les Murray, 'The 41st Year of 1968')

When 87 fires sparked by lightning joined together, they burnt out over a million hectares of the high country in northeastern Victoria (Figure 9.1). A devastating event, but one that then provided some opportunities, among them a chance for archaeologists to explore heritage places in the highland and alpine regions – for few had ventured much into these often inaccessible high hills and deep valleys of the Victorian Alps (Figures 9.2, 9.3). It is a diverse and variable land, with winter snows covering the grasslands and heath above 1300 metres, and thicker woodland at lower altitude. The weather, too, is variable, always liable to sudden changes bringing cold winds, rain and fog.

Surveying the Victorian Alps

Starting a year after the fires, Joanna Freslov and her teams of archaeologists and members of Aboriginal communities set out to look at 14 broad regions ranging in size from 70 square kilometres to over 3000 square kilometres (Figure 9.4) (Freslov et al. 2004). Within each of these areas sample locations were selected for detailed survey on the basis of the few previous archaeological reports, Aboriginal knowledge, the severity of fires and the associated impact of fire-fighting. They needed to include both those places where sites were most likely to occur and also those where they were not expected. It was also always necessary for them to make sure to include all the varied landforms and types of environment, ranging from thick forests to exposed alpine fields.

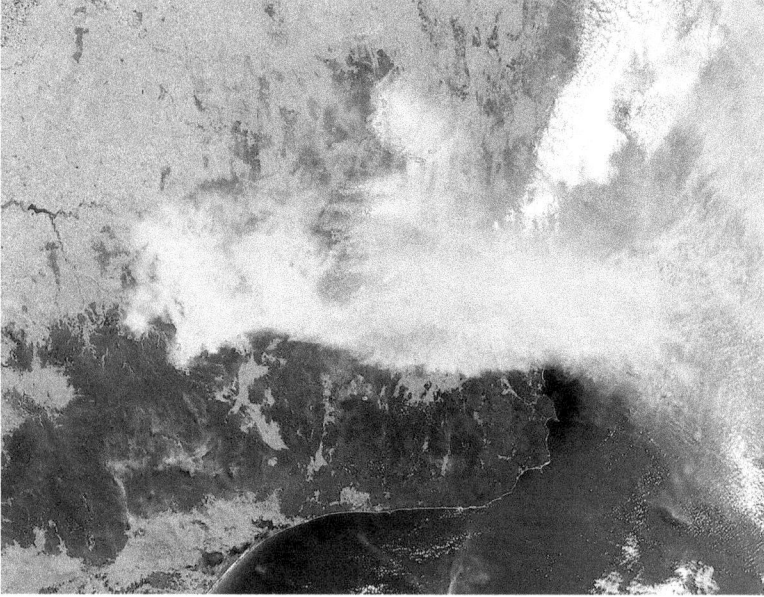

Figure 9.1 Satellite image of bushfires in the Australian Alps, 19 January 2003 (photo: NASA).

Figure 9.2 High steep hills and deep valleys characterise the Victorian Alps.

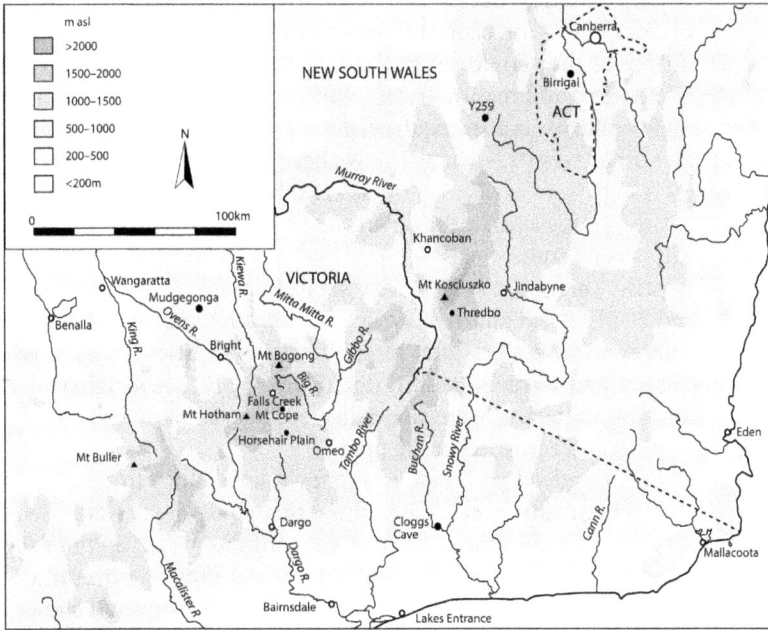

Figure 9.3 The Australian Alps.

Figure 9.4 General location of major surveys in the Victorian Alps (Hall 1992 and Freslov et al. 2004).

Every day each team would go out to explore their selected search area. They would then walk – or scramble – or clamber – over the ground, closely inspecting as much of the surface as they could see through the undergrowth and litter, as well as all the rocky outcrops and mature trees. While keeping up a uniform approach, a high degree of flexibility was also required, given the difficult terrain, problems of accessibility, and other factors, such as the wishes of the Indigenous participants. Later, the initial results were used to set out additional testing, including a focus on travel routes between large sites lower down the rivers and those far higher up the valleys in the sub-alpine zone.

It is no surprise, then, that only a very small fraction of any of the 14 areas could be looked at in any detail. It may not sound a lot, but the teams spent a good deal of energy to assess the total of 435 hectares of heavily vegetated steep slopes, ridges, spurs and terraces, and to document the 322 Aboriginal sites that they found. The stone artefacts were not collected, but as many as possible were examined, measured and recorded in the field.

Each survey area, indeed each site, has its own local story to tell. The varied quantities of artefacts or numbers of sites show that some areas were used more often or by more people than others. So, too, some of the routes up the valleys or along ridgelines were used more frequently than others. But the overall patterns are no less interesting, with consistent use of different landforms and climatic and vegetation zones (Figure 9.5). There are more isolated artefacts as well as 'sites' (where several artefacts occur together) per hectare on slopes, crests and terraces than on other landforms (Figures 9.6, 9.7). The mid and lower slopes close to valley bottoms and rivers were attractive, for there is greater shelter and plant foods are more clustered. The valley bottoms themselves were generally avoided, as these tend to be damper and trap colder air. The density of sites on exposed crests seems a little more surprising, but these overall figures are slightly misleading, as the sites at lower altitudes are bigger than those in the alpine and sub-alpine zones above 1400 metres above sea level. Most of the substantial sites are between about 600–700 metres above sea level, in the upper river valleys of the Gibbo, Big, Dargo, Mitta Mitta and Snowy. While there are a few large sites at higher altitudes (1200–1300 metres) at Dinner Plain and Dargo High Plain, and at 1600 metres (Tawonga Huts), the sites on these high, exposed ridgelines and crests are generally small. They are best seen as stopping points on access routes along narrow ridges or campsites near the rocky outcrops where bogong moths were collected. The sites on the highest peaks with panoramic views are very small, with between six and ten artefacts. Did these places have some special significance and function for Aboriginal people, not so closely tied to the availability of food or shelter?

In an earlier survey in three sections of East Gippsland, Roger Hall addressed some of the same issues, but did so in a slightly different way, avoiding the concept of 'sites' (Hall 1992). Convenient though it is for us to think of specific places in this way, these groups of artefacts were built up through many visits over very long periods of time. One alternative is to look at the relative density of artefacts across the landscape, using this as the measure of how frequently or how intensely people used different areas. Roger's small team of four people spent 85 days in 1989 and 1990 trudging 178 kilometres across the varied terrain. The results are not so dissimilar to those of the post-bushfire survey, with artefacts spread

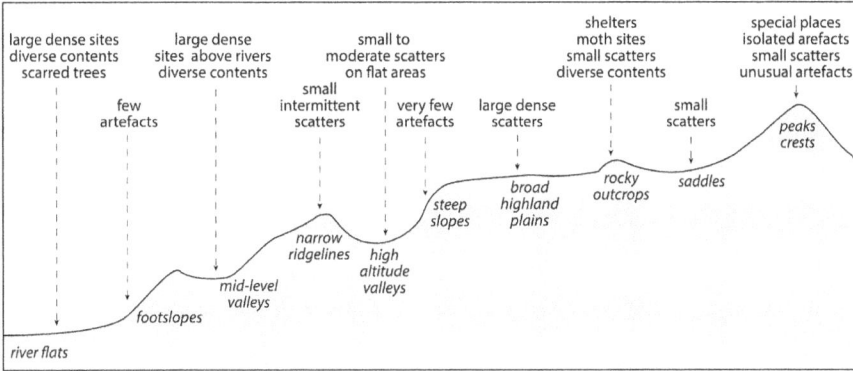

Figure 9.5 General model of site types and locations in the highlands (following Freslov et al. 2004: figure 25).

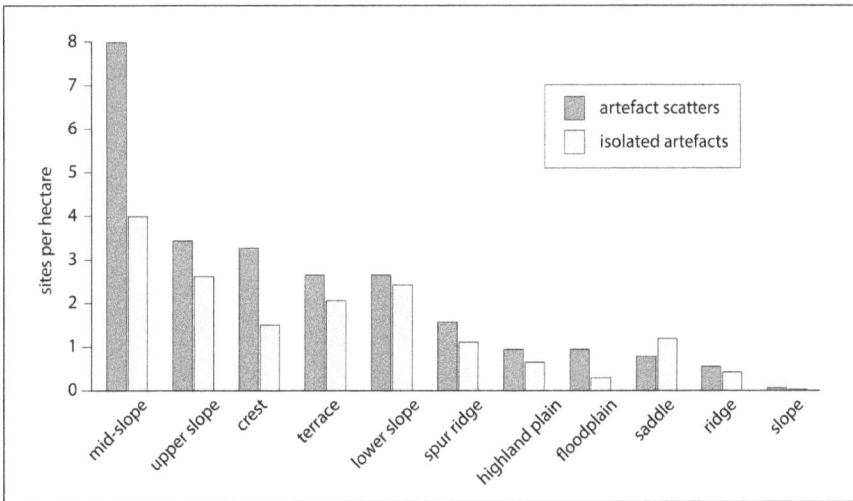

Figure 9.6 Relative density of sites in various landforms found during the post-bushfire survey (after Freslov et al. 2004: figure 19).

everywhere, although naturally unevenly distributed (Figure 9.8). The most dense concentrations were on flat land or lower slopes beside drainage lines or on nearby spurs – once again emphasising those with access to the greatest variety of forest resources. The ridgelines have a far lower density of artefacts, doubtless discarded during short stays at occasional campsites along trackways or access routes. Spurs have a high density of artefacts because they are conveniently located: well placed to rest or camp after traversing a ridgeline while also serving as useful vantage points from which to make use of the surrounding country. There are variations within these broad landforms, largely related to particular aspects of topography.

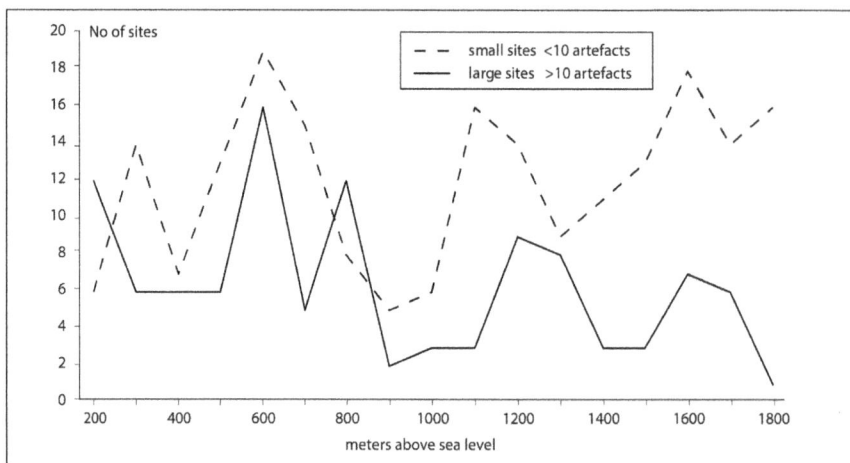

Figure 9.7 Relative numbers of small and larger sites at different altitudes (data from Freslov et al. 2004: figure 20).

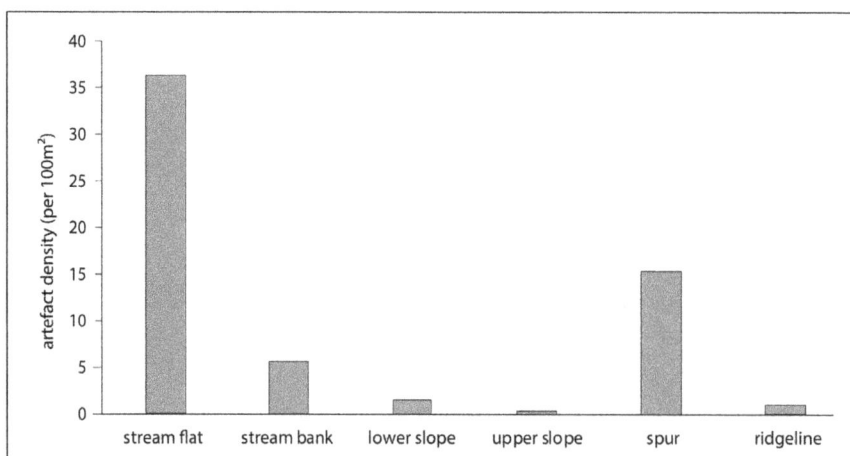

Figure 9.8 Relative density of artefacts on various landforms seen in the east Gippsland survey (after Hall 1992: figure 3).

Where plant foods are concentrated and space more limited, as in narrow steeper valleys, so too is the density or concentration of artefacts. But this is not the case where the valley floors are wider and resources more broadly available. Although these areas as a whole were well used, the artefacts are more thinly spread across them as no single spot was preferred to any other – we have seen something similar in the way people used parts of the Wimmera (Chapter 7).

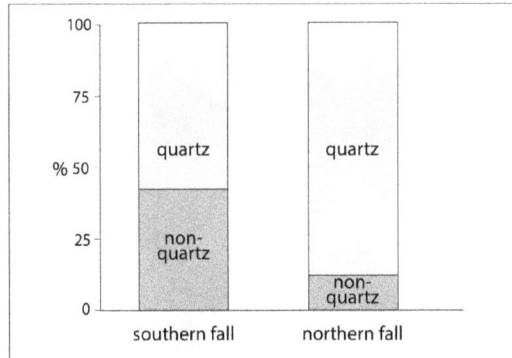

Figure 9.9 Proportions of quartz and other stone types
north and south of the divide (data from Freslov et al.
2004: figure 21).

During the post-bushfire field survey, 2476 artefacts were recorded – a small
sample of the total found, but enough to provide several insights. Everywhere
quartz was commonly used, for it is readily available, convenient to hand (Figure
9.9). There is, however, a clear difference between the sites on either side of the
watershed separating rivers that run southward towards the coast from those
flowing towards the Murray basin to the north. Sites on the Southern Fall, linked to
the valleys running up from the coast, include many more artefacts made of other
types of stone than quartz. Much of this would also have been collected locally,
for the underlying geology is complex, so that a wide variety of rocks, including
silcrete and rhyolite, can be found in the beds and banks of the south-flowing
rivers. Other types, including chert and hornfels, may have been carried in from
further away. In contrast, at sites on the Northern Fall, stone other than quartz
was far less common and with a more restricted array of types. The small amounts
of fine-grained siliceous stone most suited to making neat small tools must have
been carried up the mountains from some distance away. Taking this further, the
presence of these exotic stones even on the highest peaks of the Southern Fall and
their absence from north-oriented sites only a few kilometres away represents a
cultural as much as a geological and topographic divide, correlating with group
affiliations and language boundaries mapped by Sue Wesson (2000).

Perhaps, too, we can link the highland evidence with some from lower down
the valleys. Mudgegonga 2 is one of a group of small granite rock-shelters, known
for their rock art, set on the side of a valley running from the north up towards
Mount Beauty and Mount Bogong (Figure 9.10). There are some charcoal
drawings, but most of the motifs were painted using red ochre, along with a few
white and yellow paintings: these broadly fall into a sequence, similar to that noted
for sites in Gariwerd (Chapter 2) (Gunn 2002). There may also be an equivalent
change from motifs associated with rituals to more general and public art, for the

171

Figure 9.10 Mudgegonga Shelter 2.

earlier, red paintings include figures wearing ritual costume. These may date from as early as 4000 years ago. Here, Ben Gunn adds a further level of interpretation, suggesting not that ceremonies took place in the shelter, but that it was used by men as they made their way to or returned from ceremonies high up in the mountains. Not only would rituals have been at the forefront of their minds, but the paintings could have served an important role in preparing young men for initiation or in revealing esoteric knowledge to them once they had been put through the law.

Back in the more mundane world of everyday archaeological remains, we find that at Mudgegonga 2, quartz was very much the standard raw material, although other, better quality stone was very occasionally used for small backed points (Perham 1985). Over 97 per cent of all the tools and fragments excavated at this site were made of quartz, probably obtained from sources along the nearby Barwidgee Creek. It is then not hard to imagine Jaimathang or other people visiting this or similar sites on their way up the valleys into the high country, perhaps even carrying quartz and very small amounts of other stone with them: the characteristic raw materials of the Northern Fall.

The same could be said for Cloggs Cave on the other side of the Divide, where, as might be expected, a wider array of stone was found. As we have seen in Chapter 1, this site was used in far earlier times, but it seems that afterwards no one visited it for many thousands of years until the last millennium (Flood 1980). It too may also have served as a staging point as people made their way from near the coast up the Buchan River towards the high country.

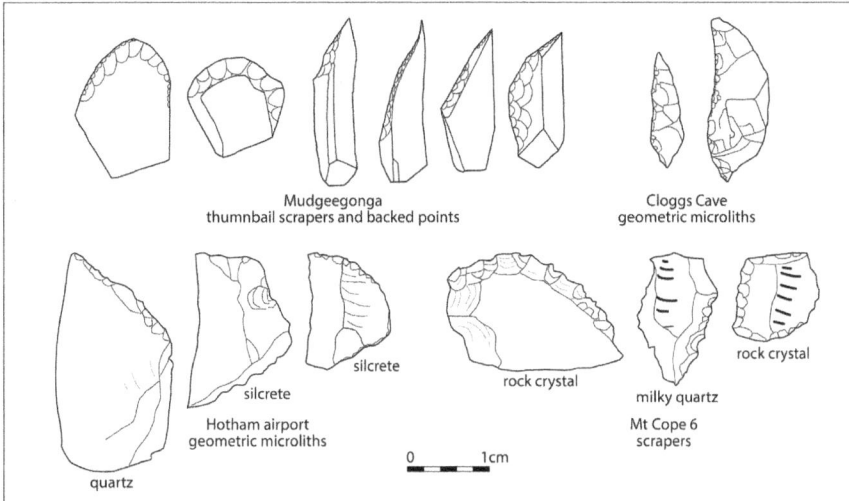

Figure 9.11 Microlithic stone tools from Mudgegonga, Cloggs Cave, Hotham airport and Mount Cope Shelter 6 (after Perham 1985: figures 5.3, 5.6; Flood 1980: figure 57; Shawcross 2000: figure 3; Shawcross et al. 2006: figure 5).

None of the sites found in either of the main surveys in Victoria provide independent dates, but there is no reason to believe that any of the stone tools are older than a few thousand years. The more standardised points and scrapers, like those excavated at Mudgegonga and Cloggs Cave (Figure 9.11), are types which, as we have seen elsewhere, become most common in the last 4500 years.

Graders at the airport

At 1298 metres above sea level, the airport on Horsehair Plain is the highest in Australia, serving the ski resorts at nearby Dinner Plain and Mount Hotham (Figure 9.12). During its construction in 1989–90, a group of Aboriginal people representing the native title claimants of the Gunai/Kurnai People were monitoring progress (Shawcross 2000). No one expected to find anything much; perhaps a few small scatters of stone tools, such as had been noted during earlier surveys. But there are always surprises. As the bulldozers began to work on the access road from the Great Alpine Road, dozens of artefacts appeared. And there were signs that there were many others buried by the peaty soil accumulated across the area. It became very clear that the very small number of artefacts visible on the ground surface was an unreliable guide to what lay below. The extent of the site was a shock to everyone, especially the developers. Fortunately for them – and the future of the airport – the Aboriginal community decided that if the site could be adequately salvaged and documented, the work could go ahead as planned, without undue delay. They brought in an archaeologist, Wilfred Shawcross, to oversee the project.

Figure 9.12 Mount Hotham airport at Horsehair Plain (image: Google Earth).

The strategy he followed made use of the skills of the grader-drivers. Experimental tests showed how they could scrape off very thin slices of soil, leaving in place the artefacts they uncovered. Together with the Aboriginal monitors, Wilfred then worked alongside the construction crews, plotted the location of the finds and collected them for further analysis. More than 40,000 pieces of stone were documented across an area of about 40 hectares, revealing the overall pattern of distribution (Figure 9.13).

Artefacts were most common in drier areas where there would have been stands of trees. Lower-lying soft and damp places were, for obvious reasons, less attractive camping places. There was therefore little or nothing to be found in the area now covered by the airport apron, buildings and carpark. Many more artefacts appeared on the higher ground along the line of the scarp beside the access road and on the slight rise just east of the buildings, near where the planes now taxi out to the main runway. Here, and on another similar rise a little further east, were the greatest concentrations of finds. Elsewhere, again where the levelling graders cut through slightly raised ground once sheltered by trees, more finds were made. And, of course, we should envisage equivalent distributions in all the other suitable places away from those cleared for the runway.

Within the general spreads of artefacts there were some small, discrete patches where waste flakes were scattered around and about the cores from which they had been stuck. As usual, there was far more waste material than cores; had a finer collection strategy been used, even more of the very smallest chips would have been found. These scatters were working areas where tools were made. One example near the northwest end of the runway – the first of the working areas to be recognised – had 373 fragments of quartz within an oval area about 1.5 metres long. Some of these workshops were grouped together, clearly favourite places to sit and make tools. The stone workers used a small amount of silcrete, which they

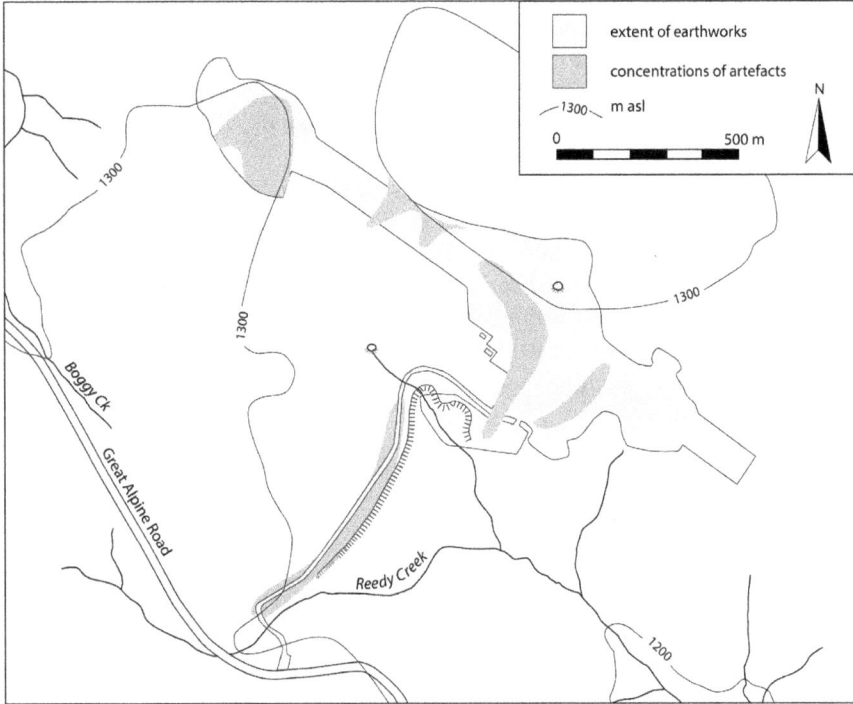

Figure 9.13 Areas investigated and main artefact concentrations found during construction of the Hotham Airport in 1998 and 1989 (after Shawcross 2000: figure 1).

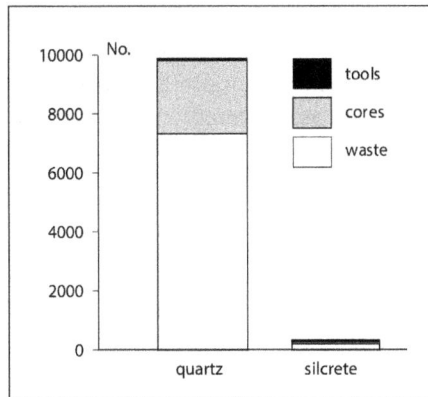

Figure 9.14 Numbers of quartz and silcrete artefacts from Horsehair Plain (data from Shawcross 2000: table 1).

must have brought from quite far away. But almost all of the material (about 98 per cent) was quartz, as at other sites on the Northern Fall. Although quartz is not available on the Horsehair Plain itself, it could easily have been collected not far away on the banks or gravels of the Cobungra River.

While it is hard to estimate just how much this one place was used, or for how long, there is no reason to think that any of the tools are more than a few thousand years old, and one radiocarbon sample gives a date of 2500 years ago (Shawcross et al. 2006). And, while 40,000 pieces of stone does sound a lot, this could be as few as 40 per year when spread over a millennium. Even so, this place does signal that the high plateaus were used consistently, at least during the summer months. The people – perhaps even sizeable numbers of people – who camped at Horsehair Plain could take advantage of the local mix of plants, animals and fish, and use this place as a base from which to make excursions higher up into the mountains to collect bogong moths.

Bogong moths, feasts and ceremonies

The Waverong natives say that they have the Boogong fly at Tarerewait in their country; it is the only place and is on the highest rocks and are not numerous. They call it *teberer*, from Teberer the plains now occupied by Andrew Erwin under south side of Mount Buller, the Alps, this belongs to the Yowenillum. The Omeo blacks call the fly olleong, the Yowenillum call it teberer. The natives say that they make black fellows very fat all the natives go they put them in a bag and shake them to break their wings and legs; then tie them up in a piece of bark and roast them: are very good. I am not certain that the women go with Waverong to collect teberer. (G.A. Robinson, 14 June 1844, Clark 1998b: 101)

Residents of Canberra are all too familiar with sudden plagues of bogong moths, either blown off course or attracted by the lights during their spring migrations into the Snowy Mountains. Each year more than two billion of them gradually move to higher, cooler altitudes as temperatures rise. Over the summer, the moths cluster by their thousands or tens of thousands in dark, cold and moist crevices and rocky shelters (Figure 9.15). As autumn approaches, they return to breed in the lowlands. This pattern of movement would not have been necessary, or indeed possible, during glacial times, but as temperatures increased these insects needed to escape the summer heat. Perhaps by 10,000 years ago, if not earlier, they were already resorting to the dense 'camps' seen today.

By all accounts great quantities of moths could easily be scraped or brushed off the rock surfaces, collected in finely woven baskets and roasted, providing great quantities of nutritious food. There is no doubt of the significance of this seasonal local abundance for

all the tribes from Gipps Land, the Dodoro, Omeo, Maneroo and others all assemble during month of ... at the Boo.gon mountains part of the Alps at Omeo and feast upon a fly which are found in that particular locality. Combing the rocks, the native women brush them off into their bags, they contain honey and

Figure 9.15 A mass of bogong moths (photo: CSIRO).

are called the Boogon fly. The Alps are called the Boogon mountains but is one mountain at Omeo where the fly is so abundant. Large numbers of blacks go thither, they are in general very thin but return stout, it is fine feasting for them. (G.A. Robinson, 1 June 1844, Clark 1998b: 88)

There is, however, no direct archaeological evidence at all of either moth collection or consumption. Analysis of smooth river cobbles found in the highlands indicates residues of proteins: could these cobbles have been used when moths were 'ground into a paste by the use of a smooth stone and hollow piece of bark, and made into cakes' (Scott 1869: 47; Flood 1980: 62)? But the evidence is still circumstantial rather than certain. We are here beyond the limits of what archaeology can show or prove; indeed, as Josephine Flood has noted, 'no ethnography, no moth hunters' (Flood 1988).

Of course, even if only travelling up to and down from the moth sites, people had to live, to hunt or gather other food and to collect stone for making tools. Despite the undeniable economic, social and cultural importance of moths, the range of sites and artefacts, like those at Horsehair Plain, shows that many other things went on in the Alps. Indeed, it is likely that people spent long periods in the highlands during the warmer months when a wide variety of plant and animal foods was available (Kamminga 1992). The moths were, however, of particular importance, especially as they provided the stimulus for large numbers of people to come together at particular times.

About the year 1840 my friend the late Mr A.M. McKeachie met two young men of the Ngarigo tribe at the Snowy River, near Barnes Crossing [now Dalgety];

one of them carried two peeled sticks, each about two feet long and with notches cut in them, which they told him reminded them of their message. The sticks were about one half inch in diameter. Their message was that they were to collect their tribe to meet those of the Tumut River and Queanbeyan, at a place in the Bogong Mountains, to eat the Bogong moths. (Howitt 1904: 693)

Elsewhere the local abundance of other seasonal foods – eels in western Victoria, cycads in Queensland – also provided the basis for major gatherings of hundreds of people. These were also occasions for important ceremonies, which must have taken place at significant sites or ceremonial grounds in the Victorian Alps as well as those known in New South Wales.

A rock-shelter at the top of the world

The conical peak of Mount Cope is one of several surrounding the Bogong High Plains. Just below its summit there are several small rock-shelters. Some, like Shelter 3, close to the cairn on the summit, are likely to have often been used by bushwalkers, caught out by sudden changes in weather. But others, Shelter 6 among them, were hidden from view by vegetation – at least until the 2003 bushfires. As we have seen, the post-bushfire surveys explored broad areas of the highlands. The team also located and excavated a few sites. Mount Cope Number 6 was selected because there were some artefacts on the surface, a thin wire probe indicated a reasonable depth of deposit and it was large enough to shelter several people. Not that the shelter was an ideal place: poorly lit, with limited headroom, uncomfortable in the past and for the excavators (Shawcross et al. 2006).

The shelter is one of the highest known Aboriginal sites in Australia, and the highest to be excavated. The team dug a small trench 50 centimetres wide and 1 metre long, exposing up to 70 centimetres of varied soil deposits. About 25 to 30 centimetres below the surface, a concentration of charcoal suggests that at one time a fire was lit against the north wall. Radiocarbon dates show that while sediment began to accumulate in the shelter some 6500 years ago, the earliest artefacts are only about 1500 years old, deposited at about the time that the fireplace was used.

Forty-three artefacts were found in the small area excavated. All were either milky or rock crystal quartz. This did not need to be brought to the site, for there are veins of quartz, including rock crystal quartz, visible in the shelter walls, so that people extracted raw material when needed. A third of the pieces show damage or resharpening: they were used for heavy-duty work, perhaps sharpening or preparing wooden tools.

The most obvious reason for people to have climbed up to this site – perhaps from main camping places like those on the Horsehair Plain – was to collect bogong moths, for the shelter is an ideal place for the insects to cluster for the summer (indeed, dead moths were observed in the shelter by the excavators). But the stone tools suggest that this was not all that went on. Perhaps, if the weather turned bad, a group of men might pass the time in the shelter, sitting beside their fire, making or repairing their spears or other equipment.

Across the border

The highlands, as we have seen, is a landscape of contrasts: a mosaic of zones defined by altitude, topography, ecology and geology. Of all the boundaries, the least relevant to the archaeological past are those separating Victoria, New South Wales and the Australian Capital Territory. The Snowy Mountains of New South Wales are, however, generally higher than the Victorian Alps, with fewer deeply dissected valleys and more open plateaus.

In the 1970s, Josephine Flood carried out extensive pioneering research in the Australian Capital Territory and the adjacent Monaro Tablelands, identifying and excavating a series of small rock-shelters, including Bogong Cave and Yankee Hat (Flood 1980). Since her original work, over a thousand archaeological surveys or studies of varied scale and quality have been carried out in the region, largely because of planned development in urban and tourist areas (Brockwell et al. 2013). The numerous sites found are, like those in the Victorian Alps, typically small scatters of stone tools. A great many, as we have seen at Horsehair Plain, are at fairly high altitudes, suggesting that people were spending time in areas up to 1200 metres above sea level, certainly during the summer, but perhaps also at other times (Kamminga 1992; Argue 1995). At a local level, surveys, such as those in the Thredbo Valley, show how sites were sensibly placed to take best advantage of local circumstances (Kamminga et al. 1989). People preferred the southern side of the valley, with its greater exposure to sunlight and warmth. They also chose raised flats, a little above the valley floor, which were protected by the trees from the cold winds sweeping down the valley.

As well as these seasonally visited everyday campsites, there are several ceremonial sites: something not yet identified on the Victorian side of the border. There are art sites, stone arrangements and ceremonial grounds laid out with stones or created by clearing a central area and building a low encircling bank, as seen in other parts of eastern Australia but rarely in Victoria (Chapter 10) (Flood 1980; Kamminga 1992).

The small rock-shelter at Birrigai in the Australian Capital Territory was first used between 25,000 and 19,000 years ago (Chapter 1) (Flood et al. 1987). People continued to visit this site occasionally until, soon after 10,000 years ago, this stopped for about 7000 years. More regular visits resumed in the last 3000 years, matching the overall pattern of recent use of the uplands shown through the surveys and small excavations. Although few could be directly dated, the types of stone tools – like those at Victorian sites – are the small blades or microliths which became most common during the last few thousand years. Only one other excavation provides evidence of earlier activity.

The prosaically named Site Y259, in among boulders 1100 metres above sea level, provides little shelter (Aplin et al. 2010). Although their primary intention was to investigate the environmental rather than the human history of the area, the excavators found stone tools in the lower deposits, dated to about 9500 years ago. At that time people used the site only for occasional, short visits, for there is no evidence that tools were made there; rather, they were brought in, ready-made. This was near the beginning of a generally warmer period, seen locally in the development of wetter forests interspersed with patches of open vegetation, home to a wide range of small marsupials. What attracted people to these upland areas is very unclear; they certainly hunted a variety of animals, focusing on the medium-sized to larger species such as wallaby, rather than smaller ones. But it is also possible that the warming climate led Bogong moths to use the higher mountains during the summer. Moths certainly make use of Y259 today, but it is not possible to say when they began to do so or if visits to this site were made in order to collect them.

10
Chains of connection

At the periodical great meetings trading is carried on by the exchange of articles peculiar to distant parts of the country. A favourite place of meeting for the purpose of barter is a hill called Noorat, near Terang. In that locality the forest kangaroos are plentiful, and the skins of the young ones found there are considered superior to all others for making rugs. The aborigines from the Geelong district bring the best stones for making axes, and a kind of wattle gum celebrated for its adhesiveness. This Geelong gum is so useful in fixing the handles of stone axes and the splinters of flint in spears, and for cementing the joints of bark buckets, that it is carried in large lumps all over the Western District. Greenstone for axes is obtained also from a quarry on Spring Creek, near Goodwood; and sandstone for grinding them is got from the salt creek near Lake Boloke. Obsidian or volcanic glass, for scraping and polishing weapons, is found near Dunkeld. The Wimmera country supplies the maleen saplings, found in the mallee scrub for making spears. The Cape Otway forest supplies the wood for the bundit spears, and the grass-tree stalk for forming the butt piece of the light spear, and for producing fire; also a red clay, found on the sea coast, which is used as a paint, being first burned and then mixed with water, and laid on with a brush formed of the cone of the banksia while in flower by cutting off its long stamens and pistils. Marine shells from the mouth of the Hopkins River, and freshwater mussel shells, are also articles of exchange. (Dawson 1881: 78)

James Dawson's *Australian Aborigines*, published in 1881, was the product of a long collaboration with his daughter Isabella and with many Aboriginal informants, especially Yaruun Parpur Tarneen and her husband Wombeet Tuulawarn. No one reading this extract can be left in any doubt of just how much interaction there was between different areas and how many things were exchanged between Aboriginal groups in the recent past. People often travelled far out of their own country to meet others, to transport or acquire goods, and to participate in ceremony (McBryde 1984a). But there is precious little archaeological evidence of most of the material things, let alone the social networks, relationships, gatherings and ceremonies so fundamental to Aboriginal society. The exception, of course, is stone.

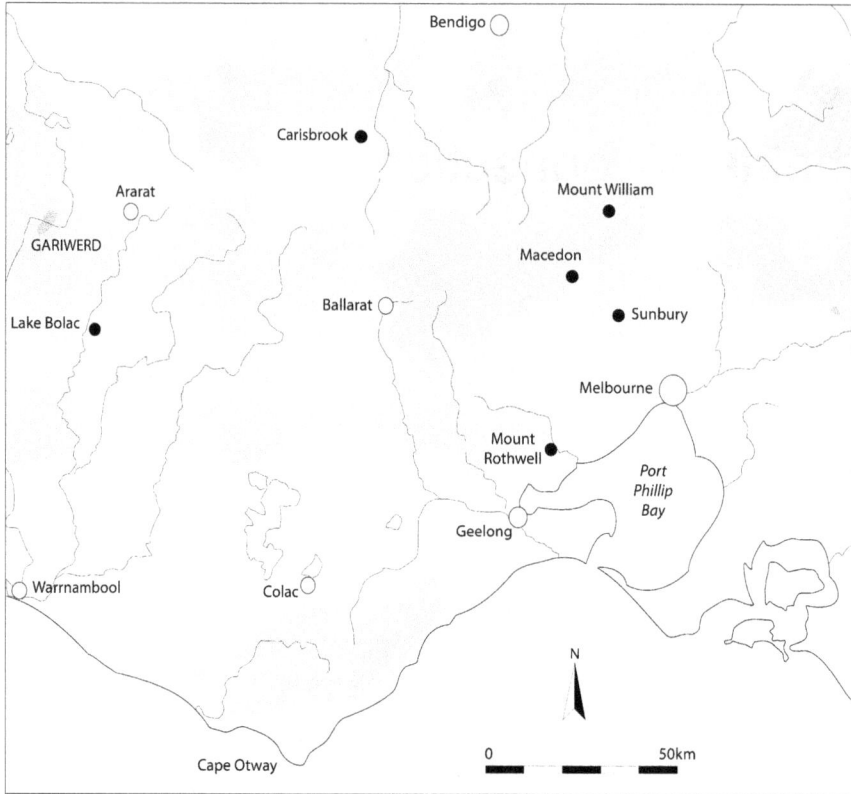

Figure 10.1 Central Victoria.

Greenstone from Wil-im-ee Moor-ring

Of all the sites we might deal with, the Mount William quarry stands out. Important to Aboriginal people in the past and in the present, it has also captured the European imagination in different ways since the mid-19th century (Paton 2005). From our archaeological perspective, the place is one of the best-known sites in Australia, partly because of the associated ethnohistorical information, partly because of the story it has to tell, and largely through the work of Isabel McBryde (1978, 1984b, 1986).

There is nothing to suggest anything special about the area as one walks up the open paddocks from the west towards the northern end of the Mount William range. The eucalypt woodland which once covered the hills began to be cleared in the 1840s, while the devastating Black Thursday bushfires of 6 February 1851 probably also swept through the area. Reaching the top of the ridge, there is now a fine view across over the hills, should one chance to be there when it is not misty and overcast, although it always seems to be windy (Figure 10.2). On the flatter top of the ridge and all down the steep slope beyond are the rocky outcrops and remnants of the quarry. Here ancient lava flows had produced the diabase (or

Figure 10.2 View of the Mount William greenstone quarry.

amphibole hornfels) locally known as 'greenstone' and which was so much sought after because its toughness and ability to hold a good, durable cutting edge without fracturing made it ideal for hatchet heads. It is a vast area of industrial activity covering at least 27 hectares, with extensive scatters and patches of greenstone chips, flakes and fragments visible on the surface – despite more than a century of visitors, curio-seekers and collectors.

Isabel McBryde was able to identify over 250 discrete areas where quarrying took place. Eighteen are deeper shaft-like cuttings dug down into the bedrock, while the others are shallower circular pits, 2 to 5 metres in diameter and still up to a metre deep (Figure 10.3). Stone was prised out of the ground or broken off the exposed vertical faces of these pits and shafts. In many pits there are still large central slabs of stone once used as anvils when smashing up larger pieces. Elsewhere in the quarry, slabs of stone were levered away from the sides of diorite outcrops. Once extracted and broken up, suitable pieces were selected to be chipped into the shape and size of hatchet heads at separate, nearby locations (Figure 10.4). There are about three dozen such flaking floors, where the waste debris was discarded, in some cases forming mounds up to 20 metres in diameter. The prepared hatchet-head blanks were then taken away to be finished elsewhere. John Green described the process well in the 1870s, although this was already at a time when the quarry had been abandoned for a generation or more and it is not clear how much of what he reported was hearsay:

The stones used for making tomahawks were dug out of the quarries with a pole of hard wood. The stones were found in blocks, not much larger than

Figure 10.3 Evidence of quarrying at Mount William.

Figure 10.4 A roughly shaped hatchet-blank among quarry debris.

the ordinary tomahawks, and the shape was given to the blocks by striking off flakes with an old tomahawk. The cutting edge was formed and polished by grinding and rubbing on a piece of sandstone. Sometimes a stone was found in the bed of a creek or river, or on the sea-shore, of the desired form, and this was ground and sharpened, and used as a tomahawk; but such a stone was considered as very inferior to the tomahawk of green stone shaped in the manner described. Pebbles were never used by the men of the Yarra tribe if they could get greenstone blocks. The greenstone was brought from a quarry near Kilmore, on a range called Mount Hope by the Europeans, and known as Wil-im-ee Moorring (Tomahawkhouse) amongst the natives. (Smyth 1878, I: 378)

An easy day's walk southwest of the quarry is a small exposed outcrop of sandstone (Figure 10.5). On its surface are 31 shallow grooves where generations of Aboriginal men ground the sharp working edges of the greenstone hatchet-head blanks brought from the quarry (West 1978) (Figure 10.6). Only the immediate cutting edge of the hatchet was ground smooth in this way; the body of the tool was left as it was after the roughing out. This was the common practice all across Australia, perhaps because the rougher surfaces were also used as anvils or for heavier hammering. The hatchet heads were then normally fitted onto a handle, generally wrapped around it and bound in place using sinews, twine and gum (Dickson 1981) (Figure 10.7), as described by Peter Beveridge:

> In putting one of these axes into a handle ... a section of a tough sapling, three feet long by an inch and a half thick, is procured; the wood preferred being a species of acacia. This piece of sapling is split down the middle, one half only being required for the handle; this half is made pliant by a process of steaming, which is achieved by judiciously mixing hot ashes with damp earth, wherein the wood is manipulated until it becomes sufficiently supple for the required purpose. It is then bent around the axe head until the two flat sides meet, when they are firmly lashed together by cord, combined with a good plaster of prepared gum. (Beveridge 1889: 68–69)

We are fortunate to have a detailed account of the social context of the Mount William quarry, although, again, one written many years after it ceased to be in active use. Alfred Howitt learnt much of this from William Barak, a senior and knowledgeable Wurundjeri elder who died in 1903, having lived through the whole period of European settlement. It is worth quoting at length as it provides an insight into the complex ties and responsibilities between people, land and resources, and hints at the significance attached to stone from Mount William.

> The right to hunt and procure food in any particular tract of country belonged to the group of people born there, and could not be infringed by others without permission. But there were places which such a group of people claimed for some special reason, and in which the whole tribe had an interest. Such a place was the 'stone quarry' at Mt William near Lancefield, from which the material for making tomahawks was procured. The family proprietorship of this quarry had wide ramifications, including more than the Wurunjerri people. On the

Figure 10.5 Sandstone outcrop with grinding grooves near Mount Macedon.

Figure 10.6 Two ground edge hatchet heads.

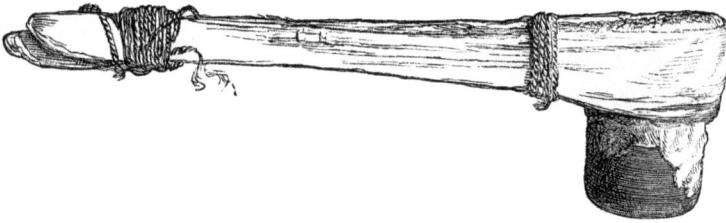

Figure 10.7 A hafted hatchet (Smyth 1878: figure 179).

one side it included the husband of Billi-billeri's sister, one of the headmen of the Kurnung-Willam, who lived at Bacchus Marsh, and who was named Nurrum-Nurrum-Biin, that is, 'moss growing on decayed wood'. On the other side it included Ningu-labul, and in another direction Bebejern, the son of an heiress in quarry rights, from whom an interest came to Berak through his father Bebejern. But it was Billi-billeri, the head of the family whose country included the quarry, and who lived on it, and took care of it for the whole of the Wurunjerri community. When he went away, his place was taken by the son of his sister, the wife of Nurrum-Nurrum-Biin, who came on such occasion to take charge, when it may be assumed, like Billi-billeri, he occupied himself in splitting stone to supply demands. The enormous amount of broken stone lying about on the mountain shows that generations of the predecessors of Billi-billeri must have laboured at this work.

When neighbouring tribes wished for some stone they sent a messenger to Billi-billeri saying that they would send goods in exchange for it, for instance, such as skin rugs. When people arrived after such a message they encamped close to the quarry, and on one occasion Berak heard Billi-billeri say to them, 'I am glad to see you and give you what you want and satisfy you, but you must behave quietly and not hurt me or each other'.

If, however, people came and took stone without leave, it caused trouble, and perhaps a fight between Billi-billeri's people and them. Sometimes men came by stealth and stole stone. (Howitt 1904: 311–12)

Past significance is matched by modern value. Mount William – *Willam-ee-mooring* – is, for present day Wurundjeri, more than an archaeological site. A large section of the area was formally returned to the community by the Australian government in 2012, and is the focus of heritage training and other cultural activities, including collecting stone for hatchets used during the *Koorong* project to manufacture a bark canoe using traditional tools and techniques (Griffin et al. 2013).

Tomahawks, hatchets, axes

Ground stone hatchets were standard equipment in many parts of Australia. The earliest example is at least 44,000 years old (Hiscock et al. 2016), but there is no evidence that this type of tool was made in Victoria until relatively recently, perhaps only in the last 5000 years or so. Few have been found in excavations: one fragment of greenstone found at Mugadgadjin in Gariwerd suggests a minimum age of 3000 years (Bird and Frankel 2005). Hatchets became essential, multi-function tools, the Swiss Army knife in each man's belt; the description of their use given by Brough Smyth 150 years ago can hardly be bettered:

> A man never leaves his encampment without his hatchet. With its help he ascends trees almost as rapidly as the native bear can climb. He cuts a notch for his toes, and placing the hatchet between his teeth, so as to set free his arms, ascends one step, cuts another notch, and so on until the height he desires to reach is attained. The rapidity with which he climbs and his dexterity would surprise a stranger. With the stone axe he cuts open limbs of trees to get opossums out of the hollows; splits open trunks to take out honey or grubs or eggs of insects; cuts off sheets of bark for his miam or for canoes; cuts down trees, and shapes the wood into shields or clubs or spears; cuts to pieces the larger animals of the chase, if necessary; and strikes off flakes of stone for inserting in the heads of spears and for skinning beasts and cleaning the skins. With an old tomahawk he will shape from the rough block of stone a new tomahawk. Its uses are so many and so various that one cannot enumerate them. It is sufficient to say that a native could scarcely maintain existence in Australia if deprived of this implement. (Smyth 1878: 1379)

In the 19th century, these tools were generally referred to as 'tomahawks' – a term Australians now rarely use or only think of in the context of Native Americans. Later, archaeologists and collectors started to refer to them as 'axes', perhaps as 'tomahawk' did not come easily to them but probably because they adopted this standard term from European archaeological terminology. Isabel McBryde followed Frank Dickson in preferring 'hatchet' and 'hatchet head' in order to emphasise a difference between the Aboriginal tools and modern axes, which have a long haft and are wielded using two hands (Dickson 1976, 1981; McBryde 1978). 'Hatchet' is indeed more appropriate as it refers to a tool with a short handle and swung with one hand, using a quite different technique. But 'axe' refuses to be displaced.

Distributing stone

Mount William was not the only source of greenstone. Other notable quarries were at nearby Mount Camel, close to Geelong, at Howqua in the high country to the east, and in the Western District at Baronga and Berrambool on the Hopkins River (Figure 10.8). There is nothing to tell the products of these apart, at least not to the naked eye. They look and feel the same, and have the same mechanical properties;

Figure 10.8 The small quarry at Berrambool on the Hopkins River.

none are any better than the others. Nevertheless, all the ethnohistorical accounts agree that the stone from Mount William was preferred above all the rest.

Archaeological confirmation of the importance and value attached to Mount William greenstone is provided by the major study of hatchet heads carried out by Isabel McBryde in the 1970s. Thousands of hatchet heads have been picked up by generations of farmers, collectors and others all across the country. Some – far from all – were later deposited in the major museums in Victoria, South Australia and New South Wales, as often as not without any indication of where they were found. Isabel McBryde was able to make use of about 1400 hatchets in a program of geological analyses to determine where the stone came from. This is not an easy task, for the geological or chemical structure of rocks from individual quarries can be quite varied while there is sometimes too great a similarity to distinguish one source from another, so that samples from Mount William could not always be distinguished from those from nearby Mount Camel.

The distribution of hatchet heads from each quarry or area could then be plotted out, revealing patterns of interaction and relationships (Figure 10.9).

Three things are immediately apparent. One is that greenstone from each quarry can be found over a considerable area; a second is that these distributions overlap, so people in any area did not only make use of one source; the third is that Mount William/Mount Camel stone is far more widespread than any of the others. Examples have been found across all of central and western Victoria and well beyond the Murray into New South Wales and South Australia. Their distribution represents the long chains of connections linking communities over hundreds of kilometres, across all lands of the Kulin Nation and beyond.

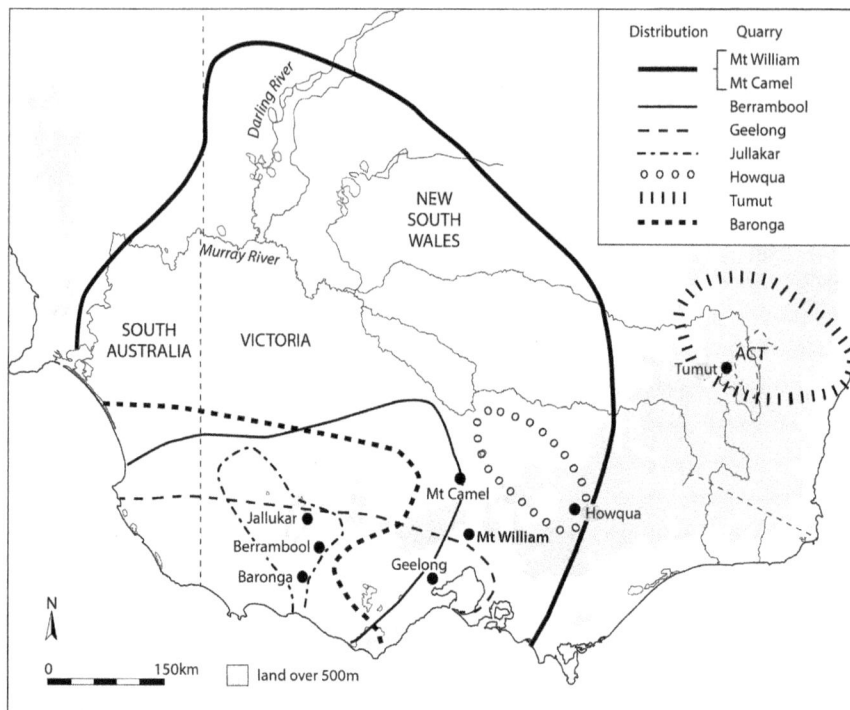

Figure 10.9 The distribution of greenstone from different quarries (after McBryde 1986: figure 6.1).

There is a relatively straightforward relationship between the number of hatchet heads and the distance from the smaller quarries – the further away, the fewer there are. This suggests a fairly direct system of distribution and of access within the local area. It is different with the Mount William/Mount Camel stone. It displays a more varied pattern, with many hatchet heads found close to the quarry, far fewer between 50 and 100 kilometres away, and then greater quantities once again further from the source: the numbers vary, but the relative density of artefacts is fairly even across hundreds of kilometres. There must have been more complex systems of distribution and redistribution, linked, perhaps, to locales where large gatherings took place (McBryde 1986; see also Frankel 1991a).

It is also clear from Figure 10.9 that the overall pattern of distribution of stone is not the same in all directions. It is skewed to the north and west, for Mount William stone did not make its way into Gippsland. In the disturbed times of the 19th century there was little connection (and none of it peaceful) between the Kulin of central and western Victoria and the Gunai/Kurnai of Gippsland. Their languages are distinctly different, so this was no new development. An ancient social boundary is here made manifest.

As suitable and functionally indistinguishable stone was available from many places, there must have been other reasons apart from utility why Mount William stone was particularly favoured over such a broad area. It must have served a social function as well – desired for its prestige or as representing connections with distant, and hence dangerous, people and places. But there is yet another dimension of value. The quarry and its products were believed to have great innate power and were part of a mythic and symbolic system which linked people of central Victoria with those in other areas (Brumm 2010; see, however, Hiscock 2013). We might also begin to appreciate something of the way in which Mount William and its stone was valued if we draw a general parallel from Ngilipitji in the far north of Australia:

> That the quarry from which these spears came was remote, I had long known, for the very few, even of the oldest men on the northern coastline, who had told me about it, had ever been there, although they knew and cherished, lovingly, the flint spearheads from it, each wrapped in its sheath of fine soft paperbark, tied with fibre string. (Donald Thomson, quoted in Jones and White 1988)

Our hatchets, however, were workaday tools: valued but regularly used. We are still left to wonder why, if they were precious, they were discarded so readily. In some circumstances, rare, imported stone tools were carefully maintained, used and reused, gradually becoming worn away by constant use and sharpening, so that the further tools are from the raw material source, the smaller they are when disposed of. There is no indication of any difference in the way people curated or looked after their greenstone tools no matter where they were. None were much worn down before falling out of use to become part of the archaeological record. It may simply be that hatchet heads needed to be a certain size or weight to function properly (western Victorian hatchets generally weigh between 500 and 600 grams). In addition, perhaps it was also that the act of acquisition, and the exchanges and social interactions involved, were of greater importance than the mere material object.

Sometimes men travelled to Mount William to collect stone for themselves, sometimes it was passed from hand to hand in individual exchanges, but, as suggested above, most would have been among the many goods that were traded or given as gifts at the periodic large gatherings which brought so many people together. Such meetings were often occasions for ceremonies, known about but seldom represented archaeologically.

Ceremonies at Sunbury and beyond

When I documented three earth circles at Sunbury in 1978 I saw them as an archaeological puzzle to be solved – what were these low earth rings and were they Aboriginal or European? (Frankel 1981a, 1991) I did not think that this, more than any of the other work I have done anywhere in the world, would have the most immediate value and significance beyond archaeology. That was strongly brought home to me years later when a Wurundjeri elder took over the explanation of their meaning to my students when we met on a field trip to the sites. For him, the

Figure 10.10 One of the earth circles at Sunbury.

Figure 10.11 Excavations in one of the Sunbury rings with a stone cairn in the centre.

circles were not an academic problem, but had become reincorporated into his cultural understanding.

Three rings are within the grounds of the Salesian College at Rupertswood, once the home of the Clarke family and famous in the cricketing world as the home of the Ashes. The more ancient ovals were handed over to the Traditional Owners some years ago and they are now managed by the Wurundjeri Land Council.

These three rings are all on the upper slopes of the hills above Jacksons Creek. They now look out across the valley but originally were surrounded by substantial trees, hiding the view and the sites from one another and from anywhere nearby. They are unevenly spaced over about 500 metres, their low, partly eroded earth banks enclosing lower, flatter interior spaces ranging from 15 to 25 metres in diameter. The ring on the west is the smallest; the largest, on the east, has two concentric circular banks. Perhaps it was refurbished on different occasions. We only excavated within the third, central ring, selected because scattered stones within it suggested some additional structure (Figure 10.10). This proved to be a neatly made stone cairn originally three or four courses (perhaps 30 to 40 centimetres) high (Figure 10.11). A second smaller cairn was found on the downslope edge of the ring. On this side the surrounding earth bank was formed by scraping back the thin soil covering down to the hard stony ground below; on the uphill side, soil from both the interior and exterior was heaped up.

Similar earth circles, commonly referred to as 'bora grounds', are well known elsewhere in Australia, especially in northern New South Wales and in Queensland (Bowdler 2005). The discovery of new examples in those areas would not be unusual. Now ceremonial grounds of this kind can be seen in Victoria. There are no descriptions of earth rings by Europeans who attended Aboriginal ceremonies or more secular 'corroborees' in the first years after the establishment of Melbourne, perhaps because they were more excited by the dramatic and exotic action and had no understanding of any deeper significance (Casey 2011; see also the selections in Frankel and Major 2015: 5–21). However, towards the end of the 19th century, Aboriginal men in the area of the Lodden, Campaspe and lower Goulburn Rivers described their initiation ceremonies to Robert Mathews. They told him that when there were enough young men of the right age, messengers were sent out to invite men from other groups to attend a ceremony. While they were away, the

> whole of the men who remain at home select a suitable place for the meeting. In close proximity to the camp, a fairly level patch of ground is cleared of all rubbish and loose sticks, by collecting them into heaps and burning them off. The grass is then chipped off and the surface made smooth this space is enclosed by a circular bank of loose earth about six inches or a foot high and is called goanga.
>
> While waiting for the invited contingents to reach this general meeting ground, there are dances and other amusements, and ceremonial songs every evening. As each contingent arrives at the goanga, it is received in a formal manner by the hosts. The novices brought by each contingent, together with those who have previously arrived, are put into the goanga about dusk and kept there in company of some strangers for a short time. (Mathews 1905: 872–73)

Figure 10.12 A ceremonial ground gradually enclosed by development on the western side of Sunbury (1990–2010).

Mathews goes on to describe the long series of secret, often frightening events which then took place over several days. At one stage the initiates had an upper incisor extracted – a common sign of initiation in this part of Australia. It is not hard to imagine all these activities taking place in and around the Sunbury rings, for, as Mathews suggested, it is

> likely that the Yarra and Murray River people would attend each other's initiation ceremonies, and, although there would perhaps be differences of detail, most of their leading features would be similar. (1898: 328)

Within the ring we found many silcrete artefacts: a dozen small cores and 150 blades struck from them. Whatever else went on in this space, we can also imagine that here older men were producing small sharp blades to be used during initiation ceremonies, for both

> men and women are ornamented with cicatrices – which are made when they come of age – on the chest, back, and upper parts of the arms, but never on the neck or face. These cicatrices are of a darker hue than the skin, and vary in length from half an inch to an inch. They are arranged in lines and figures according to the taste or the custom of the tribe. The operator cuts through the skin with a flint knife, and rubs the wounds with green grass. (Dawson 1881: 82)

A hundred and fifty years ago, Alfred Howitt noted that

so rapid was the disorganisation, for instance of the Woiworung tribe of the Yarra River that its ceremonies do not appear to have survived in a complete form more than ten years after the foundation of Melbourne. (1884: 435)

As physical reminders of this core aspect of Aboriginal culture, these earth rings have a special significance, well recognised by Wurundjeri Traditional Owners. Their preservation and management throw up particular challenges. The three at Rupertwood and a fourth further up Jacksons Creek should – ideally will – be key nodes in developing a broader cultural landscape, one that can recognise that these Aboriginal places were not isolated, enclosed sacred structures, but that their surrounds and setting were as important as the circles themselves. It is, sadly, too late to do the same for another ring on the western fringe of Sunbury. Although the feature itself is protected, it is now surrounded by suburban development, its environmental as well as its cultural context lost (Figure 10.12). The last time I visited this site I asked neighbours in the street if they knew anything about what appeared to be a piece of waste land. It was no surprise that they did not. As I came away I was strongly reminded of Judith Wright's poem 'Bora ring':

> The song is gone; the dance
> is secret with the dancers in the earth,
> the ritual useless, and the tribal story
> lost in an alien tale.

> Only the grass stands up
> to mark the dancing-ring; the apple-gums
> posture and mime a past corroboree
> murmur a broken chant.

Ceremonies often involved hundreds of people gathering together from many areas around (Mulvaney 1976; McBryde 1984a). But people need to eat, so this could only happen when there was enough food available to feed them all for at least several days. Timing and location were therefore dictated by local, often seasonal availability. In the high country, moths were the attraction; in the stony rises, as we have seen, it was eels:

> These masses are a collection of representative tribes and the eeling and whaling seasons are wisely taken advantage of by them for holding their great social and political meetings. But for this singular provision such masses could not subsist; for during the other parts of the year, there is barely support for the tribe of the locality ... Of all the places I saw, Lake Boloke was the most interesting. This spot, celebrated for its eels and its central situation, appears to have been fixed upon by general consent for the great annual meeting of the tribes of the interior. (G.A. Robinson, April 1841, Kenyon 1928: 146; see also McBryde 1984a: 139)

Elsewhere it was plant food such as the widespread staple, myrrnong – the yam daisy, *Microseris scapigira* (Gott 1983):

which somewhat resembles a small parsnip, with a flower like a buttercup, grows chiefly on the open plains. It is much esteemed on account of its sweetness, and is dug up by the women with the muurang pole. The roots are washed and put into a rush basket made on purpose, and placed in the oven in the evening to be ready for next morning's breakfast. When several families live near each other and cook their roots together, sometimes the baskets form a pile three feet high. (Dawson 1881: 19–20)

There is no doubt that there was a seasonal abundance of these tubers at Sunbury, where Issac Batey remembered that in the mid-19th century there was

rich basaltic clay evidently well fitted for the production of myrnongs. On the spot adverted to are numerous mounds with short spaces between each, and as all these are at right angles to the ridge's slope it is conclusive evidence that they were the work of human hands extending over a long series of years. This uprooting of the soil to apply the best term was accidental gardening, still it is reasonable to assume that the aboriginals were quite aware of the fact that turning the earth over in search of yams instead of diminishing that form of food supply would have had a tendency to increase it. (Frankel 1982b; Frankel and Major 2015: 97–8; Gott 2005: 1203)

These ceremonial grounds are rare enough; equally rare are stone arrangements (Lane and Fullagar 1980; Lane 2009) which may have had similar functions. One complex near Carisbrook has several associated alignments of small to medium size stones: a larger curved 'boomerang-shaped' outline, three smaller open circles and a stone pile (Massola 1963) (Figure 10.13). At the Wurdi Youang arrangement near Mount Rothwell, a hundred or so very substantial basalt blocks were placed in a pointed oval about 150 metres in circumference (Norris et al. 2013).
An even larger alignment is beside the Glenelg Highway near Lake Bolac, where over 150 big boulders were placed in a semicircle about 400 metres long (Figure 10.14). We have no idea of how long ago it was set up or how many years it took for people to manoeuvre all these stones into place. Nor of its function or meaning. As discussed in Chapter 8, the lake was

the most celebrated place in the Western District for the fine quality and abundance of its eels; and when the autumn rains induce these fish to leave the lake and go down the river to the sea, the aborigines gather there from great distances … For a month or two the banks of Salt Creek presented the appearance of a village. (Dawson 1881: 94–95)

Such large gatherings would surely have provided opportunities for major ceremonies - perhaps associated with this extensive stone arrangement.

Figure 10.13 The stone arrangement at Carisbrook.

Figure 10.14 Part of the large stone arrangement at Lake Bolac.

11
Approaching the present

The aborigines have been visited on several occasions by epidemics, which are very fatal. The first occasion which the natives remember was about the year 1830 and the last in 1847. The very small amount of old aborigines now alive [in 1881] who escaped the first of these epidemics describe it as an irruptive fever resembling small-pox. They called it Meen warann – 'chopped root'. They still have a very vivid recollection of its ravages, and of the great numbers cut off by it in the Western District. In remembrance of it they still chant a wail called Mallæ Mallææ, which was composed in New South Wales, when the disease first broke out, and is known to all the tribes between Sydney, Melbourne and Adelaide ... It was considered to be so infectious and deadly that when anyone sickened and refused food, and when pustules appeared on the body, the tribal doctor gave them up at once ... (Dawson 1881: 60)

At least one-third – perhaps even more – of the people in the more densely settled areas along the Murray and coast died during major epidemics in 1828–1832 and again in 1866-67 (Dowling 1997) (see also Chapter 6). As many again succumbed to other introduced diseases. It is difficult to estimate earlier populations – figures for the Western District, for example, range from 3500 to 8000 (Critchett 1990: 70–76). By the 1860s, the population had crashed to less than a tenth of what it would have been in 1800. Diane Barwick's careful tracking of individuals indicates that there were hardly more than 2000 people in Victoria classified as Aboriginal in 1863, and half that number 14 years later (Figure 11.1) (Barwick 1971). The distinction then made between 'fullblood' and 'half-caste' is now regarded as inappropriate – indeed offensive – but it was not only standard practice at the time but had serious implications for the way people were treated by officialdom: among other things, in regard to marriage or whether they were allowed to live with their families on government stations or reserves, as the Stolen Generation know to their cost.

Trauma and violence

Population collapse was one of the two severe traumas which afflicted Aboriginal people in Victoria and South Australia. The other was the combination of direct dispossession of land and the more indirect destruction of traditional life and customs brought about by the invasion of European settlers.

We have already seen some aspects of 19th-century events in many earlier chapters: continuity of occupation in Gariwerd; a new, hybrid culture on Kangaroo Island; frontier violence at Glen Aire. Along with descendants, it is historians, rather than archaeologists, who have the major role in exposing and clarifying the ensuing web of actions, reactions and interactions, making use of many kinds of documents, oral traditions and illustrations (Critchett 1990; Broome 2005; Jenkin 1979). But archaeology – primarily, although not exclusively, concerned with material things – can also contribute to this important, if sensitive, subject (Lawrence and Davies 2010).

Alongside the general disruption to Aboriginal society – is that too mild a term? – there were numerous deadly attacks on Aboriginal people by settlers. Well over a hundred massacres, with a total toll of some 800 to 1000 lives, took place in Victoria, most in the 1840s (Broome 2005: 80; Allen 2009; see also Clark 1995). The general, and sometimes the exact locations of these mainly small, local vigilante incidents are known (Figure 11.2), but there are now no identifiable traces on the ground. And why would there be? – for these actions are not of the sort to leave lasting physical, archaeological, evidence.

Even so, some archaeological evidence can be linked to those troubled times in southwestern Victoria. While some of the circular huts in the stony rises were, as we have seen in Chapter 8, used in earlier times, others with European objects or materials in them were used in the 19th century. These may well have been places where Aboriginal people retreated in the face of European settlement. The rugged, rocky and relatively inaccessible terrain provided a refuge for families and the base for Aboriginal resistance during what became known as the 'Eumeralla War' of the mid-1840s.

Thomas Browne, better known as Rolf Boldrewood, the author of *Robbery under arms*, was living in the area at the time. His descriptions in *Old Melbourne memories*, over-dramatised and self-serving as they are, are worth quoting at length as they give us some feeling of the attitudes and events as seen from the European side of the frontier:

> Sure enough we saw a plainly-marked track, with a fragment of flesh, or a blood-stain, showing the path by which they had carried in a slaughtered animal. Further we could not follow them, as the lava downs were at this spot too rough for horses, and we might also have been taken at a disadvantage …
>
> It now became a serious question how to bear ourselves in the face of the new state of matters. If the blacks persisted in a guerilla warfare, besides killing many of the best of our cattle, they would scatter and terrify the remainder, so that they would hardly stay on the run; besides which, they held us at a disadvantage. They could watch our movements, and from time to time make sorties from the Rocks, and attack our homesteads or cut us off in detail. In the

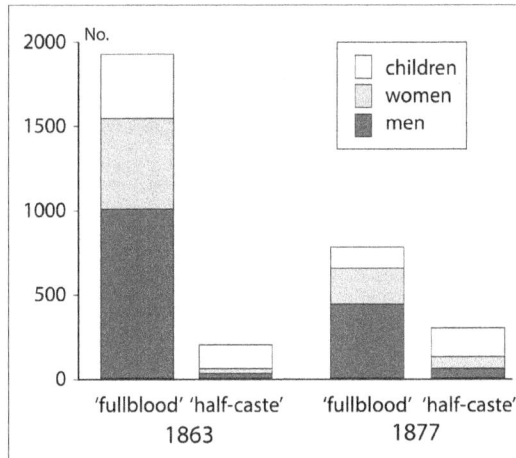

Figure 11.1 Aboriginal populations in Victoria in 1863 and 1877. The distinction between 'fullblood' and 'half-caste' was standard practice at the time and had important implications for how people were treated (data from Barwick 1971).

winter season much of the forest land became so deep and boggy that, even on horseback, if surprised and overmatched in numbers, there would be very little chance of getting away. By this time the owners of the neighbouring stations were fully aroused to the necessity of concerted action. We had reached the point when 'something must be done.' We could not permit our cattle to be harried, our servants to be killed, and ourselves to be hunted out of the good land we had occupied by a few savages.

Our difficulty was heightened by its being necessary to behave in a quasi-legal manner. Shooting blacks, except in manifest self-defence, had been always held to be murder in the Supreme Courts of the land, and occasionally punished as such. Now, there were obstacles in the way of taking out warrants and apprehending Jupiter and Cocknose, or any of their marauding braves, in the act. The Queen's writ, as in certain historic portions of the west of Ireland, did not run in those parts. Like all guerillas, moreover, their act of outrage took place sometimes in one part of a large district, sometimes in another, the actors vanishing meanwhile, and reappearing with puzzling rapidity.

We went now well armed. We were well mounted and vigilantly on guard. The Children of the Rocks were occasionally met with, when collisions, not all bloodless, took place …

A few more miles brought them up with the main body. They opened fire upon the tolerably large body of blacks in possession, directly they came within range. 'It was the first time I had ever levelled a gun at my fellow-man,' John Cox remarked. 'I did so without regret or hesitation in this instance. I never remember having the feeling that I could not miss so strong in me – except in

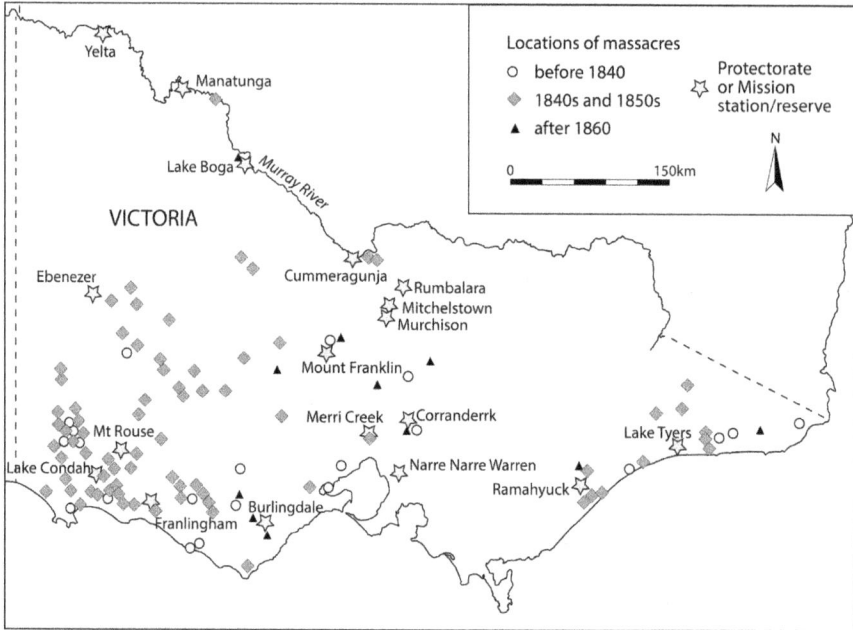

Figure 11.2 General locations of massacre sites, Protectorate and Mission stations and reserves in Victoria (adapted from Allen 2009: figures 5 and 16).

snipe-shooting. I distinctly remember knocking over three blacks, two men and a boy, with one discharge of my double barrel.'

Sou'wester had a good innings that day, which he thoroughly enjoyed. He fired right and left, raging like a demoniac. One huge black, wounded to death, hastened his own end by dragging out his entrails, meanwhile praising up the weapons of the white man as opposed to those of the black. Sou'wester cut short his death-song by blowing out his brains with the horse-pistol of the period. A few of the front-rankers were shot on this occasion; but most of the others saved themselves by precipitately taking to the lake. (Boldrewood 1896: 66–69)

As well as taking the law into their own hands in this way, Thomas Browne and other settlers called for official support. In 1843, a detachment of the Native Police Core was stationed to the area. Their drastic action helped overcome the resistance of the Gunditjmara. By 1850, the major period of violent clashes was over, and Aboriginal people in the area increasingly developed new relationships with the Europeans, many working as farmhands on what had once been their country (Critchett 1990).

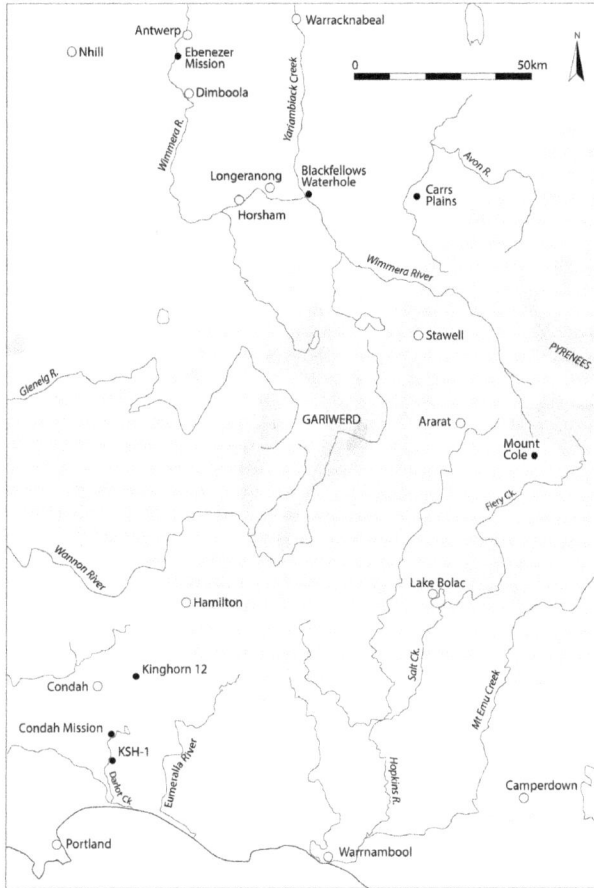

Figure 11.3 Sites and places referred to in this chapter.

Stones of resistance

Descendants of some of the Aboriginal survivors are today part of the Gunditjmara community, which owns and manages the Kurtonitj Indigenous Protected Area in the Tyrendarra lava flow and the Budj Bim cultural landscape (Gunditjmara People and Wettenhall 2010). In 2012 and 2013, Ian McNiven and his students from Monash University, again working with the local community, excavated one isolated stone hut (or house) circle in the area, which they designated KSH-1 (Kurtonij Stone House 1) (McNiven et al. forthcoming).

The structure is broadly similar to those discussed in Chapter 8: a semicircle of stones stacked three or four courses high on the bedrock to enclose an area of about 4 square metres (Figures 11.4, 11.5). As elsewhere, the stone served as the footings in which to lodge the wooden supports for a domed superstructure of branches and bark. Ian and his team excavated most of the area within two 1x1 metre squares outside the hut.

Figure 11.4 Kurtonitj Stone House 1 (photo: Ian McNiven).

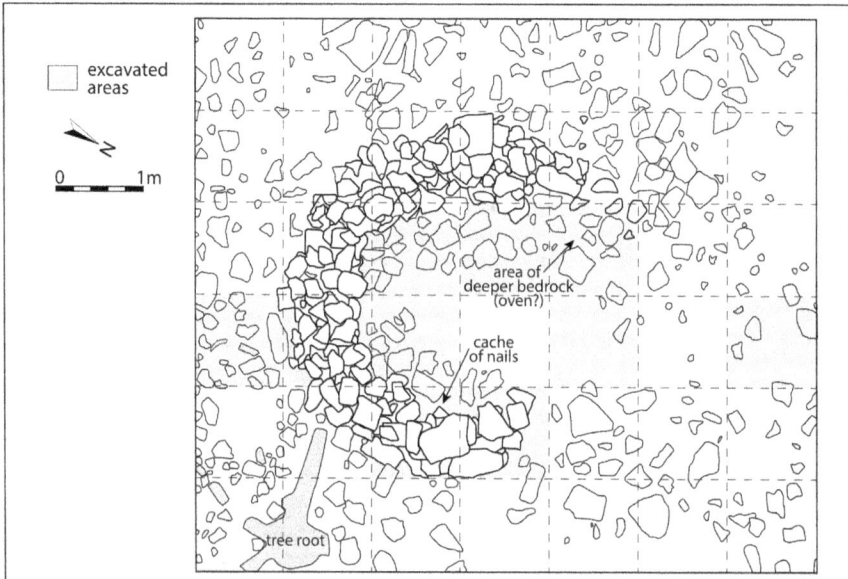

Figure 11.5 Plan of Kurtonitj Stone House 1 (adapted from McNiven et al. forthcoming: figure 6).

Just near the right-hand side of the entrance, a small section of bedrock was at a lower level, forming a natural hollow. The bottom half was filled with charcoal. Perhaps this was simply the remains of a burnt stump, where a tree had taken root in a crack in the rock; but the hollow may equally well have been used as a cooking pit. Indeed, Ian has speculated that the placement of the hut was no accident, but deliberately positioned to take advantage of the natural depression.

A hundred and six small pieces of bottle glass were found; they may all have come from only one or two bottles. Some pieces show signs of deliberate preparation and shaping as tools, others have damage which developed during use. As the fragments were more concentrated near the entrance to the hut than elsewhere, we can imagine an Aboriginal man (let's assume it was a man) sitting and working just within the shelter, picking out suitable bits of glass to carve or sharpen utensils or tools. From the time of their first contact with European goods, Aboriginal people were quick to see the advantages of glass as a substitute for fine-grained stone. Glass could readily be chipped in the old way, but both fine razor-like edges and more robust angular ones needed no modification to improve their efficiency.

We have already seen glass tools elsewhere in the stony rises at Structure 883 (Chapter 8). Both it and other similar huts were perhaps used in the same way and at the same time as KSH-1. At one of these, Kinghorn 12 (Wesson 1981; Coutts et al. 1977), few of the glass fragments have any obvious signs of either having been used or prepared for use. Despite this, Nathan Wolski and Tom Loy (1999) were able to show that the few pieces they examined were, in fact, tools. By looking at the residues left on the tools when they were used, they could tell that bits of glass had been used to scrape soft food plants and tubers and to slice harder greenwood. People at these sites were maintaining traditional practices using new materials while either actively resisting or more simply avoiding European encroachment.

There was no other particular distribution of finds within the excavated areas of KSH-1, apart from a collection of three dozen, mainly complete and perhaps unused, iron nails in a small hole in the bedrock. Nails of this particular type were imported from Britain between the late 1830s and the 1870s. These ones could have been collected and deposited at any time during these 30 years. Why they were deliberately cached in this way is, and probably will always remain, a mystery. All we can say is that whoever buried the nails never returned to collect them.

Other small fragments of rusty metal could have come from anything, apart from one possible knife handle. There was also a used percussion cap for priming a muzzle-loading firearm and 16 small lead 'birdshot' pellets of varied size that could have been fired at or across the hut. Was this someone like Boldrewood's John Cox firing at the Aboriginal occupants, or a hunter, perhaps Aboriginal, perhaps European, out after birds or small game well after the hut was no longer used?

Only 72 chipped stone artefacts were found, mostly small flakes, although there were two cores indicating stone was knapped at the site. As at other sites in the stony rises, flint was the most common raw material, collected from the beach about 13 kilometres to the south.

Although the deposits at KSH-1 were shallow and no clear layering could be identified, the distribution of the finds suggests that the stone tools found at the site were from an earlier episode of occupation, and that the glass and other

European-made materials were from a later time. But how far apart these two short episodes were cannot be determined. Nor can their precise date. KSH-1 and the other sites in the stony rises may well have been among the guerrilla bases used by Gunditjmara people during the 'Eumeralla War' of the 1840s. However, it is equally likely that they were used during the more settled times of the 1850s or 1860s when Aboriginal people who had accommodated themselves to the new realities of dispossession still maintained a degree of independence when living away from the pastoral runs, reserves or missions.

Stones of help

From the earliest period of European settlement, governments struggled to find a way to deal with Aboriginal communities. More often than not, in spite of the best intentions, the unexpected consequences of official policies did more harm than good: it is fair to say that similar mistakes continue to be made today. In the late 1830s, the Protectorate system was set up in Victoria to provide some way of assisting them and mediating conflicts, although as we have seen, with limited success. We have met George Augustus Robinson – the Chief Protector of Aborigines – on several occasions, for his reports and diaries are a major source of information about the Aboriginal people he met on his journeys. By 1849, his role, and that of the sub-Protectors, was no more. A decade later different policies began to be developed, and from 1861 the newly established Board for the Protection of Aborigines placed an increasing emphasis on encouraging Aboriginal people to settle down – in the case of Corranderrk largely as a result of representations by Kulin elders. By 1863, 23 areas were set aside for Aboriginal people: small camping places, ration depots and reserves (Broome 2005) (Figure 11.2). Five were Christian missions, organised in partnership with the government, with the added aim of religious alongside social and cultural conversion.

One of the first of these was Ebenezer Mission. It was established in 1859 by members of the small but influential Moravian Church with a reputation for charitable and missionary work around the world (Jensz 2010). In Victoria, its activities were encouraged during his time as Lieutenant-Governor by Charles Joseph La Trobe, himself from a well-regarded Moravian family. The site they chose, on the high ground above a loop of the Wimmera River, was on land known to the local Wergaia-speaking people as Bunyo-budnutt, a major ceremonial ground. This persistence of place may be matched by the placement of the mission cemetery in an area previously used for Aboriginal burials (Brown et al. 2002).

While missionaries and Aboriginal people shared this settlement, their relative status and relationships were clearly defined, in life and in death. The missionaries' graves are more substantial and formal, but there is little to mark those of the other 170 or more people who were buried in the Ebenezer Mission cemetery during and after the mission period (Brown et al. 2002). The locations of only a few of the unmarked graves are known to their descendants, and through surface and sub-surface surveys using ground magnetic and ground-penetrating radar. Oral traditions and historical accounts also suggest that some Aboriginal people who died away from the mission were brought to Ebenezer to be buried; but other

Figure 11.6 'Ebenezer Mission, Dimboola' in 1882 (*Illustrated Australasian News*, 22 March 1882: 36).

residents preferred to be buried elsewhere. One, known to Wotjobaluk elder Jack Kennedy, was in a coffin made from bark taken from a nearby tree.

An engraving published in the *Illustrated Australasian News* in 1882 gives an idealised image of the mission, with the main buildings including the mission-house and church in the upper register, with neat 'Aboriginal huts' in the register below (Figure 11.6). Apart from the church, little remains of any of these buildings today (Figure 11.7). Numerous heritage studies have been undertaken at the site over the last 20 years, with the most substantial archaeological work carried out by Jane Lydon in collaboration with the Goolum Goolum Aboriginal Cooperative and the Barengi Gadjin Land Council (2009a, 2009b; Lydon et al. 2004, 2007). Over the years, several different areas were investigated, relating to times before, during and after the mission period (Figure 11.8).

Stone artefacts – cores and flakes mainly of quartz – found in several places in Areas 1, 2 and 3 probably date from earlier times, although it is possible that people were still carrying out traditional crafts while living on the mission. Clearer evidence comes from Area 6, across the Wimmera River to the west. Here, the River Road Midden 2 provided evidence of a small fireplace where a small group of people briefly camped and cooked mussels they had collected from the river at some time between 400 and 200 years ago, a few generations before traditional use of the river was brought to an end.

Initial fieldwork in 2003 concentrated on the mission-house, which had been occupied by the missionaries and by some Aboriginal people as well. The extensive excavations revealed details of the foundations and the history of the building (Figure 11.9). Annexes were added as the missionaries chose to extend the original

Figure 11.7 Ebenezer Mission church looking across the excavations (photo: Jane Lydon).

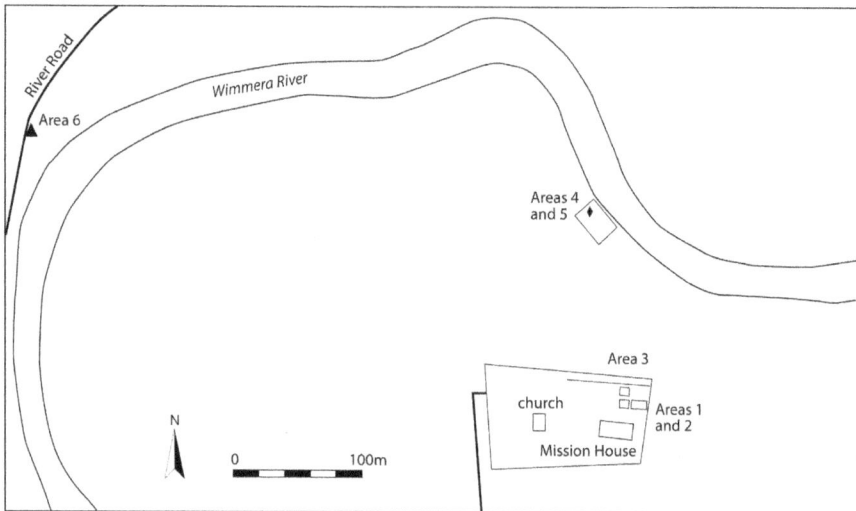

Figure 11.8 Area of Ebenezer Mission (after Lydon 2009: figure 2.3).

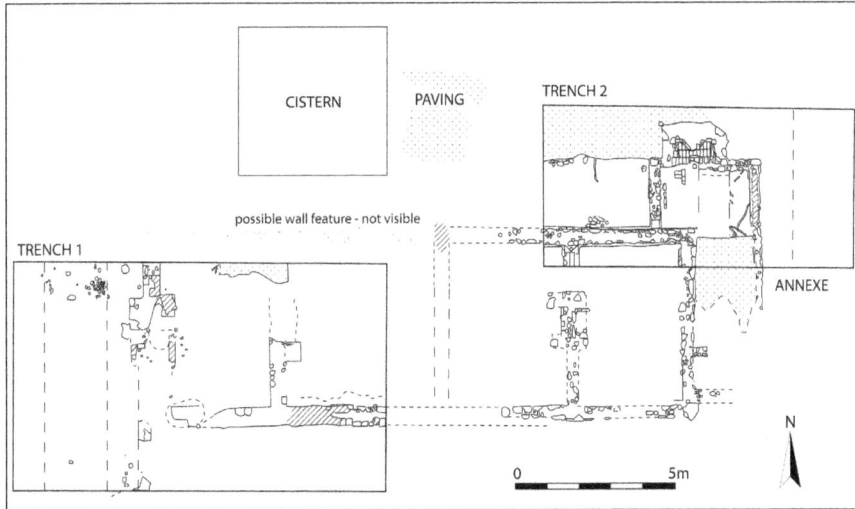

Figure 11.9 Plan of the excavated areas of the Ebenezer mission-house (after Lydon 2009: figure 4.3; Lydon et al. 2004: plan 2).

building rather than to build separate ones as needs arose, maintaining the unity of this functional and symbolic centre of the settlement. Few artefacts were found, for broken items and other waste would have been discarded elsewhere.

Subsequently, a series of smaller excavations were carried out in other areas, beside the kitchen (Area 1) and the dormitory (Area 2), again revealing details of renovation or extension of the original buildings. Areas 4 and 5, away from the central buildings and closer to the river, focused on a rubbish dump, dug within a natural hollow. Although disturbed by later clearance there were, naturally, many more artefacts and animal bones to add to the few from the other areas. They give some insight into what people used and ate, but which people, and exactly when, remains unknown.

Overall, the range and types of artefacts, bottles, kitchenware and tableware conform to those typical of the second half of the 19th century; there is nothing to suggest any particular selection or difference from other sites (Figure 11.10). And, of course, no discrimination was possible between any used by the different groups of people living in this shared space. The same goes for the food remains. Sheep bones predominate, with smaller amounts of chicken. Rabbit bones suggest hunting, but there were no native animals, such as kangaroo, possum or emu. Were they not hunted and eaten, or was rubbish from the Aboriginal activities discarded elsewhere? And even to ask the question in that way is to assume that the missionaries would not have eaten these animals. Pig bones, too, were absent, even though pigs are known to have been kept. So perhaps the small sample of bones simply does not tell the whole story. Mussels were, however, collected from the river; these, together with a single fish vertebra, suggesting a more varied diet. Apart from details of the buildings and finds, the overall layout of the settlement is significant. Elsewhere, perhaps most clearly seen at the Ramahyuck Mission in

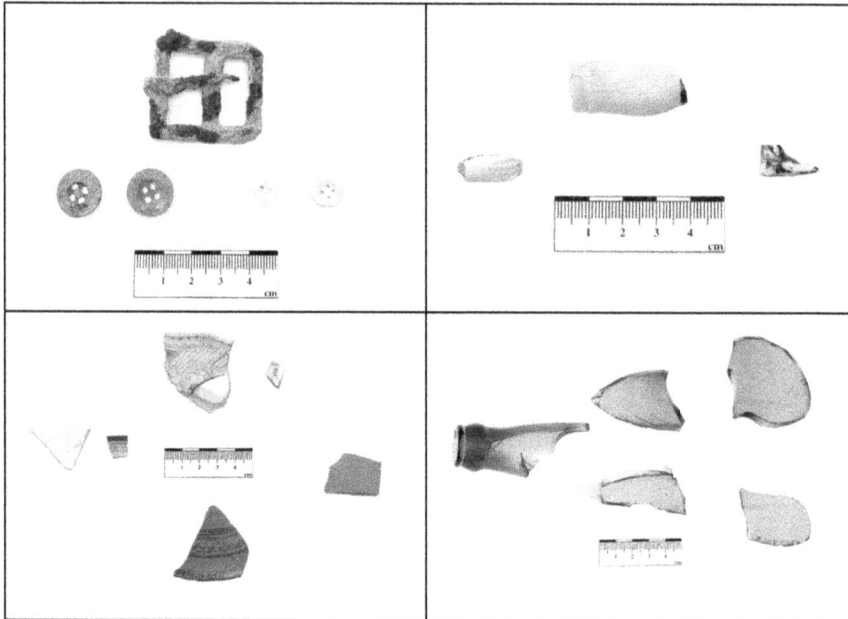

Figure 11.10 Artefacts excavated at Ebenezer Mission (photos: Jane Lydon).

Gippsland (Attwood 1989; Rhodes 1996), a formal arrangement was designed to create a built environment which reinforced Moravian principles and aspirations. Ideally, houses should have formed a square, facing inward towards the church, which, set on the highest ground, with its pointed steeple pointing heavenward, symbolically encoded and reinforced core values. The fieldwork, together with surveyors' plans made when the mission closed in 1904, indicate that the ideal plan was not closely followed at Ebenezer, as the domestic square was not complete and the mission-house, rather than the church, was the main focus of attention.

A somewhat similar arrangement of this kind is seen at Condah Mission, established by the Church of England Mission to the Aborigines in 1867 on a gentle slope above Darlot Creek, a little south of Lake Condah. Bluestone, limestone or timber cottages were arranged around a central 'village green' or sports field, with the bluestone mission-house, schoolhouse and timber dormitory on the southern side (Figures 11.11, 11.12). Just to their west was the very substantial bluestone church, once such a prominent feature of the mission but demolished in the 1950s despite local protests (Gunditjmara People and Wettenhall 2010). Many Gunditjmara people were able to continue to use the church and to live in other buildings at Condah for several decades after the mission officially closed in 1919 – about 70 were there in 1939 – and the community has always maintained an attachment to the place to which they now hold title. Meanwhile, Ebenezer and many other missions closed down and were abandoned early in the 20th century, an almost inevitable consequence of the 1886

Figure 11.11 Houses at Condah Mission, 1985.

Aborigines Protection Law Amendment Act, which required that Aboriginal people of partly European parentage and their spouses had to leave the reserves.

The wooden dormitory, with its six small bedrooms, a central dining-room and a kitchen, was originally built to house orphaned children, although clearly not in great comfort. In 1875, during an outbreak of scarlet fever, John Green reported to the Board for the Protection of Aborigines that

> The house occupied by the children had a very bad smell in it, arising from an accumulation of filth which passed through the openings between the flooring boards; on hot days especially, the odour was bad, and must be bad for the health of the children. (Board for the Protection of Aborigines 1875: 6)

It is a little comforting to know that the building was renovated soon after: floorboards were replaced and the walls lined – although archaeologists might regret the removal of the 'filth' from below the floor.

The building continued to be used well into the 20th century before it was burnt down in 1938. Nearly half a century later, David Rhodes carried out excavations on the site (Figure 11.13) (Rhodes 1986). These revealed the foundations and general layout of the dormitory (Figure 11.14), which was later used for the reconstructed building that stands on the site today. It was a rectangular building, measuring 9x12 metres, with local basalt (bluestone) used for the footings and the oven or fireplace towards the east, possibly enclosed in 1926. There were two other fireplaces with dressed bluestone bases, one facing the dining-room and the other towards the kitchen. The latter was rebuilt in 1926 when a fuel stove was fitted.

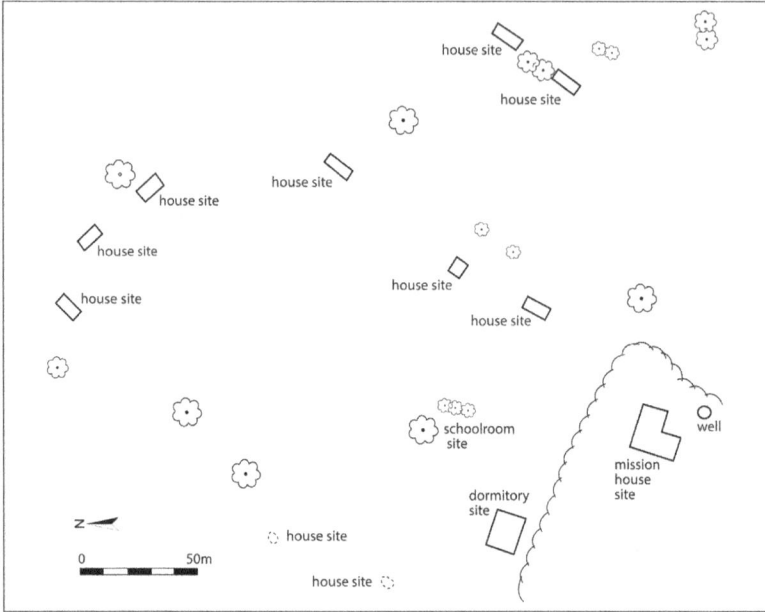

Figure 11.12 Plan of standing buildings at the Condah Mission in 1985 (adapted from Rhodes 1986: figure 2).

Figure 11.13 Excavations at the Condah Mission dormitory, 1985.

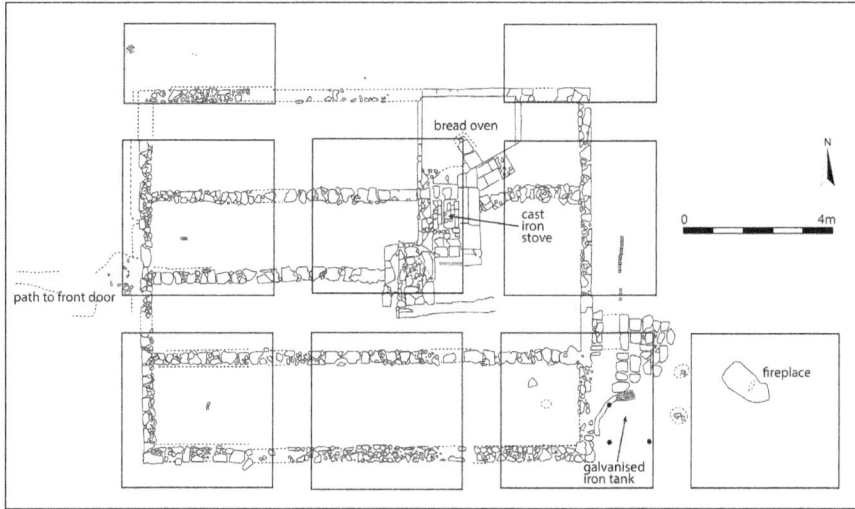

Figure 11.14 Excavation plan of the foundations and other features of the Condah Mission dormitory (adapted from Rhodes 1986: figure 13).

Outside the building, post-holes marked the line of a fence, and a firepit the site of a kerosene tin boiler.

The artefacts excavated from the burnt-out ruins come from all the different phases of the history of the building – and from before it was built. They include a wide range of things, the many miscellaneous goods that might be found at other 19th- and 20th-century sites (Lawrence and Davies 2010). There were bits of cutlery and crockery, bottles and tin cans, rifle cartridge cases and shotgun pellets, rabbit-traps and can-openers, beads and combs, toys and toothbrushes, shoes and buttons, slates and slate pencils. There were few more individual items than John King's Hamilton Football Club 1927 premiership medal, while military buttons and a Palestinian coin were probably brought home by Aboriginal servicemen who saw action abroad during the world wars.

Among the bits of leather – boots, shoes and such – were two items identified as basketry needles, for this traditional craft, now revitalised through elders such as Connie Hart (Robson 2013), was important throughout the life of the mission:

> The women continue to earn a deal of money by making and selling baskets and mats &c, and the money so realized is generally laid out for the requirements of their houses and themselves. (Board for the Protection of Aborigines 1877: 16)

While stone flakes, mainly of flint, were found mixed in with the modern refuse at the dormitory site and in test excavations elsewhere, these are most likely to be from earlier activities in the area, before – possibly well before – the mission was established:

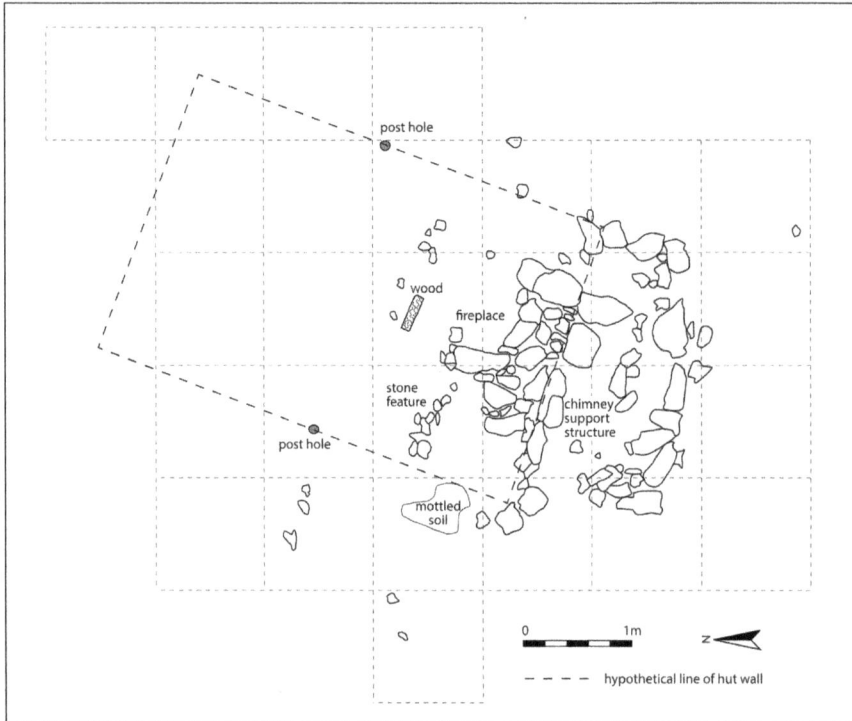

Figure 11.15 Plan of excavated area of the Campbell Outstation 1 hut (after Wolski 2000: figure 24).

Since the blacks have been allowed a little meat weekly they have not hunted after native game so much, although one day a week is allowed them for that purpose. They do, however, spend a little time in fishing, and sometimes obtain large quantities of the black-fish and eels, which they seem to enjoy with a relish. (Board for the Protection of Aborigines 1875: 16)

But no fish remains were found in the excavations, and only a very small number of kangaroo, possum or bird bones. Sheep and rabbit were most common, with far smaller amounts of cattle, dog and pig. But we cannot say how old any of these are.

Living on country

Pastoral stations, goldfields, emerging towns and institutions like Ebenezer framed the landscape in a very different way from Aboriginal traditions, where rights and obligations to broader territories were embedded in social practice and cultural beliefs. The 19th-century locations and the routes between them imposed a different way of controlling, mapping and understanding land. Aboriginal people's association to place was denied or ignored. But people still kept up these connections. Despite the pressures and mixed attractions of settled centres, many spent time or lived more permanently in fringe camps or outstations. Or, taking the emphasis off the centrality of the European world view, we might also think of people living 'on country': a more positive approach to independence and tradition. Reports to the Board for the Protection of Aborigines by Local Guardians and Honorary Correspondents responsible for distributing goods and supplies often tell a sorry tale, with few brighter events and attempts by Aboriginal people to establish permanent homes for themselves during the second half of the 19th century (Clark 1990: 245–50).

In 1840, Colin and Alexander Campbell, newly arrived from Scotland, established a pastoral run near Mount Cole, east of Ararat. The brothers, by all accounts, had a particularly good relationship with Djab wurrung people of the Beeripmo balug and Utoul balug clans (Clark 1990: 111, 135), allowing them to camp on the station as well as employing them – not only because they accepted lower wages than European workers. They were therefore able to maintain traditional practices, including ceremonies which involved visitors from other areas.

The Campbell Outstation site (CO-1) is a shepherd's hut on the Campbells' Mount Cole property, which Nathan Wolski (2000) excavated in order to explore the relationships between Aboriginal people and Europeans. The main structural remains were those of the stone fireplace and chimney, which, together with a couple of post-holes, give some idea of the size and shape of what would have been a fairly basic slab and bark hut (Figure 11.15). Unfortunately, the soil deposits were shallow and no clear layering could be identified to indicate the nature or location of the floor or other features. Nathan found 303 quartz artefacts as well as numerous glass, metal and other bits and pieces. These were generally mixed together throughout the soil deposits, above and beside the surviving structural remains, making it impossible to sort out which things were directly related to the time when the hut was occupied. It is, however, very likely that most, if not all, of this stone was older, for many of the pieces were at greater depth than other things (Figure 11.16). They probably come from Aboriginal use of the place before, long before, the hut was built, and were then dug, scuffed or churned up during its construction, use or demolition. Equally, items found above the fallen building stones may suggest that people also visited the site after the abandoned hut had collapsed. Microscopic examination of residues left on some of the quartz tools shows that they were used, as might be expected, for working wood, processing plant food and cutting up animals (Wolski 2000). Some of the fragments of glass had obviously also been deliberately shaped, while similar residues identify other unmodified pieces as tools, again used for cutting hard dry wood and processing starchy tubers, like those we have seen at Kinghorn 12 (Wolski and Loy 1999; Wolski 2001). This makes it likely that the glass artefacts were made and used by Aboriginal people. But we cannot ignore the possibility that an isolated shepherd might not occasionally have found it convenient to pick up and use bits of his broken bottles in the same way. Even if the glass tools were Aboriginal artefacts, the nature of the site makes it hard to be sure that they were not made and left there after the hut collapsed: certainly some were found on top of the collapsed chimney stones. But Nathan was confident that this was not the case, and that the glass tools provide material evidence of social interactions between people of very different backgrounds in the mid-19th century.

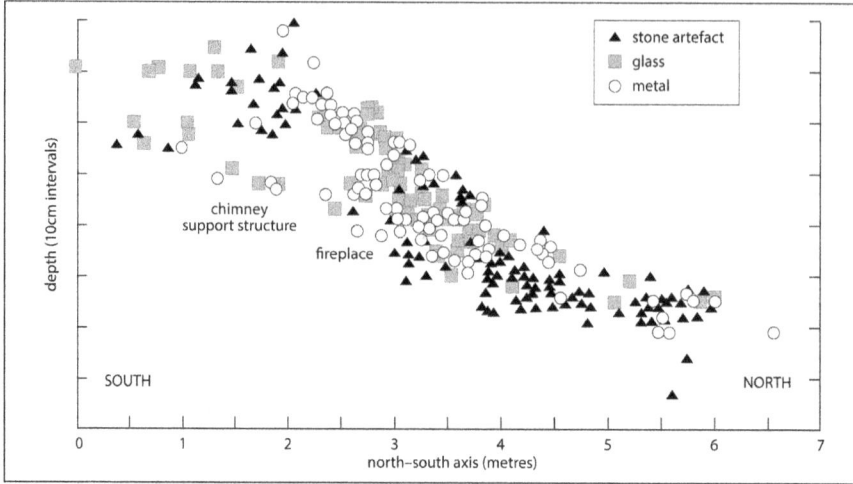

Figure 11.16 Schematic north–south profile across the Campbell Outstation site showing the depths at which artefacts were found (adapted from Wolski 2000: figure 25).

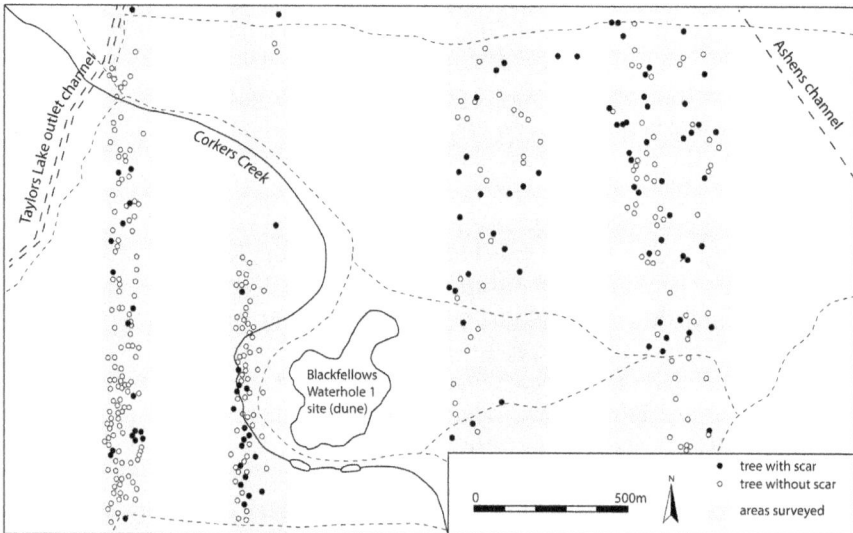

Figure 11.17 Location of scarred trees near Blackfellows Waterhole in the Berrabool Reserve (data from Webber and Burns 2004).

Near Stawell, historical records describe Jawadjali people of the Djappuminyu clan living in bark huts close to the Carrs Plains homestead, which served as an Honorary Correspondent Depot, from which rations and other supplies were provided to Aboriginal people by William Dennis, the 'Local Guardian' (Clark 1990: 261–62). Until the 1870s, Dennis employed several of them on the property as shepherds, bullock drivers and farmhands. Here again, Nathan Wolski looked for archaeological evidence of Aboriginal life in what had become a shared landscape, where, in

> good seasons the swamp, which was several acres in extent, was a beautiful sight … The natives were permanently camped here, and had good bark mia-mias. Their implements were beautifully decorated. They made them from green buloke or cherry tree, and after the whites had come, learned to use glass to smooth them. In earlier times they had used stone. (Wettenhall 1945)

The material evidence of such a fringe camp was provided by excavations beside a small, low mound. Unlike the Campbell Outstation hut, this was clearly an Aboriginal site: clay heat-retainers on the surface suggest it was an oven rather than the remains of one of the 'good bark mia-mias' described by Wettenhall. In clearing 19 square metres of topsoil over an area adjacent to the mound, Nathan found a handful of small quartz artefacts and 30 fragments of bottle glass, half of which had signs of having been modified or used: the residues on them again indicating woodworking, removing bark and scraping the soft fleshy stem from a shrub or small tree (Wolski 2000; Wolski and Loy 1999).

Jawadjali people frequenting the Carrs Plains Depot are also known to have spent time elsewhere in their traditional country, at the Longerenong Station and at Blackfellows Waterhole. In Chapter 7, we have already seen the evidence for earlier Aboriginal occupation at Blackfellows Waterhole. It continued to be a favourite camping place in the southeastern Wimmera at least until the 1880s, as is clear from a letter to the Board for the Protection of Aborigines:

> Carr Plains
> Glenorchy
> March 29, 1881
> Sir, I have the honor to ask the consideration of the Board to the following case, viz. a number of the Aborigines in this district are desirous to have a portion of land reserved for their exclusive use and they point out to me a place known as the 'Magical Water Holes' on Corkers Creek about 1½ to (2) two miles east of Longerenong Home Station, where they say they were always allowed to camp by Sir Samuel Wilson. This position would certainly be very central for them and they could always find wood around. There are not many of them left and I think they should have a place to call their own while they remain and trust you will kindly bring this matter before the Board at an early date as possible and let me know the result. I daresay Sir S. Wilson could give you more definite information re the locality of the space mentioned.
>
> I have the honor to be Holford H. Wettenhall, L.G.
> (Quoted in Webber and Richards 2004: 8–9; Porter 2004: 81)

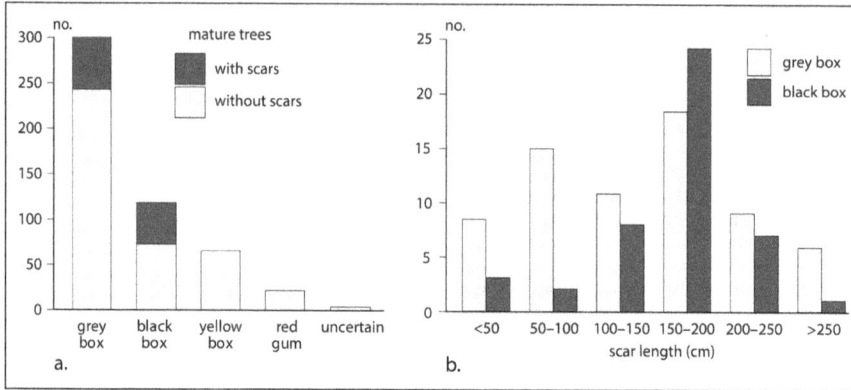

Figure 11.18 Scarred trees in the Berrabool reserve. a. number of trees of different species; b. number of scars of different sizes (data from Webber and Burns 2004: table 1 and figure 7).

The recent archaeology of the area was seen to be as important as the more ancient in the project by Aboriginal Affairs Victoria in collaboration with the Goolum Goolum Aboriginal Cooperative and Wotjobaluk Traditional Land Council (Webber and Richards 2004). This work included extensive survey of scarred trees in the reserve. Elsewhere we have considered some aspects of these immobile artefacts, noting that it is often problematic to separate natural from cultural scars, and equally so to determine who removed the bark.

Nearly 150 hectares – a substantial proportion – of the Berrabool Reserve was systematically surveyed. Four teams worked their way along wide north–south transects across the flat, wooded area, examining each tree in turn (Figure 11.17). Those at least 150 years old can be regarded as cut by Aboriginal people. As well as detailed recording of these trees they also noted the location, species and size of all other mature ones. Altogether the teams recorded 508 mature trees, most of which were grey or black box. Bark had been taken from about one-quarter of these, but none from the other, less common species (Figure 11.18).

Although people removed bark from trees all over the area, the activity was more prevalent closest to where people would have normally camped near Blackfellows Waterhole itself. Most pieces of bark were between 1.5 and 2 metres in length, an appropriate size to use in making shelters, but grey box was preferred for smaller items, perhaps for dishes or other containers. There is, however, no difference in the range of sizes where work was carried out using stone and steel hatchets; there was a continuity of practice from before European-made tools became available, as people used the new tools for traditional products. It is quite possible that some of the larger slabs of bark were cut by Aboriginal people for sale to Europeans, as James Nisbet noted in 1853 when he

met a party of a half dozen at Ballarat employed by the diggers in remote gullies to strip trees of their bark for a hut, for a day's labour at which a little bread or a English shilling is sufficient recompense. (Quoted in Cahir 2012: 68)

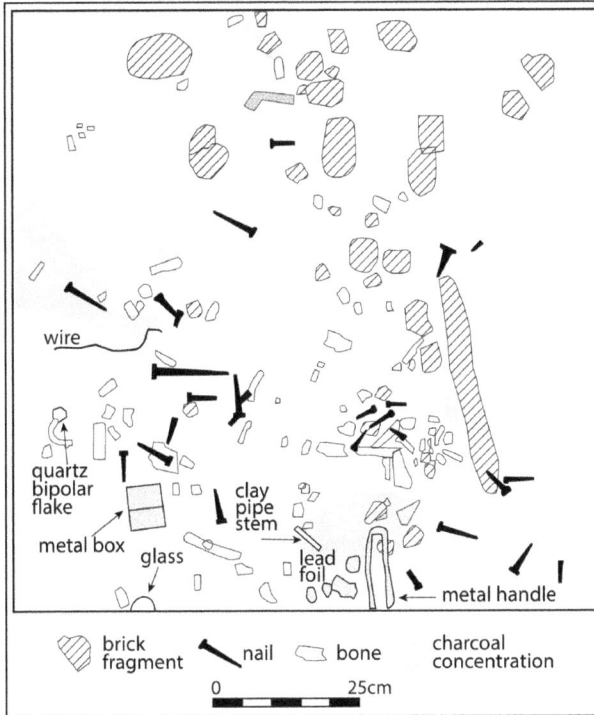

Figure 11.19 Items documented in situ during the excavation of Square 1 at Blackfellows Waterhole (after Webber and Richards 2004: figure 35).

Two small excavations were also carried out in the exposed low sandhills and hollows just north of the waterholes, where most stone tools were also found. In one of the excavated squares, 19th-century artefacts occurred above layers containing only stone tools (Chapter 7). The other, Square 2, was dug beside an area of hard-packed clay, with poor quality, locally made bricks nearby. These could be the remains of a cooking oven or hearth, where the bricks were used as heat-retainers, but it is also possible that they were once part of a firewall at the back of a fireplace of a bark hut, perhaps similar to one described in 1866:

> Some time ago the principal family among them built a comfortable log hut and fenced and trenched a small garden. But owing to the death of one they discontinued their residence in it and it is now occupied by a splitter who paid a few shillings for the place ... (quoted in Porter 2002: 28)

This raises once again a key problem on sites of this kind: there is no way of identifying either the identity or ethnicity of the people who last used and discarded the artefacts. The finds from Square 2 included things which were distributed from the Correspondents' depots or goods otherwise available in the

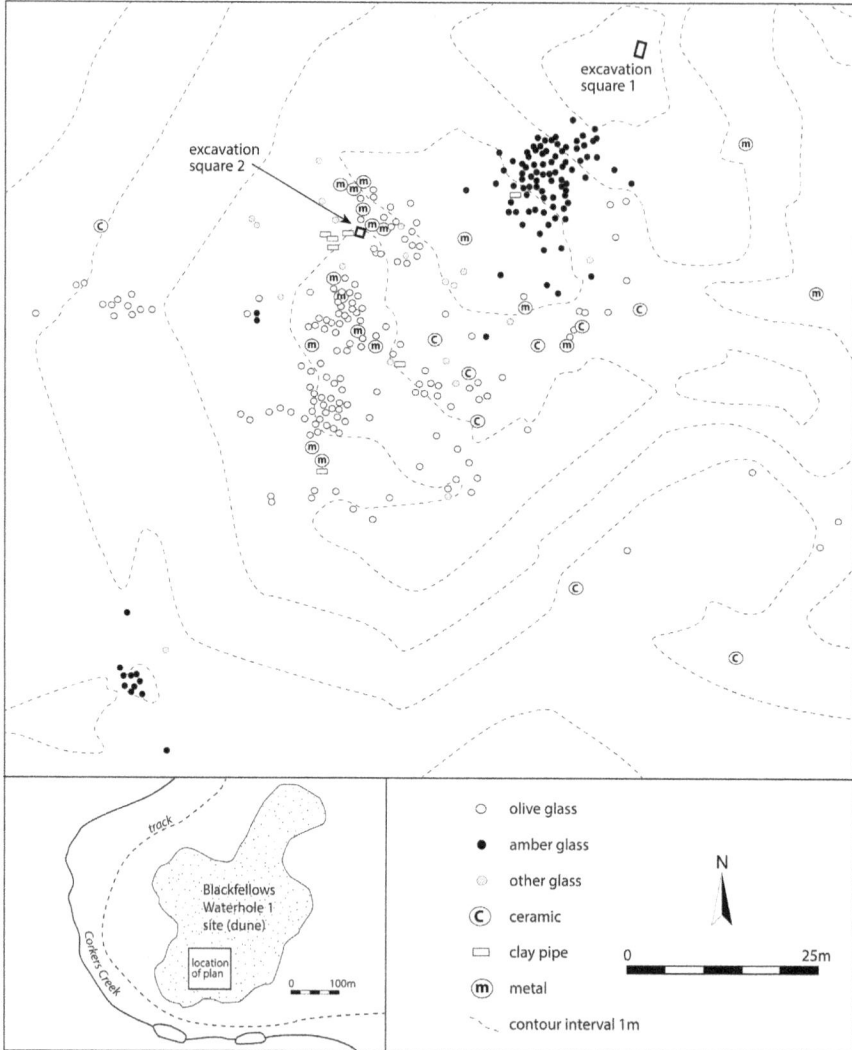

Figure 11.20 Distribution of 19th- and 20th-century artefacts across the southern part of the low sand dunes at Blackfellows Waterhole Site 1 (data from Webber and Richards: figure 26).

mid-19th century (Porter 2002, 2004; Clark 1990: 246–47) (Figure 11.19). There were fragments of bricks like those on the surface nearby. Were they heat-retainers, or, together with the nails, an indication that there was a building there? None of the small fragments of animal bone were from marsupials; most, if not all, were from sheep. There were more personal items, such as the stem of a clay pipe (the broken bowl found on the surface nearby) and a few buttons of porcelain, bone and shell. Most items could have been made at any time between about 1840 and the 1870s, although the tin box must have been a little more recent. So it is not

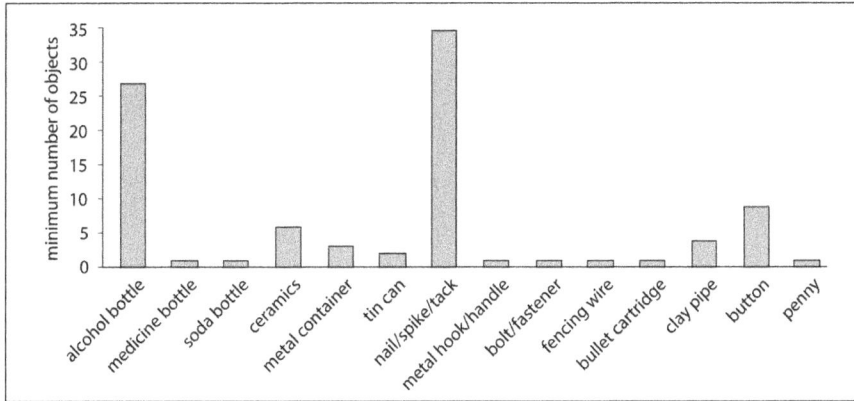

Figure 11.21 Minimum number of objects of various types from Blackfellows Waterhole (data from Porter 2004: figures 4, 6, 9).

possible to say exactly when they were used or discarded at the site. Even when something has a precise date, such as the 1857 British penny, who can say how long it was before it made its way to the Wimmera or when it was lost?

During the Berrabool project, Jenny Porter organised a broader scale surface survey in the southern part of the low dunes in the vicinity of the excavations. She recorded 1285 items of different types (Figures 11.20, 11.21). Most of the items (about 90 per cent) were fragments of glass, although of course these probably came from a relatively small number of bottles, mainly types originally used for beer, wine or spirits, although we can also see that at least some of the glass was recycled as tools. Only two pieces show deliberate chipping to form a working edge. However, it is possible that others were also used as tools, as we have seen at Carrs Plains, the Campbell Outstation, and at Kinghorn 12 in the stony rises (Chapter 7), even though they have no obvious, visible signs. The distribution of the glass fragments, however, may also suggest a structured pattern related to their possible second life as tools or raw material. While the olive glass is somewhat more widely spread, there are two distinct clusters of amber glass, one to the northeast and the other to the southwest. This cannot be random, but must represent distinct episodes or activity, perhaps related to the use of bottles as raw material rather than as containers.

Despite the recommendations to formalise the Jawadjali people's use of the Waterholes, this never took place. The number of Jawadjali people living there and in similar places in the region gradually dwindled, and many, especially the elderly and infirm, eventually, reluctantly, moved to Ebenezer Mission.

12
Changes

In the last chapter we glimpsed something of the work of the Board for the Protection of Aborigines. A key figure on the Board was Robert Brough Smyth, a civil servant and mining engineer. Mistakenly believing, along with so many others, in the Aborigines' inevitable disappearance, he compiled the two-volume *The Aborigines of Victoria* (1878), which still remains a valuable, if not always reliable, source of information. My old copy, often referred to in this book, was once owned by the Australian linguist Arthur Cappell. Perhaps if I had paid more attention to his lectures when I was an undergraduate at Sydney University I would be in a better position to understand something of Aboriginal languages. But I am not alone among archaeologists in hesitating to step into this difficult field. Language, so important to identity, is often neglected. Although many of the Aboriginal groups referred to in this book are defined by language, as much, if not more, than anything else, linking this with archaeological evidence is seldom possible.

Investigating the origin, distribution and relationships between Aboriginal languages is itself contentious (Evans and McConvell 1998; Clendon 2006; McConvell and Bowen 2011). Linguists separate out two broad families. Across almost all of Australia, the 'Pama-Nyungan' languages (an invented term using the word for 'man' in opposite corners of the continent) have some underlying, generic aspects in common. But these are all relatively new. During the last 8000 to 4000 years or so, these languages replaced older ones everywhere on the mainland except Arnhem Land, the home of the other broad group, which are lumped together as 'non-Pama-Nyungan'. How and why this happened is hotly debated by linguists, especially the extent to which it was a shift in language and not a change of population. It should not be thought of as a sudden, dramatic or noticeable process, but one where words, phrases and ways of saying things gradually shifted over many generations, perhaps patchily and in varied ways in different areas.

One line of argument connects the spread of new languages with the appearance of the small tools characteristic of the last 5000 to 4000 years; another with population restructuring caused by the loss of land as the sea advanced; a third with population expansion, as improved conditions, particularly in more arid regions, allowed the recolonisation of the interior and increases elsewhere; a fourth suggests that the diffusion of newly developed rituals and esoteric knowledge provided the context, if not driver, for the adoption of associated languages (Evans and Jones 1977; Gibbs and Veth 2002; see also Veth 2000).

Whatever the explanation, the ways in which people conceived of themselves and their cultural and natural surroundings cannot have been quite the same in their new linguistic worlds. But whether we can see any material manifestation of these changes remains very unclear. Three common suggestions are the spread or increased popularity of small tools, the development of large-scale ceremonies and the introduction of dingoes. But the connections between these developments remain tenuous: a matter of approximate contemporaneity at best.

Dingoes were brought to northern Australia from Southeast Asia by 3500 years ago (Filios and Taçon 2016). Their rapid spread across the continent may have been independent of, although perhaps made easier by, the relationships between people. Although often seen as linked, very different mechanisms would have been responsible for the increased popularity of small tools after 4500 years ago, building on more scattered earlier use of the types and techniques (Hiscock and Attenbrow 1998; McNiven 2000, 2008). These changes probably varied from place to place and time to time, both causes and results of changed toolmaking technologies, implements and perhaps access to raw materials.

Other changes during the last few thousand years are less easy to define. Many archaeologists point to an apparent increase in the number and complexity of sites (indicative of more people), the rate of sedimentation and artefact discard within sites (as measure of intensity of occupation), new sites types such as mounds (suggesting less mobility) and fish traps (intensity of resource use), and an expansion of exchange networks. These are interpreted as indicating more efficient productivity and production, population increases and more social interaction between more tightly bounded territorial groups – all indicative of a trend towards more closed or exclusive social relations in place of earlier open, inclusive systems (Lourandos 1997; see also David et al. 2006).

I am not convinced. Some of my particular reasons are more technical, such as how to quantify the number of sites given the vagaries of site survival, excavation and dating, and the extent to which our methods of excavation and analysis affect the way we perceive and explain change (Bird and Frankel 1991a, 1991b; Frankel 1988). I also have an inherent minimalist approach in other respects: less inclined to accept evidence for larger groups of people living for extended periods in 'villages' (Williams 1987, 1988), or to see fish traps – important as they are – as indicative of 'aquaculture', as strongly argued, for example, by Heather Builth (2002, 2004) and Bruce Pascoe (2014).

What is certain is that there was always diversity, resilience and adaptation. While there were long-term continuities in social structure and genetics, there were always developments and local variations in the way people lived at different times. Some differences directly reflect the availability, and the changing availability, of resources, as evolving climate and topography allowed. Some may – as cause or effect – be associated with population density. New techniques were introduced in mundane activities such as toolmaking, housing or cooking along with developments in ritual practices. The sites or places we have looked at vary in type and function. Some were used only once, others repeatedly, if intermittently, over unimaginably long periods of time, and perhaps for different reasons or in different ways. A key question is the extent to which individual and specific events and histories can be brought together into a unified narrative. Personally, I prefer to see the past as characterised by short-term adaptations and adjustments to local circumstances, whether social, technological or environmental. This view is to some extent reflected in the way I have presented the evidence in this book. It is also inherent in its structure, framing discussion around particular sites or excavations rather than broader themes.

But this does not preclude other approaches any more than my preferred explanations do. For the remains of past activities also serve other ends. Sites, artefacts and the results of research can be drawn upon in many different ways, including the promotion of Aboriginal identity, pride and aspirations. Although still a minority in this book, Aboriginal voices are increasingly important in Australian archaeology, not simply as consumers or clients, but in setting agendas and approaches for both research and management. Each state has its own political and legal frameworks in place, which define the rights, roles and responsibilities of Aboriginal communities in regard to their heritage. Most experience archaeology through heritage studies, where site surveys and rescue excavations precede development. Hundreds, if not thousands, of these studies are carried out each year. I have used only a tiny fraction of them; indeed, one of the biggest challenges facing archaeology in Australia is to find ways to access, understand and integrate this enormous volume of disparate information and use it to write new histories.

However we identify them, diversity and change characterise all periods of the Australian past. They also characterise the way we study it and the explanations we prefer. My approach in this book has been from an academic archaeological perspective: my interests are in the nature of the archaeological record and how we can use it to explore the past. I have tried here to give a flavour of both aspects, bringing together for the first time much primary evidence for this one region, and in doing so exposing the vitality of both Aboriginal society and those who study it.

Dates and a timeline

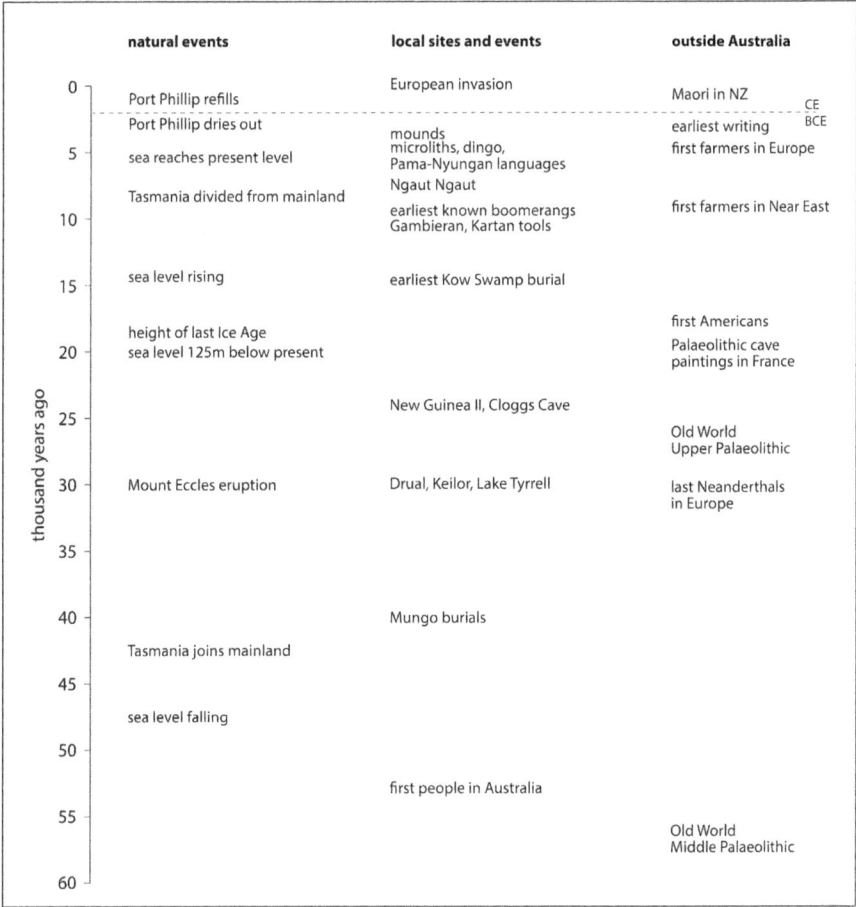

thousand years ago	natural events	local sites and events	outside Australia
0	Port Phillip refills	European invasion	Maori in NZ CE
	Port Phillip dries out		earliest writing BCE
5	sea reaches present level	mounds microliths, dingo, Pama-Nyungan languages	first farmers in Europe
	Tasmania divided from mainland	Ngaut Ngaut	
10		earliest known boomerangs Gambieran, Kartan tools	first farmers in Near East
15	sea level rising	earliest Kow Swamp burial	
20	height of last Ice Age sea level 125m below present		first Americans Palaeolithic cave paintings in France
25		New Guinea II, Cloggs Cave	Old World Upper Palaeolithic
30	Mount Eccles eruption	Drual, Keilor, Lake Tyrrell	last Neanderthals in Europe
35			
40		Mungo burials	
45	Tasmania joins mainland		
50	sea level falling		
55		first people in Australia	
60			Old World Middle Palaeolithic

Figure a.1 Timeline of key events during the last 60,000 years.

The timeline places a few key sites or developments in their environmental and global context, compacting 2000 generations of history onto a single page.

Almost all the dates used in this book are based on radiocarbon estimates, which, while accurate, are probability ranges, not precise dates. I have generally rounded these out to whole numbers and referred to them as 'years ago', where the technical literature would use 'BP' (before the present) or 'kya' (thousands of years ago). The dates are sometimes older than those quoted in some earlier studies, mainly because I have calibrated them using OxCal 4.2.

For a valuable discussion and a list of radiocarbon and other dates from all parts of Australia, see Williams et al. 2014.

Further reading

The in-text references give the primary sources of information and ideas. This list includes only a few of the more recent and accessible general books. There is a considerable and growing specialist literature and innumerable heritage management reports that provide additional evidence and discussion. Reliable information on heritage and archaeology is available on the websites of Aboriginal Victoria and the South Australian Museum: http://www.dpc.vic.gov.au/index.php/aboriginal-affairs/aboriginal-affairs-overview; http://www.samuseum.sa.gov.au/.

Allen, Harry, ed (2010). *Australia. William Blandowski's illustrated encyclopaedia of Aboriginal Australia*. Canberra: Aboriginal Studies Press.

Broome, Richard (2005). *Aboriginal Victorians: a history since 1800*. Sydney: Allen & Unwin.

Cane, Scott (2013). *First footprints: the epic story of the first Australians*. Crows Nest: Allen & Unwin.

Clark, Ian D. (1990). *Aboriginal languages and clans: an historical atlas of western and central Victoria, 1800–1900*. Monash Publications in Geography 37. Melbourne: Monash University.

Eidelson, Meyer (2014). *Melbourne dreaming: a guide to important places of the past and present*. Canberra: Australian Institute of Aboriginal and Torres Strait Island Studies.

Flood, Josephine (2010). *Archaeology of the dreamtime: the story of prehistoric Australia and its people*. Revised edition. Marleston: Gecko Books.

Frankel, David (1991). *Remains to be seen: archaeological insights into Australian prehistory*. Melbourne: Longman Cheshire.

Frankel, David and Janine Major, eds (2014). *Kulin and Kurnai: Victorian Aboriginal life and customs*. Melbourne: Messmate Press.

Gammage, Bill (2011). *The biggest estate on earth: how Aborigines made Australia*. Crows Nest: Allen & Unwin.

Hiscock, Peter (2008). *Archaeology of ancient Australia*. Abingdon: Routledge.

Holdaway, Simon and Nicola Stern (2004). *A record in stone: the study of Australia's flaked stone artefacts*. Melbourne: Museum Victoria and Aboriginal Studies Press.

Jones, Philip (2007). *Ochre and rust: artefacts and encounters on Australian frontiers*. Adelaide: Wakefield Press.

Keen, Ian (2004). *Aboriginal economy and society: Australia at the threshold of colonisation*. Oxford: Oxford University Press.

Lawrence, Susan and Peter Davies (2010). *An archaeology of Australia since 1788*. New York: Springer.

Lourandos, Harry (1997). *A continent of hunter-gatherers*. Cambridge: Cambridge University Press.

Mulvaney, John (1989). *Encounters in place: outsiders and Aboriginal Australians*. St Lucia: University of Queensland Press.

Mulvaney, John and J. Peter White, eds (1987). *Australians to 1788*. Sydney: Fairfax, Syme & Weldon.

Mulvaney, John and Johan Kamminga (1999). *Prehistory of Australia*. Sydney: Allen & Unwin.

Pascoe, Bruce (2014). *Dark emu black seeds: agriculture or accident?* Broome: Magabala Books.

Presland, Gary (2010). *First people: the eastern Kulin of Melbourne, Port Phillip and central Victoria*. Melbourne: Museum Victoria, Melbourne.

Wettenhall, Gib (1999). *The people of Gariwerd: the Grampians' Aboriginal heritage*. Melbourne: Aboriginal Affairs Victoria.

Zola, Nellie and Beth Gott (1992). *Koorie plants Koorie people: traditional Aboriginal food, fibre and healing plants of Victoria*. Melbourne: Koorie Heritage Trust.

Works cited

Allen, Harry (1996). Ethnography and prehistoric archaeology in Australia. *Journal of Anthropological Archaeology* 15: 137–59.

Allen, Harry and Kim Akerman (2015). Innovation and change in northern Australian Aboriginal spear technologies: the case for reed spears. *Archaeology in Oceania* 50 (Supplement): 82–92.

Allen, Jim, Geoff Hewitt and Josara de Lange (2008). *Bend Road 1 phases 1 to 3: report on the Bend Road archaeological investigations prepared for Theiss John Holland.* Melbourne: La Trobe University.

Allen, Molly (2009). *An analysis of Victoria's Aboriginal massacre sites.* BA(Hons) thesis, La Trobe University.

Almeida, Francesco and Tya Lovett (2016). At the distance of a snapshot (well, maybe more than one): affordable 3D modelling of Aboriginal cultural heritage through photogrammetry. *Excavations, Surveys and Heritage Management in Victoria* 5: 35–44.

Angas, George F. (1847). *South Australia illustrated.* London: Thomas M'Lean.

Aplin, Ken, Fred Ford and Peter Hiscock (2010). Early Holocene human occupation and environment of the southeast Australian Alps: new evidence from the Yarrangobilly Plateau, New South Wales. In *Altered ecologies: fire, climate and human influence on terrestrial landscapes.* Simon Haberle, Janelle Stevenson and Matthew Prebble, eds. 187–212. Terra Australis 32. Canberra: ANU ePress.

Argue, Debbie (1995). Aboriginal occupation of the southern highlands: was it really seasonal? *Australian Archaeology* 41: 30–36.

Attwood, Bain (1989). *The making of the Aborigines.* Sydney: Allen & Unwin.

Barwick, Diane (1971). Changes in the Aboriginal population of Victoria, 1863–1966. In *Aboriginal man and environment in Australia.* John Mulvaney and Jack Golson, eds. 288–315. Canberra: Australian National University Press.

Bednarik, Robert G. (1986). Parietal finger makings in Australia and Europe. *Rock Art Research* 3(1): 30–61.

Bednarik, Robert G. (1992). Early subterranean chert mining. *The Artefact* 15: 11–24.

Bell, David, Annie Ross and Rex Silcox (1981). *An archaeological survey of Lake Wahpool and Lake Timboram in northwestern Victoria. A report to ICI Australia Ltd.* Victoria Archaeological Survey Occasional Report 4.

Berndt, Ronald M. (1940). Some aspects of Jaralde culture, South Australia. *Oceania* 11(2): 164–85.

Berndt, Ronald M. and Catherine H. Berndt (1993). *A world that was: the Yaraldi of the Murray River and the lakes, South Australia.* Melbourne: Melbourne University Press.

Berryman, Annette J. and David Frankel (1984). Archaeological investigations of mounds on the Wakool River, near Barham, New South Wales: a preliminary account. *Australian Archaeology* 19: 21–30.

Beveridge, Peter (1869). Aboriginal ovens. *Journal of the Anthropological Society of London* 7: clxxxvii–clxxxix.

Beveridge, Peter (1883). Of the Aborigines inhabiting the great lacustrine and Riverina depression of the lower Murray, lower Murrumbidgee, lower Lachlan, and lower Darling. *Journal and Proceedings of the Royal Society of New South Wales* 17: 19–74.

Beveridge, Peter (1889). *The Aborigines of Victoria and Riverina*. Melbourne: Hutchinson.

Bird, Caroline F.M. (1987). Mount Talbot 1: a rockshelter in the southern Wimmera, Victoria. *The Artefact* 18: 12–21.

Bird, Caroline F.M. (1989). *Archaeological field survey in the Grampians National Park*. A report to Parks Victoria, Melbourne.

Bird, Caroline F.M. and David Frankel (1991a). Chronology and explanation in Western Victoria and southeast South Australia. *Archaeology in Oceania* 26: 1–16.

Bird, Caroline F.M. and David Frankel (1991b). Problems in constructing a prehistoric regional sequence: Holocene southeast Australia. *World Archaeology* 23: 179–92.

Bird, Caroline F.M. and David Frankel (1998). Pleistocene and early Holocene archaeology in Victoria: a view from Gariwerd. *The Artefact* 21: 48–62.

Bird, Caroline F.M. and David Frankel (2001). Excavations at Koongine cave: lithics and land use in the terminal Pleistocene and Holocene of South Australia. *Proceedings of the Prehistoric Society* 67: 49–83.

Bird, Caroline F.M. and David Frankel (2005). *An archaeology of Gariwerd: from Pleistocene to Holocene in western Victoria*. Tempus 8. St Lucia: University of Queensland.

Bird, Caroline F.M., David Frankel and Nora van Waarden (1998). New radiocarbon determinations from the Grampians-Gariwerd region, western Victoria. *Archaeology in Oceania* 33: 31–36.

Bird, Caroline F.M. and James W. Rhoads (2011). Topographic archaeology revisited: regional archaeological structure in the southern Wimmera, Victoria, Australia. *Records of the Western Australian Museum* Supplement 79: 109–22.

Bird, Eric C.F. (1993). *The coast of Victoria: the shaping of scenery*. Carlton: Melbourne University Press.

Blackwood, Robert and Kenneth N.G. Simpson (1973). Attitudes of Aboriginal skeletons excavated in the Murray Valley region between Mildura and Renmark, Australia. *Memoirs of the National Museum of Victoria* 34: 99–150.

Bland, Catherine, Amy Roberts, Isobelle Campbell and the Mannum Aboriginal Community Association Inc (MACAI) (2012). New interpretations for the stone artefact assemblage from Ngaut Ngaut (Devon Downs), South Australia. *Journal of the Anthropological Society of South Australia* 36: 47–65.

Board for the Protection of Aborigines (1873). *Ninth report of the Board for the Protection of the Aborigines in the colony of Victoria*. Melbourne: Government Printer. http://aiatsis.gov.au/sites/default/files/catalogue_resources/24604.pdf.

Board for the Protection of Aborigines (1875). *Eleventh report of the Board for the Protection of the Aborigines in the colony of Victoria*. Melbourne: Government Printer. http://aiatsis.gov.au/sites/default/files/docs/digitised_collections/remove/24682.pdf.

Boldrewood, Rolf (1896). *Old Melbourne memories* (2nd edition). London: Macmillan.

Bonhomme, Theresa (1990). *An archaeological survey of the Barmah Forest*. Victoria Archaeological Survey Occasional Report 34.

Bowdler, Sandra (1976). Hook, line and dilly bag: an interpretation of an Australian coastal shell midden. *Mankind* 10(4): 248–58.

Bowdler, Sandra (1981). Hunters in the highlands: Aboriginal adaptations in the eastern Australian uplands. *Archaeology in Oceania* 16(2): 99–111.

Bowdler, Sandra (2005). Movement, exchange and the ritual life in southeastern Australia. In *Many exchanges: archaeology, history, community and the work of Isabel McBryde*. Ingereth Macfarlane, ed. 131–46. Aboriginal History Monograph 11. Canberra: Aboriginal History.

Bowdler, Sandra (2010). The empty coast: conditions for human occupation in southeast Australia during the late Pleistocene. In *Altered ecologies: fire, climate and human influence on terrestrial landscapes*. Simon Haberle, Janelle Stevenson and Matthew Prebble, eds. 177–185. Terra Australias 32. Canberra: ANU ePress.

Bowler, James M., Harvey Johnston, Jon M. Olley, John R. Prescott, Richard G. (Bert) Roberts, Wilfred Shawcross and Nigel A. Spooner (2003). New ages for human occupation and climatic change at Lake Mungo, Australia. *Nature* 421(6925): 837–40.

Bride, Thomas F. (1898). *Letters from Victorian pioneers* (revised edition, 1983). Melbourne: Trustees of the Public Library, Museums and National Gallery of Victoria.

Brockwell, Sally, Keryn C. Kefous, H. Cooke and Anne M. Constantine (2013). *ACT grey literature v2: an annotated bibliography of unpublished reports relating to archaeological and palaeoecological survey and research in the ACT and neighbouring highlands regions*. Canberra: Canberra Archaeological Survey.

Broome, Richard (2005). *Aboriginal Victorians: a history since 1800*. Sydney: Allen & Unwin.

Brown, Oliver J.F. (2006). Tasmanian devil (*Sarcophilus harrisii*) extinction on the Australian mainland in the mid-Holocene: multicausality and ENSO intensification. *Alcheringa. An Australasian Journal of Palaeontology* 30(sup1): 49–57.

Brown, Steve, Steven Avery and Megan Goulding (2004). Recent investigations at the Ebenezer mission cemetery. In *After Captain Cook: the archaeology of the recent Indigenous past in Australia*. Rodney Harrison and Christine Williamson, eds. 147–70. Sydney: Sydney University Archaeological Methods 8.

Brumm, Adam (2010). 'The falling sky': symbolic and cosmological associations of the Mt William greenstone axe quarry, central Victoria, Australia. *Cambridge Archaeological Journal* 20(2): 179–96.

Builth, Heather C. (2002). *The archaeology and sociology of Gunditjmara: a landscape analysis from southwest Victoria*. PhD thesis, Flinders University.

Builth, Heather C. (2004). Mt Eccles lava flow and the Gunditjmara connection: a landform for all seasons. *Proceedings of the Royal Society of Victoria* 116(1): 163–82.

Burke, Christine (1990). *Analysis of the lithic assemblage from the Keilor archaeological site (site number 7822/010)*. Victoria Archaeological Survey Occasional Report 30.

Byrt, Pauline N. (2004). *The Thomas papers in the Mitchell Library: a comprehensive index*. Melbourne: Monash University.

Cahir, Fred (2012). *Black gold: Aboriginal people on the goldfields of Victoria, 1850–1870*. Canberra: ANU ePress.

Cahir Fred and Ian Clark (2013). The historic importance of the dingo in Aboriginal society in Victoria (Australia): a reconsideration of the archival record. *Anthrozoös* 26:2: 185–98. http://dx.doi.org/10.2752/175303713X13636846944088.

Cairns, John (1858). On the weir malleè, a water-yielding tree, the bulrush, and porcupine grass of Australia. *Transactions of the Philosophical Institute of Victoria* 3: 32–35.

Campbell, Judy (2002). *Invisible invaders: smallpox and other diseases in Aboriginal Australia 1780–1889*. Carlton South: Melbourne University Press.

Campbell, Thomas D., John B. Cleland and Paul S. Hossfeld (1946). Aborigines of the lower southeast of South Australia. *Records of the South Australian Museum* 8(3): 445–502.

Canning, Shaun (2009). Broad-scale palaeoenvironmental reconstructions of southern Victoria, Australia. *The Artefact* 32: 4–14.

Canning, Shaun, Darren Griffin, Pamela Ricardi and Vanessa Flynn (2010). Recent archaeological excavations of Pleistocene deposits at Brimbank Park, Keilor, Victoria. *Archaeological Heritage* 2(1): 25–35.

Casey, Maryrose (2011). Cross-cultural encounters: Aboriginal performers and European audiences in the late 1800s and early 1900s. *Double Dialogues* 14. http://www.doubledialogues.com/article/cross-cultural-encounters-aboriginal-performers-and-european-audiences-in-the-late-1800s-and-early-1900s/

Chauncy, Philip (1878). Appendix A. Notes and anecdotes of the Aborigines of Australia. In *The Aborigines of Victoria: with notes relating to the habits of the natives of other parts of Australia and Tasmania*. R. Brough Smyth, ed. 221–84. Melbourne: Victorian Government Printer.

Clark, David J. (1979). *The Gambieran stone tool industry*. BA(Hons) thesis, La Trobe University.

Clark, Ian D. (1990a). *Aboriginal languages and clans: an historical atlas of western and central Victoria, 1800–1900*. Monash Publications in Geography 37. Melbourne: Department of Geography, Monash University.

Clark, Ian D. (1990b). In quest of the tribes: G.A. Robinson's abridged report of his 1841 expeditions among western Victoria Aboriginal tribes: Kenyon's 'condensation' reconsidered. *Memoirs of the Museum of Victoria (Anthropology and History)* 1(1): 97–130.

Clark, Ian D. (1995). Scars in the landscape: a register of massacre sites in western Victoria, *1803–1859*. Canberra: Australian Institute of Aboriginal and Torres Strait Islander Studies.

Clark, Ian D. ed (1998a). *The journals of George Augustus Robinson, Chief Protector, Port Phillip Aboriginal Protectorate, vol. 2, 1 October 1840–31 August 1841*. Melbourne: Heritage Matters.

Clark, Ian D. ed (1998b), *The journals of George Augustus Robinson, Chief Protector, Port Phillip Aboriginal Protectorate, vol. 4, 1 January 1844–24 October 1845*. Melbourne: Heritage Matters.

Clark, Ian D. and Lionel L. Harradine (1990). *The restoration of Jardwadjali and Djabwurrung names for rock art sites and landscape features in and around the Grampians National Park*. Unpublished report, Koorie Tourism Unit, Victoria.

Clark, Peter and Jeannette Hope (1985). Aboriginal burials and shell middens at Snaggy Bend and other sites on the Central Murray River. *Australian Archaeology* 20: 68–89.

Clarke, Anne (1991). *Lake Condah project Aboriginal archaeology resource inventory*. Melbourne: Victoria Archaeological Survey Occasional Report 36.

Clarke, Anne (1994). Romancing the stones: the cultural construction of an archaeological landscape in the western district of Victoria. *Archaeology in Oceania* 29: 1–15.

Clarke, Philip A. (1995). Myth as history? The Ngurunderi Dreaming of the lower Murray, South Australia. *Records of the South Ausralian Museum* 28(2): 143–147.

Clendon, Mark (2006). Reassessing Australia's linguistic prehistory. *Current Anthropology* 47(1): 39–61.

Cosgrove, Richard, David Frankel and David Thomas (2013). From the moat to the Murray: teaching practical archaeology at La Trobe University. *Australian Archaeology* 74: 44–51.

Coutts, Peter F.J. (1970). *The archaeology of Wilson's Promontory*. Australian Aboriginal Studies 28. Canberra: Australian Institute of Aboriginal Studies.

Coutts, Peter J.F. (1982). Victoria Archaeological Survey activities report 1979–80. *Records of the Victorian Archaeological Survey* 13: 1–28.

Coutts, Peter J.F., ed. (1984). Coastal archaeology in southeastern Victoria. *Records of the Victoria Archaeological Survey* 14.

Coutts, Peter J.F., Rudy K. Frank and Philip Hughes (1978). Aboriginal engineers of the Western District, Victoria. *Records of the Victorian Archaeological Survey* 7.

Coutts, Peter F.J., Peter Henderson and Richard L. Fullagar (1979). A preliminary investigation of Aboriginal mounds in northwestern Victoria. *Records of the Victorian Archaeological Survey* 9.

Coutts, Peter J.F. and Michel Lorblanchet (1982). Aboriginals and rock art in the Grampians, Victoria, Australia. *Records of the Victorian Archaeological Survey* 12.

Coutts, Peter J.F. and Dan C. Witter (1977). New radiocarbon dates for Victorian archaeological sites. *Records of the Victorian Archaeological Survey* 4: 59–73.

Coutts, Peter J.F., Dan C. Witter, Murray McIlwraith and Rudy Frank (1976). The mound people of western Victoria: a preliminary statement. *Records of the Victorian Archaeological Survey* 1.

Coutts, Peter J.F., Dan C. Witter and Deborah M. Parsons (1977). Impact of European settlement on Aboriginal society in Victoria. *Records of the Victorian Archaeological Survey* 4: 17–58.

Critchett, Jan (1990). *A 'distant field of murder': Western District frontiers 1834–1848.* Melbourne: Melbourne University Press.

Crowley, Gabriel M. and A. Peter Kershaw (1994). Late Quaternary environmental change and human impact around Lake Bolac, western Victoria, Australia. *Journal of Quaternary Science* 9: 367–377.

Dawson, James (1881). *Australian Aborigines: the languages and customs of several tribes of Aborigines in the Western District of Victoria, Australia.* Melbourne: George Robinson.

Dickson, Frank P. (1976). Australian ground stone hatchets: their design and dynamics. *Australian Archaeology* 5: 33–48.

Dickson, Frank P. (1981). *Australian stone hatchets: a study in design and dynamics.* Sydney: Academic Press.

Dingli, Gillian (1995). *Karremarter: a Holocene site in southeast South Australia.* BA(Hons) thesis, La Trobe University.

Dodson, John, Richard L. Fullagar and Lesley Head (1992). Dynamics of environment and people in the forested crescents of temperate Australia. In *The native lands: prehistory and environmental change in Australia and the southwest Pacific.* John Dodson, ed. 115–59. Melbourne: Longman Cheshire.

Donlon, Denise (1994). Aboriginal skeletal collections and research in physical anthropology: an historical perspective. *Australian Archaeology* 39: 73–82.

Dortch, Charles E. (2002). Modelling past Aboriginal hunter-gatherer socio-economic and territorial organisation in Western Australia's lower southwest. *Archaeology in Oceania* 37: 1–21.

Dortch, Joe, Matt Cupper, Rainer Grün, Bernice Harpley, Kerrie Lee and Judith Field (2016). The timing and cause of megafauna mass deaths at Lancefield Swamp, southeastern Australia. *Quaternary Science Reviews* 145: 161–82.

Dowling, Peter J. (1997). *'A great deal of sickness': introduced diseases among the Aboriginal people of colonial southeast Australia 1788–1900.* PhD thesis, Australian National University.

Downey, William S. and David Frankel (1992). Radiocarbon and thermoluminescence dating of a Central Murray mound. *The Artefact* 15: 31–34.

Draper, Neale (1987). Context for the Kartan: a preliminary report on excavations at Cape du Couedic, Kangaroo Island. *Archaeology in Oceania* 22: 1–8.

Draper, Neale (1992). The history of Aboriginal land use on Kangaroo Island. In *A biological survey of Kangaroo Island, South Australia in November 1989 and 1990.* Anthony C. Robinson and David M. Armstrong, eds. 33–46. Adelaide: Heritage and Biodiversity Section, Department for Environment, Heritage and Aboriginal Affairs.

Draper, Neale (2006). Mid-Holocene hunters of Kangaroo Island: the perspective from Cape du Couedic rockshelter. In *An archaeological life: papers in honour of Jay Hall.* Sean Ulm and

Ian Lilley, eds. 27–46. University of Queensland Aboriginal and Torres Strait Islander Studies Unit Research Report Series 7.

Draper, Neale (2015). Islands of the dead? Prehistoric occupation of Kangaroo Island and other southern offshore islands and watercraft use by Aboriginal Australians. *Quaternary International* 385: 229–42.

Durband, Arthur C. (2014). Brief communication: artificial cranial modification in Kow Swamp and Cohuna. *American Journal of Physical Anthropology* 155: 173–78.

Durband, Arthur C., Judith Littleton and Keryn Walshe (2014). Patterns in ritual tooth avulsion at Roonka. *American Journal of Physical Anthropology* 154: 479–85.

Edmonds, Vanessa (1995). *An archaeological survey of the Serra Range, Grampians (Gariwerd) National Park, southwest Victoria*. Report to Aboriginal Affairs Victoria, Melbourne.

Edwards, Robert (1972). *Aboriginal bark canoes of the Murray valley*. Adelaide: Rigby.

Environment Protection Authority (2007). *A review of historic western Victorian lake conditions in relation to fish deaths*. Melbourne: EPA Publication 1108. http://www.epa.vic.gov.au/~/media/Publications/1108.pdf.

Essling, Jacinta (1999). *Analysis of the lithic assemblage from Lake Wartook, Gariwerd, Victoria*. BA(Hons) thesis, La Trobe University.

Eyre, Edward J. (1845). *Journal of expeditions of discovery into central Australia*. London: T & W Boone.

Fels, Marie H. (2011). *'I succeeded once': the Aboriginal protectorate on the Mornington Peninsula, 1839–1840*. Canberra: ANU ePress.

Evans, Nick and Rhys Jones (1997). The cradle of the Pama–Nyungans: archaeological and linguistic speculations. In *Archaeology and linguistics: Aboriginal Australia in global perspective*. Patrick McConvell and Nick Evans, eds. 385–417. Melbourne: Melbourne University Press.

Evans, Nick and Patrick McConvell (1998). The enigma of Pama–Nyungan expansion in Australia. *Archaeology and language II: archaeological data and linguistic hypotheses*. Roger Blench and Matthew Spriggs, eds. 174–91. London: Routledge.

Filihia, Meredith, Paul Kucera, Rachel Minos and Kym Oataway (2016). Salvage excavations at VAHR 7921-1151 'Lyndhurst Inland Port 6', Carrum Swamp: analysis of an archaeological assemblage. *Excavations, Surveys and Heritage Management in Victoria* 5: 7–15.

Fillios, Melanie A., Mathew S. Crowther and Mike Lentic (2012). The impact of the dingo on the thylacine in Holocene Australia. *World Archaeology* 44(1): 118–34.

Filios, Melanie A. and Paul S.C. Taçon (2016). Who let the dogs in? A review of the recent genetic evidence for the introduction of the dingo to Australia and implications for the movement of people. *Journal of Archaeological Science: Reports* 7: 782–92.

Fison, Lorimer and Alfred W. Howitt (1880). *Kamilaroi and Kurnai*. Melbourne: George Robertson.

Fitzsimmons, Kathryn E., Nicola Stern, Colin V. Murray-Wallace, William Truscott and Cornel Pop (2015). The Mungo mega-lake event, semi-arid Australia: non-linear descent into the last Ice Age, implications for human behaviour. *PLoS ONE* 10(6): e0127008. doi: 10.1371/journal. pone.0127008.s.

Flood, Josephine (1980). *The moth hunters: Aboriginal prehistory of the Australian Alps*. Canberra: Australian Institute of Aboriginal Studies.

Flood, Josephine (1987). Moth hunters of the southeastern highlands. In *Australians to 1788*. John Mulvaney and J. Peter White, eds. 275–92. Sydney: Fairfax, Syme & Weldon.

Flood, Josephine (1988). No ethnography, no moth hunters. In *Archaeology with ethnography: an Australian approach*. Betty Meehan and Rhys Jones, eds. 270–76. Canberra: Australian National University.

Flood, Josephine (2010). *Archaeology of the Dreamtime: the story of prehistoric Australia and its people*. Revised edition. Marleston: Gecko Books.

Frankel, David (1982a). Earth rings at Sunbury, Victoria. *Archaeology in Oceania* 17(2): 89–97.

Frankel, David (1982b). An account of Aboriginal use of the yam daisy. *The Artefact* 7: 43–45.

Frankel, David (1986). Excavations in the lower southeast of South Australia, November 1985. *Australian Archaeology* 22: 75–87.

Frankel, David (1988). Characterising change in prehistoric sequences: a view from Australia. *Archaeology in Oceania* 23: 41–48.

Frankel, David (1991a). *Remains to be seen: archaeological insights into Australian prehistory.* Melbourne: Longman Cheshire.

Frankel, David (1991b). First-order radiocarbon dating of Australian shell-middens. *Antiquity* 65: 571–74.

Frankel, David and Caroline F.M. Bird (2013). Integrating hunter-gatherer sites, environments, technology and art in western Victoria. In *Archaeology in environment and technology: intersections and transformations.* David Frankel, Jennifer M. Webb and Susan Lawrence, eds. 69–83. New York and London: Routledge.

Frankel, David and Janine Major, eds (2017). *Victorian Aboriginal life and customs through early European eyes.* Melbourne: La Trobe University Ebureau.

Frankel, David and Nicola Stern (2011). Karremarter: mid- to late Holocene stone artefact production and use in the lower southeast of South Australia. In *Changing perspectives in Australian archaeology.* Jim Specht and Robin Torrence, eds. *Technical Reports of the Australian Museum, Online* 23(5): 59–71. doi: 10.3853/j.1835-4211.23.2011.1565 to 1576. http://australianmuseum.net.au/journal/Frankel-2011-tech-rep-aust-mus-online-235-5971.

Fresløv, Joanna and David Frankel (1999). Abundant fields? A review of coastal archaeology in Victoria. In *Australian coastal archaeology.* Jay Hall and Ian J. McNiven, eds. 239–54. Canberra: Australian National University, Research Papers in Archaeology and Natural History No. 31.

Fresløv, Joanna, Phillip Hughes and Russell Mullett (2004). *Post wildfire Indigenous heritage survey. A Report to Parks Victoria, the Department of Sustainability and Environment, and Aboriginal Affairs Victoria.* Hurstbridge: Perspectives Heritage Solutions.

Fullagar, Richard (2011). Burins, bones and base camps: a re-analysis of Aire Shelter 2, Glenaire, southern Victoria. In *Changing perspectives in Australian archaeology.* Jim Specht and Robin Torrence, eds. *Technical Reports of the Australian Museum, Online* 23(8): 103–31. doi: 10.3853/j.1835-4211.23.2011.1573. http://australianmuseum.net.au/journal/fullagar-2011-tech-rep-aust-mus-online-238-103131.

Fullagar, Richard (2015). The logic of visitation: tool-use, technology and economy on Great Glennie Island, southeastern Australia. *Quaternary International* 385: 219–28.

Fullagar, Richard (2016). Uncertain evidence for weapons and craft tools: functional investigations of Australian microliths. In *Multidisciplinary approaches to the study of Stone Age weaponry.* Radu Iovita and Katsuhiro Sano, eds. Dordrecht: Springer. doi: 10.1007/978-94-017-7602-8_11.

Fullagar, Richard, Josephine McDonald, Judith Field and Denise Donlon (2009). Deadly weapons: backed microliths from Narrabeen. In *Archaeological science under a microscope: studies in residue and ancient DNA analysis in honour of Thomas H. Loy.* Michael Haslam, Gail Robertson, Alison Crowther, Sue Nugent and Luke Kirkwood, eds. Canberra: ANU ePress. *Terra Australis* 30: 248–60.

Gallus, A. (1974). A summary of the results of excavations at Keilor. *The Artefact* 1: 1–9.

Garvey, Jillian (2013). Palaeoenvironments and human adaptation in the semi-arid Murray River Valley of northwestern Victoria. *Excavations, Surveys and Heritage Management in Victoria* 2: 119–24.

Garvey, Jillian (2015). Australian Aboriginal freshwater shell middens from late Quaternary northwest Victoria: prey choice, economic variability and exploitation. *Quaternary International* (2015), http://dx.doi.org/10.1016/j.quaint.2015.11.065.

Garvey, Jillian and Darren Perry (2015). Lessons from freshwater middens: archaeology and Traditional Owner perspectives of the importance of these cultural sites from the Central Murray River valley, northwestern Victoria. *Excavations, Surveys and Heritage Management in Victoria* 4: 39–42.

Gaughwin, Denise and Hilary Sullivan (1984). Aboriginal boundaries and movements in Western Port, Victoria. *Aboriginal History* 8: 80–98.

Gaughwin, Denise and Richard L. Fullagar (1995). Victorian offshore islands in a mainland coastal economy. *Australian Archaeology* 40: 38–49.

Gerritsen, Rupert (2001). Aboriginal fish hooks in southern Australia: evidence, arguments and implications. *Australian Archaeology* 52: 18–28.

Gibbs, Martin and Peter Veth (2002). Ritual engines and the archaeology of territorial ascendancy. In *Barriers, borders, boundaries: proceedings of the 2001 Australian Archaeological Association Conference*. Tempus 7. Sean Ulm, Catherine Westcott, Jill Reid, Anne Ross, Ian Lilley, Jonathan Prangnell and Luke Kirkwood, eds. 11–19.

Gill, Edmund D. (1977). Evolution of the Otway coast, Australia, from the last interglacial to the present. *Proceedings of the Royal Society of Victoria* 89(1): 7–18.

Gillespie, Richard, David R. Horton, Phil Ladd, Philip G. Macumber, Tom H. Rich, Robert Thorne and Richard V.S. Wright (1978). Lancefield Swamp and the extinction of the Australian megafauna. *Science* 200(4345): 1044–48.

Godfrey, Michael C.S. (1980). *An archaeological survey of the Discovery Bay Coastal Park*. MA thesis, La Trobe University.

Godfrey, Michael C.S. (1989). Shell midden chronology in southwestern Victoria: reflections of change in prehistoric population and subsistence? *Archaeology in Oceania* 24(2): 65–69.

Godfrey, Michael C.S. (1994). *The archaeology of the invisible. Seasonality and shellfishing at Discovery Bay, Victoria: the application of oxygen isotope analysis*. PhD thesis, La Trobe University.

Godfrey, Michael C.S., Caroline F.M. Bird, David Frankel, James W. Rhoads and Stewart Simmons (1996). From time to time: radiocarbon determinations on Victorian archaeological sites held by Aboriginal Affairs Victoria. *The Artefact* 19: 3–51.

Gott, Beth (1982a). Ecology of root use by the Aborigines of southern Australia. *Archaeology in Oceania* 17(1): 59–67.

Gott, Beth (1982b). Kunzea pomifera – Dawson's 'nurt'. *The Artefact* 7(1–2): 13–17.

Gott, Beth (1983). Murnong – *Microseris scapigera*: a study of a staple food of Victorian Aborigines. *Australian Aboriginal Studies* 1983: 2–17.

Gott, Beth (2005). Aboriginal fire management in southeastern Australia: aims and frequency. *Journal of Biogeography* 32: 1203–8.

Gott, Beth and John Conran (1981). *Victorian Koorie plants*. Hamilton: Yanennanock Women's Group.

Griffin, Darren, Delta L. Freedman, Bill Nicholson, Fiona McConachie and Alexander Parmington (2013). The Koorong project: experimental archaeology and Wurundjeri continuation of cultural practices. *Excavations, Surveys and Heritage Management in Victoria* 2: 59–65.

Griffiths, Tom (1996). *Hunters and collectors: the antiquarian imagination in Australia*. Cambridge: Cambridge University Press.

Grist, Mark J. (1995). *An archaeological investigation into the 'no stone saga' of far northwest Victoria: a study of the Berribee Quarries in the landscape*. BA(Hons) thesis, Australian National University.

Gunditjmara People and Gib Wettenhall (2010). *The people of Budj Bim: engineers of aquaculture, builders of stone house settlements and warriors defending country.* Ballarat: em Press Publishing.

Gunn, Robert G. (1983). Aboriginal rock art in the Grampians. *Records of the Victorian Archaeological Survey* 16.

Gunn, Robert G. (1987). *Aboriginal rock art of Victoria.* Report to the Victoria Archaeological Survey, Melbourne.

Gunn, Robert G. (2002). Mudgegonga-2 and the rock art of northeast Victoria. *Rock Art Research* 19(1): 1–17.

Gunn, Robert G. (2003). Three more pieces to the puzzle. Aboriginal occupation in Gariwerd (Grampians), western Victoria. *The Artefact* 26: 32–50.

Gunn, Robert G. (2008). Dry-pigment drawings within Gariwerd, Australia. *Rock Art Research* 25(2): 183–200.

Gunn, Robert G. (2009). Wooden artefacts from Gariwerd rockshelters, western Victoria. *Australian Archaeology* 68: 23–30.

Hale, Herbert M. and Norman B. Tindale (1930). Notes on some human remains in the lower Murray valley, South Australia. *Records of the South Australian Museum* 4: 145–218.

Hall, Roger (1992). Artefact density patterns in areas of high relief: a case study from far east Gippsland. In *Cultural heritage of the Australian Alps.* Babette Scougall, ed. 125–40. Canberra: Australian Alps Liaison Committee.

Hamm, Giles et al. (2016). Cultural innovation and megafauna interaction in the early settlement of arid Australia. *Nature* doi: 10.1038/nature20125.

Hawdon, Joseph (1952). *The journal of a journey from New South Wales to Adelaide (the capital of South Australia) performed in 1838.* Melbourne: Georgian House.

Head, John, Rhys Jones and Jim Allen (1983). Calculation of the 'marine reservoir effect' from the dating of shell-charcoal paired samples from an Aboriginal midden on Great Glennie Island, Bass Strait. *Australian Archaeology* 17: 99–112.

Head, Lesley (1983). Environment as artefact: a geographic perspective on the Holocene occupation of southwestern Victoria. *Archaeology in Oceania* 18: 73–80.

Head, Lesley (1987). The Holocene prehistory of a coastal wetland system: Discovery Bay, southeastern Australia. *Human Ecology* 15(4): 435–62.

Head, Lesley (1988). Holocene vegetation, fire and environmental history of the Discovery Bay region, southwestern Victoria. *Australian Journal of Ecology* 13: 21–49.

Head, Lesley (1989). Using palaeoecology to date Aboriginal fishtraps at Lake Condah, Victoria. *Archaeology in Oceania* 24: 106–15.

Head, Lesley and Iain M. Stuart (1980). *Change in the Aire: palaeoecology and the prehistory of the Aire basin, southwestern Victoria.* Melbourne: Monash Publications in Geography 24, Monash University.

Hewitt, Geoff and Jim Allen (2010). Site disturbance and archaeological integrity: the case of Bend Road, an open site in Melbourne spanning pre-LGM Pleistocene to late Holocene periods. *Australian Archaeology* 70: 1–16.

Hewitt, Geoff and Josara de Lange (2007). *Bend Road 2 phases 1 to 4: report on Bend Road archaeological investigations prepared for Thiess John Holland.* Melbourne: La Trobe University.

Hill, Jeffrey C. (2006). *Lithic utilisation in the central Murray valley: the distributional archaeology of surface material.* BA(Hons) thesis, La Trobe University.

Hiscock, Peter (2013). Beyond the Dreamtime: archaeology and explorations of religious change in Australia. *World Archaeology* 45(1): 124–36.

Hiscock, Peter and Val Attenbrow (1998). Early Holocene backed artefacts from Australia. *Archaeology in Oceania* 33(2): 49–62.

Hiscock, Peter, Sue O'Connor, Jane Balme and Tim Maloney (2016). World's earliest ground-edge axe production coincides with human colonisation of Australia. *Australian Archaeology* 82(1): 2–11.

Hofmaier, Keith C. (1957). Aborigines in the southern Mallee of Victoria. *Victorian Historical Magazine* 31(1): 63–80.

Holdgate, Guy, Barbara E. Wagstaff, and Stephen J. Gallagher (2011). Did Port Phillip bay nearly dry up between ~2800 and 1000 cal. yr BP? Bay floor channeling evidence, seismic and core dating. *Australian Journal of Earth Sciences* 58: 157–75.

Horton, David R. (1984). Red kangaroos: last of the Australian megafauna. In *Quaternary extinctions: a prehistoric revolution*, Paul S. Martin and Richard G Klein, eds. 639–80. Tucson: University of Arizona Press.

Horton, David R. and Richard V.S. Wright (1981). Cuts on Lancefield bones: carnivorous thylacoleo, not humans, the cause. *Archaeology in Oceania* 16(2): 73–80.

Hotchin, Kieran L. (1990). *Environmental and cultural change in the Gippsland Lakes region, Victoria, Australia.* PhD Thesis, Australian National University.

Howitt, Alfred W. (1884). On some Australian ceremonies of initiation. *Journal of the Royal Anthropological Institute* 13: 432–59.

Howitt, Alfred W. (1904). *The native tribes of southeast Australia.* London: MacMillan.

Ingold, Tim (1993). The temporality of the landscape. *World Archaeology* 25(2): 152–74.

Jenkin, Graham (1979). *The conquest of the Ngarrindjeri: the story of the Lower Murray tribes.* Adelaide: Rigby.

Jensz, Felicity (2010). *German Moravian missionaries in the British colony of Victoria, Australia, 1848–1908: influential strangers.* Leiden, the Netherlands: Brill.

Jones, Philip (2004). *Boomerangs: behind an Australian icon.* Kent Town: Wakefield Press.

Jones, Rhys and Jim Allen (1979). A stratified archaeological site on Great Glennie Island, Bass Strait. *Australian Archaeology* 9: 1–11.

Jones, Rhys and Neville White (1988). Point blank: stone tool manufacture in the Ngiliptji quarry, Arnhem Land, 1981. In *Archaeology with ethnography: an Australian approach.* Betty Meehan and Rhys Jones, eds. 51–87. Canberra: Australian National University.

Jordan, Bill and members of Gunditj Mirring Traditional Owners Aboriginal Corporation (2011). *Engineering works of the Gunditjmara at Lake Condah (Tae Rak) and Tyrendarra. Nomination under Heritage Recognition Program of Engineering Heritage Australia.* Newcastle: Engineering Heritage Australia. http://bit.ly/2mRxo0v.

Jurisich, Mark and David Davies (1976). The palaepathology of prehistoric Aboriginal skeletal remains excavated by the Victoria Archaeological Survey. *The Artefact* 1(4): 194–218.

Kamminga, Johan (1992). Aboriginal settlement and prehistory of the Snowy Mountains. In *Cultural heritage of the Australian Alps.* Babette Scougall, ed. 101–24. Canberra: Australian Alps Liaison Committee.

Kamminga, Johan and Mark Grist (2000). *Yariambiack Creek Aboriginal heritage study.* Report to Aboriginal Affairs Victoria.

Kamminga, Johan, Robert Paton and Ingereth MacFarlane (1989). *Archaeological investigations in the Thredbo valley, Snowy Mountains.* Canberra: ANUTECH.

Kayandel Archaeological Services (2009). *Subsurface archaeological salvage, Cranbourne extension: Victorian desalination project, Cranbourne. Report vol.1.* Report prepared for the Department of Sustainability and Environment, Melbourne.

Kefous, Keryn C. (1982). Prehistoric site patterning in the Victorian Mallee. *Archaeology in Oceania* 17: 98–99.

Kefous, Keryn C. (1983). *Riverain: water availability and Aboriginal prehistory of the Murray River, Lake Victoria area, western New South Wales.* MA thesis, Australian National University.

Kefous, Keryn C. (1988). Butlin's bootstraps: Aboriginal population in the pre-contact Murray-Darling region. In *Archaeology with ethnography: an Australian approach*. Betty Meehan and Rhys Jones, eds. 225–37. Canberra: Australian National University.

Kenyon, Alfred S. (1912). Camping places of the Aborigines of southeast Australia. *The Victorian Historical Magazine* 2(3): 97–110.

Kenyon, Alfred S. (1928). The Aboriginal Protectorate of Port Phillip. Report of an expedition to the Aboriginal tribes of the Western District by the Chief Protector, George Augustus Robinson. *Victorian Historical Magazine* 12(8): 134–71.

Korumburra and District Historical Society (1998). *The land of the lyrebird: a story of early settlement in the great forest of South Gippsland*. Korumburra, Vic.: Korumburra and District Historical Society.

Lambeck, Kurt and John Chappell (2001). Sea level change through the last glacial cycle. *Science* 292: 679–86.

Lampert, Ronald (1981). *The great Kartan mystery*. Terra Australis 5. Canberra: Research School of Pacific Studies, Australian National University.

Lane, Louis and Richard L. Fullagar (1980). Previously unrecorded Aboriginal stone alignments in Victoria. *Records of the Victorian Archaeological Survey* 10: 134–51.

Lane, Sharon (2008). *Shifting stones: the Aboriginal stone-based huts of the Mt Eccles stony rises, southwestern Victoria*. PhD thesis, Sydney University.

Lane, Sharon (2009). *Aboriginal stone structures in southwestern Victoria: report to Aboriginal Affairs Victoria*. Collingwood: Quality Archaeological Consulting. http://www.vic.gov.au/system/user_files/Documents/av/Stone-Structures-in-Southwestern-Victoria.pdf.

Lang, Gideon S. (1865). *Aborigines of Australia in their original condition and their relations with whitemen*. Melbourne: Wilson & Mackinnon.

Lawler, Martin and Ilya Berelov (2013). A stratified LGM to mid-Holocene sequence at Thompsons Road, Cranbourne North, Victoria. *Excavations, Surveys and Heritage Management in Victoria* 2: 67–83.

Lawrence, Susan and Peter Davies (2010). *An archaeology of Australia since 1788*. New York: Springer.

Lewis, Kirsty (2000). *Fred Morton 1 revisited: archaeological investigations into the nature of mound sites in western Victoria*. BA(Hons) thesis, La Trobe University.

Lewis, Stephen E., Craig R. Sloss, Colin V. Murray-Wallace, Colin D. Woodroffe and Scott G. Smithers (2013). Post-glacial sea-level changes around the Australian margin: a review. *Quaternary Science Reviews* 74: 115–38.

Lilley, Jane M., Gillian Stroud, Don R. Brothwell and Mark H. Williamson (1994). *The Jewish burial ground at Jewbury*. London: Council for British Archaeology.

Littleton, Judith (1999). East and west: burial practices along the Murray River. *Archaeology in Oceania* 34: 1–14.

Littleton, Judith (2007a). Time and memory: historic accounts of Aboriginal burials in southeastern Australia. *Aboriginal History* 2007: 103–21.

Littleton, Judith (2007b). From the perspective of time: hunter-gatherer burials in southeastern Australia. *Antiquity* 81: 1013–28.

Littleton, Judith and Harry Allen (2007). Hunter-gatherer burials and the creation of persistent places in southeastern Australia. *Journal of Anthropological Archaeology* 26: 283–98.

Lourandos, Harry (1977). Aboriginal spatial organization and population: southwestern Victoria reconsidered. *Archaeology and Physical Anthropology in Oceania* 12: 202–25.

Lourandos, Harry (1980a). *Forces of change: Aboriginal technology and population in southwestern Victoria*. PhD thesis, University of Sydney.

Lourandos, Harry (1980b). Change or stability? Hunter-gatherers and population in temperate Australia. *World Archaeology* 11: 245-64.

Lourandos, Harry (1983). Intensification: a late Pleistocene-Holocene archaeological sequence from southwestern Victoria. *Archaeology in Oceania* 18: 81–97.

Lourandos, Harry (1987). Swamp managers of southwestern Victoria. In *Australians to 1788*. John Mulvaney and J. Peter White, eds. 293–307. Sydney: Fairfax, Syme & Weldon.

Lourandos, Harry (1997). *A continent of hunter-gatherers*. Cambridge: Cambridge University Press.

Lourandos, Harry, Bruno David, Bryce Barker and Ian J. McNiven (2006). An interview with Harry Lourandos. In *The social archaeology of Australian Indigenous societies*. Bruno David, Bryce Marker and Ian J. McNiven, eds. 20–39. Canberra: Aboriginal Studies Press.

Luebbers, Roger A. (1978). *Meals and menus*. PhD thesis, Australian National University.

Luebbers, Roger A. (2015a). *The Coorong report: an archaeological survey of the northern Coorong, South Australia* (revised edition). Adelaide: Department of Planning and Environment.

Luebbers, Roger A. (2015b). *The archaeology of Chinamans Wells and Hacks Station: the Coorong, South Australia* (revised edition). Adelaide: Department of Environment and Natural Resources, South Australia.

Lydon, Jane (2009a). *Fantastic dreaming: the archaeology of an Aboriginal mission*. Plymouth: Altamira.

Lydon, Jane (2009b). Imagining the Moravian mission: space and surveillance at the former Ebenezer Mission, Victoria, southeastern Australia. *Historical Archaeology* 43(3): 5–19.

Lydon, Jane, Alisdair Brooks and Zvonka Stanin (2004). *Archaeological investigations of the mission-house, Ebenezer Mission, Victoria*. Report prepared for Aboriginal Affairs Victoria and Heritage Victoria.

Lydon, Jane, Bruno David and Zvonka Stanin (2007). *Archaeological investigations of the former Ebenezer Mission, Victoria: stage II*. Report prepared for Aboriginal Affairs, Victoria.

Marshall, Larry G. (1974). Late Pleistocene mammals from the 'Keilor Cranium Site', southern Victoria, Australia. *Memoirs of the National Museum of Victoria* 35: 63–86.

Martin, Sarah (2011). Palaeoecological evidence associated with earth mounds of the Murray Riverine Plain, southeastern Australia. *Environmental Archaeology* 16(2): 162–72.

Massola, Aldo (1956). Australian fish hooks and their distribution. *Memoirs of the National Museum of Victoria* 22(1): 1–16.

Massola, Aldo (1957). The wooden shovels of the Aborigines of southeastern Australia. *Mankind* 5(7): 289–96.

Massola, Aldo (1962). The native fish traps at Toolondo in the Wimmera. *The Victorian Naturalist* 79: 162–66.

Massola, Aldo (1963). Native stone arrangement at Carisbrook. *The Victorian Naturalist* 80: 177–80.

Massola, Aldo (1966). Notes on Aboriginal antiquities of the Colac district. *The Victorian Naturalist* 73: 125–36.

Massola, Aldo (1969a). *Journey to Aboriginal Victoria*. Adelaide: Rigby.

Massola, Aldo (1969b). Aboriginal campsites on Wyperfeld National Park and Pine Plains Station. *The Victorian Naturalist* 86: 71–76.

Massola, Aldo (1973). An Avoca River – Wirrengren Plain Aboriginal trade route. *The Victorian Naturalist* 90: 126–32.

Mathews, Robert H. (1898). The Victorian Aborigines: their initiation ceremonies and divisional systems. *American Anthropologist* 11(11): 325–43.

Mathews, Robert H. (1905). Some initiation ceremonies of the Aborigines of Victoria. *Zeitschrift für Ethnologie* 37(6): 872–79.

McBryde, Isabel (1977). Determinants of assemblage variation in New England prehistory. In *Stone tools as cultural markers*. Richard V.S. Wright, ed. 225–50. Canberra: Australian Institute of Aboriginal Studies.

McBryde, Isabel (1978). Wil-im-ee Moor-ring: or, where do axes come from? Stone axe distribution and exchange patterns in Victoria. *Mankind* 11(3): 354–82.

McBryde, Isabel (1984a). Exchange in southeastern Australia: an ethnohistorical perspective. *Aboriginal History* 8(1–2): 132–53.

McBryde, Isabel (1984b). Kulin greenstone quarries: the social contexts of production and distribution for the Mount William site. *World Archaeology* 16(2): 267–85.

McBryde, Isabel (1986). Artefacts, language and social interaction: a case study from southeastern Australia. In *Stone Age prehistory: studies in memory of Charles McBurney*. Geoff N. Bailey and Paul Callow, eds. 77–93. Cambridge: Cambridge University Press.

McCrae, Hugh (1934). *Georgiana's journal: Melbourne a hundred years ago [Diary of Georgiana McCrae]*. Sydney: Angus & Robertson.

McCourt, Tom (1975). *Aboriginal artefacts*. Adelaide: Rigby.

McConnell, Anne (1985). *Archaeological site investigation, Blackfellows Waterhole, Barrabool State Forest, western Victoria*. Unpublished report, Victoria Archaeological Survey, Ministry for Planning and Environment, Victoria.

McConvell, Patrick and Claire Bowern (2011). The prehistory and internal relationships of Australian languages. *Language and Linguistics Compass* 5(1): 19–32.

McNiven, Ian J. (1998). Aboriginal settlement of the saline lake and volcanic landscapes of Corangamite Basin, western Victoria. *The Artefact* 21: 63–94.

McNiven, Ian J. (2000a). Backed to the Pleistocene. *Archaeology in Oceania* 35(1): 48–52.

McNiven, Ian J. (2000b). Treats or retreats? Aboriginal island use along the Gippsland coast. *The Artefact* 23: 22–34.

McNiven, Ian J. (2008). Colonial diffusionism and the archaeology of external influences on Aboriginal culture. In *The social archaeology of Australian Indigenous societies*. Bruno David, Bryce Marker and Ian J. McNiven, eds. 85–106. Canberra: Aboriginal Studies Press.

McNiven, Ian and Damien Bell (2010). Fishers and farmers: historicising the Gunditjmara freshwater fishery, western Victoria. *The La Trobe Journal* 85: 83–105.

McNiven, Ian J., Joe Crouch, Thomas Richards, Nic Dolby, Geraldine Jacobsen and Gunditj Mirring Traditional Owners Aboriginal Corporation (2012). Dating Aboriginal stone-walled fishtraps at Lake Condah, southeast Australia. *Journal of Archaeological Science* 39: 268–286.

McNiven, Ian J., Joe Crouch, Thomas Richards, Kale Sniderman, Nic Dolby and the Gunditj Mirring Traditional Owners Aboriginal Corporation (2015). Phased redevelopment of an ancient Gunditjmara fish trap over the past 800 years: Muldoons Trap Complex, Lake Condah, Southwestern Victoria. *Australian Archaeology* 81: 44–58.

McNiven, Ian J., Julian Dunn, Joe Crouch and the Gunditj Mirring Traditional Owners Aboriginal Corporation (forthcoming). Kurtonitj stone house: excavation of a mid-nineteenth century Aboriginal frontier site from Gunditjmara country, southwest Victoria.

Meyer, Heinrich E.A. (1843). *Vocabulary of the languages spoken by the Aborigines of the southern and eastern portions of the settled districts of South Australia*. Adelaide: James Allen.

Meyer, Heinrich E.A. (1879). Manners and customs of the Aborigines of the Encounter Bay Tribe, South Australia. In *The native tribes of South Australia* (2nd edition). James D. Woods, ed. 183–206. Adelaide: Wigg & Son.

Mitchell, Stanley R. (1949). *Stone Age craftsmen: stone tools and camping places of the Australian Aborigines*. Melbourne: Tait Book Co.

Mitchell, Scott (1988). *Chronological change in intensity of site use at Seal Point: a technological analysis*. BA(Hons) thesis, University of Queensland.

Morphy, Howard (1995). Landscape and the reproduction of the ancestral past. In *The anthropology of landscape*. Eric Hirsch and Michael O'Hanlon, eds. 184–209. Oxford: Clarendon Press.

Mulvaney, D. John (1962). Archaeological excavations on the Aire River, Otway Peninsula, Victoria. *Proceedings of the Royal Society of Victoria* 75: 1–15.

Mulvaney, D. John (1976). 'The chain of connection': the material evidence. In *Tribes and boundaries in Australia*. Nicholas Peterson, ed. 72–94. Canberra: Australian Institute of Aboriginal Studies.

Mulvaney, D. John (1991). Past regained, future lost: the Kow Swamp Pleistocene burials. *Antiquity* 65: 12–21.

Mulvaney, D. John, Graham H. Lawton and Charles R. Twidale (1964). Archaeological excavation of Rock Shelter No. 6, Fromm's Landing, South Australia. *Proceedings of the Royal Society of Victoria* 77: 479–94.

Munroe, Margaret (1998). The stone artefact assemblage from Keilor. *The Artefact* 21: 19–34.

Niewójt, Lawrence (1990). Gadubanud society in the Otway Ranges, Victoria: an environmental history. *Aboriginal History* 33: 175–99.

Norris, Ray P., Cilla Norris, Duane W. Hamacher and Reg Abrahams (2013). Wurdi Youang: an Australian Aboriginal stone arrangement with possible solar indications. *Rock Art Research* 30(1): 55–65.

Nunn, Patrick D. and Nicholas J. Reid (2015). Aboriginal memories of inundation of the Australian coast dating from more than 7000 years ago. *Australian Geographer* 47(1): doi 10.1080/00049182.2015.1077539.

Ossa, Paul, Brendan Marshall and Cathy Webb (1995). New Guinea II cave: a Pleistocene site on the Snowy River, Victoria. *Archaeology in Oceania* 30(1): 22–35.

Pardoe, Colin (1988). The cemetery as symbol: the distribution of prehistoric Aboriginal burial grounds in southeastern Australia. *Archaeology in Oceania* 23(1): 1–16.

Pardoe, Colin (1989). *Archaeology of the western Lindsay Island meander scroll*. A report to the Victoria Archaeological Survey.

Pardoe, Colin (1990). The demographic basis of human evolution in southeastern Australia. In *Hunter-gatherer demography past and present*. Oceania Monograph 39. Betty Meehan and Rhys Jones, eds. 9–70.

Pardoe, Colin (1988). The Mallee Cliffs burial (central river Murray) and population based archaeology. *Australian Archaeology* 27: 45–62.

Pardoe, Colin (1993). Wamba Yadu, a later Holocene cemetery of the central River Murray. *Archaeology in Oceania* 28(2): 77–84.

Pardoe, Colin (1994). Bioscapes: the evolutionary landscape of Australia. *Archaeology in Oceania* 29(3): 182–90.

Pardoe, Colin (1995). Riverine, biological and cultural evolution in southeastern Australia. *Antiquity* 69: 696–793.

Pardoe, Colin (2006). Becoming Australian: evolutionary processes and biological variation from ancient to modern times. *Before Farming* 2006/1: 1–21.

Pascoe, Bruce (2014). *Dark emu black seeds: agriculture or aquaculture?* Broome: Magbala Books.

Pate, F. Donald (1997). Bone chemistry and paleodiet: reconstructing prehistoric subsistence-settlement systems in Australia. *Journal of Anthropological Archaeology* 16: 103–20.

Pate, F. Donald (1998). Stable carbon and nitrogen isotope evidence for prehistoric hunter-gatherer diet in the Lower Murray River Basin, South Australia. *Archaeology in Oceania* 33(2): 92–99.

Pate, F. Donald (2000). Bone chemistry and palaeodiet: bioarchaeological research at Roonka Flat, lower Murray River, South Australia 1983–1999. *Australian Archaeology* 50: 67–74.

Pate, F. Donald (2006). Hunter-gatherer social complexity at Roonka Flat, South Australia. In *The social archaeology of Australian Indigenous societies*. Bruno David, Bryce Marker and Ian J. McNiven, eds. 226–41. Canberra: Aboriginal Studies Press.

Paton, Robert (2005). Trading places: changing social values of the Mount William stone quarry. In *Many exchanges: archaeology, history, community and the work of Isabel McBryde*. Aboriginal History Monograph 11. Ingereth Macfarlane, ed. 271–86. Canberra: Aboriginal History.

Paton, Steaphan (2013). *Boorun's canoe: a journey of connection*. Melbourne: Museum Victoria.

Penny, Jan and David Rhodes (1990). *Lake Condah project: post-contact archaeological component, Melbourne*. Victoria Archaeological Survey Occasional Report 35.

Perham, Graham F. (1985). *MUD and stone: a technological analysis of a quartz industry in northeast Victoria*. BA(Hons) thesis, La Trobe University.

Pickering, Michael P. (1979). *Aboriginal bone tools from Victoria*. BA(Hons) thesis, La Trobe University.

Pickering, Michael P. (1994). The physical landscape as a social landscape: a Garawa example. *Archaeology in Oceania* 29: 149–61.

Pike-Tay, Anne, Richard Cosgrove and Jillian Garvey (2008). Systematic seasonal land use by late Pleistocene Tasmanian Aborigines. *Journal of Archaeological Science* 35: 2532–44.

Porter, Jenny (2002). *Blackfellows Waterhole: the study of an Aboriginal contact period site in western Victoria*. BA(Hons) thesis, La Trobe University.

Porter, Jenny (2004). Blackfellows Waterhole: a study of culture contact. *The Artefact* 27: 77–90.

Presland, Gary, ed. (1977). Journals of George Augustus Robinson, March to May 1841. *Records of the Victorian Archaeological Survey* 6.

Presland, Gary, ed. (1980). Journals of G.A. Robinson, May to August 1841. *Records of the Victorian Archaeological Survey* 11.

Presland, Gary (1998). A.S. Gallus and the Archaeological Society of Victoria. *The Artefact* 21: 9–13.

Pretty, Graeme L. (1977). The cultural chronology of the Roonka Flat. In *Stone tools as cultural markers: change evolution and complexity*. Richard V.S. Wright, ed. 288–331. Canberra: Australian Institute of Aboriginal Studies.

Pretty, Graeme L. and Morrie E. Kricun (1989). Prehistoric health status of the Roonka population, *World Archaeology*, 21(2): 198–224.

Rhoads, James W. (1992). Significant sites and non-site archaeology: a case-study from southeast Australia. *World Archaeology* 24(2): 198–217.

Rhodes, David (1986). *The Lake Condah Aboriginal Mission dormitory: an historical and archaeological investigation*. MA(Prelim) thesis, La Trobe University.

Rhodes, David (1996). *The history of Ramahyuck Aboriginal Mission and a report on the survey of the Ramahyuck Mission cemetery*. Aboriginal Affairs Victoria Occasional Report 47.

Rhodes, David (2004). *Report on an archaeological excavation of pre-contact Bunurong campsite, Lakeside Estate, Pakenham*. Report to Delfin Lendlease. Melbourne: Heritage Insight.

Richards, Thomas (1998). *A predictive model of Aboriginal archaeological site distribution in the Otway Ranges*. Melbourne. Aboriginal Affairs Victoria Occasional Report 49.

Richards, Thomas (2004). The Aboriginal community heritage investigations program. *The Artefact* 27: 11–22.

Richards, Thomas (2011). A late nineteenth-century map of an Australian Aboriginal fishery at Lake Condah. *Australian Aboriginal Studies* 2011(2): 64–87.

Richards, Thomas (2012). An Early-Holocene Aboriginal coastal landscape at Cape Duquesne, southwest Victoria, Australia. In *Peopled landscapes: archaeological and biogeographic approaches to landscapes*. Simon G. Haberle and Bruno David, eds. 65–102. Terra Australis 34. Canberra: ANU ePress.

Richards, Thomas and Rochelle Johnson (2004). Chronology and evolution of an Aboriginal landscape at Cape Bridgewater, southwest Victoria. *The Artefact* 2004: 97–112.

Richards, Thomas, Christina Pavlides, Keryn Walshe, Harry Webber and Rochelle Johnston (2007). Box Gully: new evidence for Aboriginal occupation of Australia south of the Murray River prior to the last glacial maximum. *Archaeology in Oceania* 43: 1–11.

Richards, Thomas and Harry Webber, eds (2004). *Cape Bridgewater Aboriginal cultural heritage field school*. Melbourne: Aboriginal Affairs Victoria.

Richman, Jennifer R. (1996). *Food for thought: late Holocene subsistence in the Mallacoota Inlet area of east Gippsland, Victoria*. MA thesis, La Trobe University.

Richman, Jennifer R. (1999). East Gippsland coastal archaeology: past present, and future. In *Australian coastal archaeology*. Jay Hall and Ian J. McNiven, eds. 255–61. Canberra: Australian National University, Research Papers in Archaeology and Natural History No. 31.

Roberts, Amy L., Natalie Franklin, Isobelle Campbell and the Mannum Aboriginal Community Association Inc (2014a). Ngaut Ngaut (Devon Downs) petroglyphs reconsidered. *Rock Art Research* 31(1): 36–46.

Roberts, Amy L., Isobelle Campbell and the Mannum Aboriginal Community Association Inc (2014b). *The Ngaut Ngaut interpretive project: providing culturally sustainable online interpretive content to the public (South Australia). IPinCH case study – final report*. http://www.sfu.ca/ipinch/sites/default/files/resources/reports/ngautngaut_final_report_2014.pdf.

Roberts, Amy L., F. Donald Pate and Richard Hunter (1999). Late Holocene climatic changes recorded in macropod bone collagen stable carbon and nitrogen isotopes at Fromms Landing, South Australia. *Australian Archaeology* 49: 48–49.

Robertson, Gail, Val Attenbrow and Peter Hiscock (2009). Multiple uses for Australian backed artefacts. *Antiquity* 83: 296–308.

Robertson, Sarah (2007). Sources of bias in the Murray Black collection: implications for palaeopathological analysis. *Australian Aboriginal Studies* 2007/1: 116–30.

Robson, Merryl K. (1986). *Keeping the culture alive: an exhibition of Aboriginal fibrecraft featuring Connie Hart, an elder of the Gunditjmara people, with significant items on loan from the Museum of Victoria* (reprinted edition, 2013). Hamilton: Hamilton City Council.

Ross, Anne (1981). Holocene environments and prehistoric site patterning in the Victorian Mallee. *Archaeology in Oceania* 16: 145–55.

Ross, Anne (1982). Absence of evidence: reply to Kefous. *Archaeology in Oceania* 17: 99–101.

Ross, Anne (1985). Archaeological evidence for population change in the middle to late Holocene in southeastern Australia. *Archaeology in Oceania* 20: 81–89.

Ross, Anne (1986). Aboriginal archaeology in southeastern Australia. In *Planning for Aboriginal site management: a handbook for local government planners*. Anne Ross, ed. 4–16. Sydney: New South Wales National Parks and Wildlife Service.

Ross, Anne (1988). Archaeology and ethnography in the Victorian Mallee. In *Archaeology with ethnography: an Australian approach*. Betty Meehan and Rhys Jones, eds. 260–69. Canberra: Australian National University.

Russell, Lynette (2005). Kangaroo Island sealers and their descendants: ethnic and gender ambiguities in the archaeology of a creolised community. *Australian Archaeology* 60: 1–5.

Russell, Lynette (2012). *Roving mariners: Australian Aboriginal whalers and sealers in the southern oceans, 1790–1870*. Albany: State University of New York Press.

Scarlett, Neville H. (1977). The Aborigines of the Otway region. *Proceedings of the Royal Society of Victoria* 89(1): 1–6.

Scott, Alexander W. (1869). On the 'Ayrotis vastaior,' a species of moth, now infesting the sea-board of New South Wales. *Transactions of the Entomological Society of New South Wales* 2: 40–48.

Scott-Virtue, Lee (1982). *Flint: the foundation of an hypothesis*. BA(Hons) thesis, La Trobe University.

Shawcross, Wilfred (2000). *The Aboriginal people of the mountains: an exhibition of archaeological finds made during construction of this airport*. Unpublished document. Perspective Heritage Solutions.

Shawcross, Wilfred, Russell Mullett, Joanna Freslov and John Tunn (2006). *Mt Cope No. 6 Rockshelter*. Report to Parks Victoria on the archaeological investigation carried out 4–9 April 2005 as part of the Indigenous recovery program. Hurstbridge, Vic.:: Perspective Heritage Solutions.

Sherwood, John, Ben Oyston and Peter Kershaw (2004). The age and contemporary environments of Tower Hill volcano, southwest Victoria, Australia. *Proceedings of the Royal Society of Victoria* 116(1): 69–76.

Sheard, Harold L. (1927). Aboriginal rock art at Devon Downs, River Murray, South Australia. *Transactions of the Royal Society of South Australia* 51: 18–19.

Sloss, Craig R., Colin V. Murray-Wallace and Brian G. Jones (2007). Holocene sea-level change on the southeast coast of Australia: a review. *The Holocene* 17(7): 999–1014.

Smith, B.W. and John R. Prescott (1987). Thermoluminescence dating of the eruption at Mt Schank, South Australia. *Australian Journal of Earth Sciences* 34(3): 335–42.

Smith, Christina (Mrs James) (1880). *The Booandik Tribe of South Australian Aborigines*. Adelaide: Government Printer.

Smith, Diana and Racquel Kerr (2016). Djaara tachylite: resource and distribution on Dja Dja Wurrung Country. *Excavations, Surveys and Heritage Management in Victoria* 5: 17–21.

Smith, Michael A. (1982). Devon Downs reconsidered: changes in site use at a Lower Murray rockshelter. *Archaeology in Oceania* 17: 109–16.

Smith, Michael A. (1989). The case for a resident human population in the Central Australian Ranges during full glacial aridity. *Archaeology in Oceania* 24: 93–105.

Smith, Michael A. (2000). 'The opening chapters of the romance of excavation in Australia': reflections on Norman Tindale's archaeology. *Historical Records of Australian Science* 13: 151–60.

Smith, Michael A. (2013). *The archaeology of Australia's deserts*. Cambridge: Cambridge University Press.

Smyth, R. Brough (1878). *The Aborigines of Victoria: with notes relating to the habits of the natives of other parts of Australia and Tasmania*. Melbourne: Victorian Government Printer.

Stern, Nicola, Jacqueline Tumney, Kathryn E. Fitzsimmons and Paul Kajewski (2013). Strategies for investigating human responses to changes in landscape and climate at Lake Mungo in the Willandra Lakes, southeast Australia. In *Archaeology in environment and technology: intersections and transformations*. David Frankel, Jennifer M. Webb and Susan Lawrence, eds. 31–50. New York: Routledge.

Stern, Nicola (2015). The archaeology of the Willandra: its empirical structure and narrative potential. In *Long history, deep time: deepening histories of place*. Ann McGrath and Mary Anne Jebb, eds. 221–40. Canberra: ANU Press.

Stone, Tim and Matthew L. Cupper (2003). Last Glacial Maximum ages for robust humans at Kow Swamp, southern Australia. *Journal of Human Evolution* 45: 99–111.

Stuart, Iain M. (1981). Ethnohistory in the Otway Ranges. *The Artefact* 6(1–2): 79–88.

Sullivan, Hilary (1981). *An archaeological survey of the Mornington Peninsula, Victoria*. Victoria Archaeological Survey Occasional Report 6.

Taplin, George (1879). The Narrinyeri. In *The native tribes of South Australia* (2nd edition). James D. Woods, ed. 1–156. Adelaide: Wigg & Son.

Thiele, Colin (1963). *Storm boy*. Adelaide: Rigby.

Thorne, Alan G. and Philip G. Macumber (1972). Discoveries of late Pleistocene man at Kow Swamp, Australia. *Nature* 238: 316–19.

Tindale, Norman B. and Charles P. Mountford (1936). Results of the excavation of Kongarati Cave near Second Valley. *Records of the South Australian Museum* 5(4): 487–502.

Tindale, Norman B. (1957). Culture succession in southeastern Australia from late Pleistocene to the present. *Records of the South Australian Museum* 13: 1–49.

Tindale, Norman B. (1974). *Aboriginal tribes of Australia*. Berkeley: University of California Press.

Tindale, Norman B. (1982). A South Australian looks at some beginnings of archaeological research in Australia. *Aboriginal History* 6(2): 92–110.

Tindale, Norman B. (1937). Tasmanian Aborigines on Kangaroo Island South Australia. *Records of the South Australian Museum* 6: 29–37.

Tindale, Norman B. and Brian G. Maegraith (1931). Traces of an extinct Aboriginal population on Kangaroo Island. *Records of the South Australian Museum* 4: 275–89.

Tochler, Helen (2006). 'In search of the Ngaiwang'. In *Roonka: fugitive traces and climatic mischief*. Keryn Walshe, ed. 33–158. Adelaide: South Australian Museum.

Tunn, John (1998). Pleistocene landscapes of Brimbank Park, Keilor, Victoria. *The Artefact* 21: 35–47.

Tunn, John (2006). An Aboriginal campsite on the Maribyrnong River: new dates for Keilor. *The Artefact* 29: 14–21.

Vanderwal, Ron, ed. (1994). *Victorian Aborigines: John Bulmer's recollections 1855–1908*. Melbourne: Museum of Victoria.

Van Huet, Sanja (1999). The taphonomy of the Lancefield swamp megafaunal accumulation, Lancefield, Victoria. *Records of the Western Australian Museum Supplement* 57: 331–40.

Van Huet, Sanja, Rainer Grun, Colin V. Murray-Wallace, Nicola Redvers-Newton and J. Peter White (1998). Age of the Lancefield megafauna: a reappraisal. *Australian Archaeology* 46: 5–11.

Veth, Peter (2000). Origins of the Western Desert language: convergence in linguistic and archaeological space and time models. *Archaeology in Oceania* 35(1): 11–19.

Victoria Archaeological Survey (no date). *Location of sites: Willaura map sheet*. Melbourne: Government Printer.

Walshe, Keryn, ed. (2006). *Roonka: fugitive traces and climatic mischief*. Adelaide: South Australian Museum.

Walters, Ian (1988). Evidence for dual social systems in southeastern Australia? *Australian Archaeology* 27: 98–114.

Warren, Louis M. (1985). *Collectors and collections*. BA(Hons) thesis, La Trobe University.

Weaver, Fiona (1985). *Goanna Bay Top Lake 18: an example of life in the far reaches of Mallacoota Inlet*. MA(Prelim) thesis, La Trobe University.

Webb, Cathy (1987). *Use-wear on bone tools: an experimental program and three case studies from southeast Australia*. BA(Hons) thesis, La Trobe University.

Webb, Stephen (1989). *Prehistoric stress in Australian Aborigines: A palaeopathological study of a hunter-gatherer population*. Oxford: British Archaeological Reports S490.

Webb, Stephen (1995). *Palaeopathology of Aboriginal Australians: health and disease across a hunter-gatherer continent*. Cambridge: Cambridge University Press.

Webber, Harry and Alan Burns (2004). Seeing the forest through the trees: Aboriginal scarred trees in Barrabool Flora and Fauna Reserve. *The Artefact* 27: 36–45.

Webber, Harry and Thomas Richards (2004). *Barrabool Flora and Fauna Reserve Aboriginal heritage investigation and training project*. Melbourne: Aboriginal Affairs Victoria.

Wesson, Jane (1981). *Excavations of stone structures in the Condah area, western Victoria*. MA(Prelim) thesis, La Trobe University.

Wesson, Sue (2000). *An historical atlas of the Aborigines of eastern Victoria and far southeastern New South Wales*. Monash Publications in Geography and Environmental Science 53.

West, Alan L. (1972). An Aboriginal axe-grinding rock near Mount Macedon, Victoria. *The Victorian Naturalist* 89(2): 198–200.

West, Alan L. (1977). Aboriginal man at Kow Swamp, northern Victoria: the problem of locating the burial site of the KS1 skeleton. *The Artefact* 2(1): 19–30.

Wettenhall, Roland R. (1945). *Carrs Plains (twenty-three miles north of Stawell), Richardson Valley, Victoria, 1836–1945: a retrospect and a sketch*. Malvern: McKellar Press.

Wheeler, Jim, Alan N. Williams, Stacey Kennedy, Phillip S. Toms and Peter Mitchell (2014). A Pleistocene date at Chelsea Heights, Victoria: evidence for Aboriginal occupation beneath the Carrum Swamp. *Excavations, Surveys and Heritage Management in Victoria* 3: 33–42.

Wilby, Caroline R.A. (2000). *Deciphering Malangine's rocky past: an investigation of the origins and status of the lithic assemblage from Malangine cave, South Australia*. BA(Hons) thesis, La Trobe University.

Williams, Alan N., Sean Ulm, Andrew R. Cook, Michelle C. Langley and Mark Collard (2013). Human refugia in Australia during the Last Glacial Maximum and terminal Pleistocene: a geospatial analysis of the 25–12 ka Australian archaeological record. *Journal of Archaeological Science* 40: 4612–25.

Williams, Alan. N., Sean Ulm, Michael Smith and Jill Reid (2014). AustArch: a database of ^{14}C and non-^{14}C ages from archaeological sites in Australia – composition, compilation and review (data paper). *Internet Archaeology* 36. http://dx.doi.org/10.11141/ia.36.6.

Williams, Elizabeth (1984). Documentation and archaeological investigation of an Aboriginal 'village' site in southwestern Victoria. *Aboriginal History* 8: 173–88.

Williams, Elizabeth (1985). Estimation of prehistoric populations of archaeological sites in southwestern Victoria: some problems. *Archaeology in Oceania* 20: 73–80.

Williams, Elizabeth (1987). Complex hunter-gatherers: a view from Australia. *Antiquity* 61: 310–21.

Williams, Elizabeth (1988). *Complex hunter-gatherers: a Late Holocene example from temperate Australia*. Oxford: British Archaeological Reports S423.

Wolski, Nathan (2000). *Brushing against the grain: excavating for Aboriginal–European interaction on the colonial frontier in western Victoria, Australia*. PhD thesis, University of Melbourne.

Wolski, Nathan (2001). All's not quiet on the western front: rethinking resistance and frontiers in Aboriginal history. *In Colonial frontiers: Indigenous–European encounters in settler societies*. Lynette Russell, ed. 216–36. Manchester: Manchester University Press.

Wolski, Nathan and Thomas H. Loy (1999). On the invisibility of contact: residue analyses on Aboriginal glass artefacts from western Victoria. *The Artefact* 22: 65–73.

Worsnop, Thomas (1897). *The prehistoric arts, manufactures, works weapons etc. of the Aborigines of Australia*. Adelaide: Geographical Society of Australasia.

Zobel, Daniel E., David Frankel and Ron L. Vanderwal (1984). The Moonlight Head rockshelter. *Proceedings of the Royal Society of Victoria* 96(1): 1–24.

Index

www.ingramcontent.com/pod-product-compliance
Lightning Source LLC
Chambersburg PA
CBHW080233270326
41926CB00020B/4217